Tales from an Old Hack

Tales from an Old Hack

Memoir of a Local Reporter

Betty
Very best wishes
Barbara Fisher
13·11·2019.

Barbara Fisher

The Book Guild Ltd

First published in Great Britain in 2018 by
The Book Guild Ltd
9 Priory Business Park
Wistow Road, Kibworth
Leicestershire, LE8 0RX
Freephone: 0800 999 2982
www.bookguild.co.uk
Email: info@bookguild.co.uk
Twitter: @bookguild

Typeset in Garamond

Printed and bound in Great Britain by CPI Group (UK) Ltd, Croydon, CR0 4YY

ISBN 978 1912575 237

British Library Cataloguing in Publication Data.
A catalogue record for this book is available from the British Library.

Mum and Dad
Mike, Zoë and Nick
for love and support always
xxxxx

And friends – for being there

And for the fun!

Contents

Terry Pratchett was once asked in an interview if he thought he'd 'done good', for a former hack – a reference to the author's early days as a local newspaper reporter.

'I'm still a hack,' the Discworld author insisted, with no small measure of pride, and a pinch of defiance.

The Glory Days

In 2002 the *Uxbridge Gazette* series won a top award for its news coverage. The paper scooped the Best News Pages prize at the Trinity Mirror* Regionals' Editorial Awards in a competition run by the paper's publishers, Trinity Mirror. A panel of top judges agreed that the *Gazette* had the best news pages out of all of its weekly titles across the UK. Its citation said: 'The paper displays evidence that the news coverage is a result of thought and planning, rather than mere reaction, and has a clear awareness of the concerns of its community.'

TM chairman Sir Victor Blank presented the award to *Gazette* editor Anthony Longden at a ceremony in London. Anthony had edited the *Gazette* for eight years, and had swapped roles with Adrian Seal, Editor of Berkshire Regional Newspapers, earlier that year. At that time TM employed around 14,000 staff and produced more than 250 titles, making it the biggest newspaper publisher in the UK.

---

* Trinity Mirror plc changed its name to Reach plc in May 2018.

1

First Things

Most people know me from my weekly column in the *Uxbridge Gazette*. Bm@il started in 2008 but I'd already clocked up twenty years as a reporter by then. Before that I was a teacher. I'd been an acting deputy head before I left to have my daughter in 1974, but went back part-time when she was five. When offered the chance to work full-time at the newspaper I had no problems with starting again at the bottom, even accepting a slight pay cut. Luckily my husband Mike, a civil servant, earned a good salary, and supported my move. Now, familiar to readers of my column as Mr F, Mike has his own cult following (he says).

My change of career came about because I'd written a school page for five years, but I certainly wasn't eased in, and on my first day I was expected to find a front page for my edition. Although given the title of senior reporter because I was older, I still had to learn the ropes the hard way – on the job – with the help of successive editors, some of whom probably rued the day they'd taken on an untrained rookie.

People often ask me why I never wanted to move on, maybe to national papers, but I always loved writing about where I live, going back to the same people, celebrating or being concerned about the same things as our readers. Though I was born, bred and educated in Birmingham, Hillingdon borough has been my home for more than 40 years and I'm very fond of it.

At one point, I did work briefly for a national – as a freelance for the *Times Educational Supplement* – but travelling to other places such as Bristol, and writing about a school there, did not affect me, or interest me, in the same way. I was glad to return to writing about Hillingdon schools. I know some journalists are not too keen on this approach and prefer to be arms-length but being a big fish(er) in a small pond has produced some unexpected results. I've twice had lunch with the Queen (once sitting at her table) and was made an honorary fellow of Brunel University in 2005. This year (2017) Mike and I were invited to a garden party at Buckingham Palace. All were complete surprises and only happened because of strong community links.

We've certainly not been short of big stories here. I've covered a plane crash on the A40, an IRA bomb in Hayes and a mortar attack at Heathrow Airport.

Possibly the biggest surprise for me came on a Sunday in August 1997, the day we all woke up to hear that Diana had died.

It wasn't long before my phone began to ring...

2

Death of Diana

Everyone knows what they were doing on Sunday August 31 1997, the day that Diana died. For me, it started as an innocuous summer day. I had plugged in the kettle, switched on the radio, and was considering popping out to buy the papers.

When I caught the words 'princess' and 'died' on the radio, I thought the news item was going to be about Princess Margaret. Then the announcer mentioned 'two sons'.

Unlikely as it seemed, it had to be the Princess of Wales who had died in a car crash in France. After staring at the radio for a few seconds, I phoned my mother in Birmingham (a Diana fan), and then woke the rest of the household.

My husband and daughter thought at first I'd been dreaming, but the dog knew something was up and decided to stick close. We switched on the TV to try and piece together what had happened, and learned that paparazzi had allegedly chased the princess's car, which had crashed in a tunnel.

So many thoughts crowded into my head. How would Diana's young sons cope? What was the fall-out likely to be for the Royal Family? How would it affect the optimism surrounding the new Labour government, which was riding high; all the country was euphoric about having a new leader and a new start. I had interviewed Tony Blair only a few weeks earlier when he had come to Uxbridge to support his candidate in a parliamentary by-election.

Then the phone rang. It was my editor saying he had arranged for a reporter to go inside RAF Northolt, the airport to which Diana's body was to be brought home. He wanted me to go as well, to talk to the crowds outside. I thought 'crowds, what crowds? She's only just died. There'll be no-one there'. It couldn't have been further from the truth. It was on our patch in West London that the nation's immediate grief and anger revealed itself.

Only hours after her death I turned up to find a 5,000-strong crowd already lining the A40 route to London. I was nonplussed by the bouquets, plants, and teddy bears already left at the gates of the aerodrome. Most of the tributes were unsigned. Others left notes with messages such as 'a light has been extinguished today'. One intriguingly said: 'We were to meet you on Thursday – obviously it was not meant to be'.

Many in the crowd were clearly distressed, some shocked into silence. Most said they just had a compulsion to be near her. What I wasn't prepared for was the hostility towards the press – and that meant anyone with a camera or a notebook.

Spells of sobbing and silence were broken only by insults, hurled at us as we turned up to do our job. A police officer was requested by a woman in the crowd to 'arrest any press', there were cries of 'scum', first at a BBC camera crew, then at all journalists. Our chief photographer was advised for his own safety to stay inside the gates of the airport.

One woman shouted at me: 'Can't you leave her alone? She was the only one to do any good for this country.' As I interviewed people in the crowd, one man asked whether I had a photographer with me. 'If so, I don't think I'll be able to restrain myself,' he said.

I remember a very puzzled reporter from ProSieben Television, then Germany's second biggest channel, being very confused by the backlash. She told me that people in her country loved Diana, and they too were upset by her death.

As one group became very irate, we were all advised to move inside the gates of the airport, and it was then, having walked away from the rest of the press, that I found myself alone, just as the plane landed.

As the red and white BAe 16 taxied along the runway, and the coffin was removed from the hold by six pall-bearers and four escorts, there followed an eerie silence that spread to the crowds outside the gates. Amongst those watching the coffin being transferred to a waiting hearse were Prince Charles, who had accompanied her body, and Tony Blair. The Prince of Wales then returned to the plane and flew back to Scotland to be with his sons.

All alone on the perimeter road I saw the sad procession approach. The first car contained her sisters, Lady Sarah McCorquodale and Lady Jane Fellowes, who had accompanied Diana's body on the flight. They were naturally sombre, but worse, close up they looked like waxworks, frozen by raw grief.

It finally became real for me when I found myself only a few feet away from the hearse that followed. The coffin was draped with the Princess's standard but it was hard to accept the evidence of my own eyes. I had never seen Diana in the flesh, but that casket held her body. I drove home, writing the story in my head, little knowing how the incredible public reaction was to escalate over the next few days and weeks. And how the monarchy itself was to be threatened by the public's perception of the Queen's apparent coolness.

At the paper – as newspapers all over the country were doing – we searched our files and combed our contacts for stories of the princess. One local school revealed a story of a secret trip Diana had made to them to make up for her visit which was marred by a roaring press pack.

It was in November 1993 and the first public engagement since controversial pictures of her working out in the gym appeared in a national newspaper.

Buckingham Palace had described these photographs of a leotard-clad princess as a 'gross intrusion' into her private life, but she was apparently calm and chatty as she met pupils at the Roman Catholic school for children with moderate learning difficulties.

The princess was apparently more concerned about the school being besieged by hordes of press photographers than about herself, so after the visit she rang the school and asked if she could return secretly and 'muck in and relax'. It was just a few weeks later and close to Christmas – always the best time in schools. Diana took William and Harry back to the school where the boys queued up for their lunch like everyone else, saw Father Christmas and stayed for the disco. After her death many more of these local secret visits came to light for newspapers all over the country.

One man who was deeply affected by Diana's death was the then Director-General of The British Red Cross, who knew her very well. Mike Whitlam, who lives in our area, was the man seen constantly at her side during fact-finding trips to places like Zimbabwe, and most famously her visit to Angola where she was photographed walking through a minefield in protective gear to publicise the anti-landmine campaign.

The terrible news of the princess's death was broken to Mike in a phone call from his brother in Australia at 4am. By 6am his answerphone was jammed with about a dozen calls from journalists requesting comments, and he spent the whole day doing television and newspaper interviews.

He told me he found it very difficult to pick out a particular memory, but Angola was special because it put the landmine problem in the public eye, and showed the princess's passion and care for victims.

Diana, who was the charity's vice-president, often confided in Mike, but he was always very discreet, in spite of my probing. The princess often came secretly to our borough and we later learned that Harefield Hospital and Royal Brompton heart surgeon Hasnat Khan was the magnet. After she died, people told us how she had donned a brown wig to drink in local pubs and eat in restaurants with him. This was later borne out in the film Diana, when actress Naomi Watts, as the princess, was seen at Ronnie Scott's jazz club in Soho, wearing a long, dark wig that completely transformed her appearance. It was very frustrating to discover what had been going on under our noses.

Andrew Morton mentions in his book, that Mike was part of Diana's inner circle, and that he arranged to meet her at a go-kart track near Heathrow. There they discussed – as William and Harry crashed about in their go-karts – her intention to give up some of her charities. The following day it made big headlines when, accompanied by Jeffrey Archer, she announced that she would be paring back.

There were big bucks to made for stories about Diana and for her own reasons, not financial, she sometimes manipulated these herself. It is testimony to the loyalty she inspired that so many people in our area, including Mike, kept these visits a secret. She strongly supported the Chain of Hope Charity which operates on children from third world and developing countries – without payment – and she was present at one of these operations carried out by Professor Magdi Yacoub. Staff at Harefield Hospital honoured her requests for privacy and no unofficial photographs, as far as I know, were taken during her visits here.

Following our newspaper's coverage of Diana's death, I, like most people, devoured the national coverage which became more and more astonishing. I travelled with my daughter and a fellow reporter to see the tributes outside Kensington Palace. The Underground train was packed with people clutching flowers. After the silent journey, everyone spilled zombie-like on to escalators, as if ascending from the underworld. Outside the station, we were swept along by an even bigger tide of mourners who shuffled miserably along over-crowded pavements. Hastily set up candle stalls were doing a roaring trade, echoing newspaper reports that the Diana factor was seeing florists all over London selling out of bunches, sprays and plants.

There was no sign of the bitterness then that I'd witnessed when her body was returned to London; instead a mass outpouring of grief had resulted in a gigantic shrine outside her home. That the 'reserved' English had turned a vast grassy area into an ocean of candles, flowers and cuddly toys worthy of Eva Peron's followers was a surprise to many people around the world. For the press, it was a relief that the desire to punish them had, at least temporarily, abated. We could never have dreamt that so many years later, the stories and conspiracy theories surrounding Diana's death would still be circulating.

3

In the Beginning

My earliest memory is of sneaking a tiny hand from under a warm blanket to feel the rain I could see splashing on umbrellas and puddling on pavements. Though still young enough to be in a pram, I'd like to think that under my knitted bonnet I was giving my existence serious thought. Was life going to be better out there, or would it be preferable to stay warm and dry and safe? I still haven't decided.

Born a month early, I must have looked surprised when I surfaced, as my father had been told that it was unlikely my mother and I would both survive the birth. Asked by the doctor which of us to save, if he had to choose, Dad quite rightly had said my mother, Nora. In spite of being an unplanned baby – conceived on my parents' honeymoon and then causing a horrible pregnancy – I was unaccountably always very loved by them both.

Nora had suffered toxaemia (eclampsia) and I must admit to being a little freaked out in recent years when I watched Lady Sybil in ITV's *Downton Abbey* die during childbirth from the same condition. It may have been fictional but it hammered home to me that I, or my mum, might never have made it past first base.

My introduction to the world at Dudley Road Hospital

in Birmingham, now called City Hospital, was particularly impressive in that it was over the road from Winson Green Prison. But, unlike Fred West who, many years later, was to commit suicide there, I was alive, both parents were intact, and I was ready to rumble.

OK, I was underweight at 5lbs, but I had all my fingers and toes and against all the odds, I was here, so... time to celebrate?

Clearly not. Popped into an oxygen tent where they hoped I'd try a spot of breathing, my mother lay back, made the decision to never have any more children, and stuck to it. Although she did consent to a budgie when I was seven.

Beauty sadly came to a sticky end when, while stretching her wings around the living room, she tried to follow my mum to the kitchen. They were very close – too close as it happens.

Poor old devoted Beauty, who had clearly imprinted on my mother as her parent in that animaly/birdy attachment kind of way, crashed against the door trying to get to her, and died instantly as a result. Beauty however fared slightly better though than a pet mouse I had years before which I believed had exploded. This was probably my interpretation of adult conversations about nasty evacuations leaving its body rather forcefully. No real explosions were involved.

While she recovered in hospital (my mum, not the budgie – Beauty came much later), Nora's father Joe got married again. He was a veteran of WW1, including the Battle of the Somme, but he lived well into his 80s. This was despite serious respiratory problems caused by a mustard gas attack. His first wife Ethel, Nora's mother, had died the previous year when she was only 42, from heart failure, following years of illness caused by rheumatic fever as a child.

His new wife, whom he knew from work, apparently cried when it was announced at her wedding that the bridegroom had just become a grandfather. They weren't tears of joy. Yes, I'd done it again and put a spanner in the works, having turned her dashing new husband into an old grandad. I don't think she ever forgave me, or my mum, who was also an only child.

My home was Birmingham, Britain's second city, where I was to spend the next 23 years before marrying Mike, and moving to the bigger smoke. He was a civil servant, born within the sound of Bow Bells, at Bart's Hospital, London – nowhere near any prisons – although we were both students when we first met. Part of a bigger crowd of friends from around the country, we regularly showed up at the same parties. Well, it was the 1960s. These days, as I mentioned earlier, Mike ('Mr F') features regularly in my weekly column, taking it all in his stride that I parade some of our foibles in public. Readers seem to like the bizarre mixture of Fisher family tales with local events and general comment: I have just written about the playground fighting of North Korea's Kim Jong-Un and US president Donald Trump and their silly 'my nuclear weapon is bigger than yours' argument. People often stop me in the street to agree or disagree with my ramblings, which is great.

My first job was as a teacher which, when I was at home with a young baby, wasn't always an advantage when it came to looking for casual work. I will always remember the moment when, after filling in endless forms and being interviewed at Hayes Job Centre, I was told I was over-qualified to get a part-time evening job stacking shelves in a local supermarket.

There was no maternity leave in those days and I had been looking forward to getting some pin money while Mike babysat. He assured me he was happy to take over the responsibilities of a baby and a dog, after he returned from work as a civil servant in London.

As a student, I'd always enjoyed trying different things, from chalet maid and coffee bar assistant at Butlin's Holiday camp, to post office casual work (night work experience), and a shop assistant in a big store.

Lewis's in Birmingham was a huge store, though my products didn't attract many customers. How many fur, leather and suede coats do you buy in a lifetime? (If you're vegan or an animal rights campaigner, none obviously.)

Perhaps at the Hayes Job Centre, I should have asked them to consider my experience helping Mrs Johnson in the grocer's shop when I was a child. My mum worked there part-time, and I loved standing behind the counter with her, breathing in the smell of bacon, cheese, bread and coffee. The 'ladies' – they were all ladies, never women, and very rarely men – would come into Mrs Johnson's with their lists, from which they would read out their requirements. It was my job to get the quarter of tea, tin of Spam, or Rowntree's jelly off the shelves, while she, or my mum, cut cheese and ham and totted up the total IN THEIR HEADS.

My failure at the Sainsbury's interview was obviously because of the final job on my CV. It troubled them that I was a qualified teacher who had been an acting deputy head before I left to have Fisher Junior. Did that really leave me unemployable – apart from the world of education, which didn't offer much evening work? I could have done supply teaching (I did a bit later), but at this stage, before she started school herself, I didn't want to leave my new daughter during the day. Little did I know then that I would never go back to teaching full-time, as a whole new career in journalism was waiting around the corner.

But first – hurrah – I eventually got an evening job (so there, Sainsbury's – ha!). It was at Richmond Ice Rink where the clientele were no trouble and happy to be skating, or more often falling over, to music. On two evenings a week I could be seen peering out of the sweet kiosk overlooking the vast stretch of ice. I saw Robin Cousins (later to appear as a judge on *Dancing on Ice*) skate there; I once sold Pete Townsend of The Who some fags; and I was surrounded by chocolate bars. What more could anyone want?

Fast forward a few years and I am sitting in a newsroom – as a reporter. Probably pinching myself. More about my early life, and the unusual road to writing for a living (yes PAID to write) later. Feel free to skip those bits if you are more interested in tales from an old hack – the people I wrote about in the *Gazette* – which may be the main reason you bought this book.

Working for a newspaper proved to be very different to anything else I'd experienced. The strict timetable in a school contrasted dramatically with a reporter's daily dealings with the unknown. I found myself – instead of taking assembly – trying to find a crashed plane on the A40. Rather than shivering on playground duty I'd be driving to RAF Northolt to meet Nelson Mandela. Both of these stories will appear later; only one of them saw me discharge my duty with honour!

My favourite example of the bizarreness of the job came when we heard about a possible hostage situation. A man had barricaded himself into his house and was chucking mattresses out of the bedroom window. We were told he may have a child with him, and could be armed.

Arriving in good time – the advantage of being a local reporter – I was shunting my car through the gawping crowds when a boiling hot geyser erupted from under the bonnet. Great timing.

Gritting my teeth, I rang my breakdown service Britannia Rescue. I begged them to come and sort my car out so that I could get back to the office as soon as I'd got my story. A concerned operator asked the routine question, 'Are you a woman alone?' I tried not to laugh as I looked at the rows of police in riot gear – helmets, shields, batons – that now surrounded me, particularly when he added, 'Do you feel safe?'

4

Scones, Typewriters,
Making Contacts, Schools

A local paper isn't all about prize-winning parsnips and car boot sales and in two decades we've not been short of big stories. Mine have included murders, rapes, plane crashes, sex abuse and IRA bombs, and an amazing tale of an Uxbridge plane spotter who ended up in a Greek jail. We've had political shenanigans and celebrity interviews, but best of all some great yarns about ordinary people, including positive stories with (gasp) happy endings.

On my first day in January 1989 I was assigned to a three-strong team which covered Uxbridge, but the other two reporters were still on holiday after Christmas. Thrown in at the deep end, I was told that, amongst other things, I had to find a front page for that week's Uxbridge edition. I tried not to panic. I could do this – couldn't I?

Interviewing and making contacts was right up my street, but style, newspaper practice and law, were whole new areas which needed to be absorbed into my bloodstream. Fast. One of the hardest lessons was learning to slice through the health and local government jargon in numerous wordy reports. Definitely not for the faint-hearted.

The newsroom didn't mirror a classroom – it was much stricter. We were writing about people's lives so it was drummed into us to get things right, never mind the legal implications. This bullishness – and at times it was very harsh – was accepted newspaper culture, which reduced many to tears. However, the training was good and most youngsters passed through the pain barrier to make successful careers. One of them, long before my time, was Greg Dyke who hasn't done too badly! (His CV includes being Director-General of the BBC and chairman of the Football Association). In time, I got to love the job, and was let loose as chief reporter, and later deputy news editor.

As we are geographically close to the people we are writing about on a local newspaper, they often came to us for help. A shy first approach can lead to a big lead story or an unexpected chain of events with several follow-ups. Sometimes it was difficult, such as in neighbours' disputes, but if we printed both sides of the argument, the story could often be told. There were numerous queries about housing problems, some genuine including problems of damp or rats which we would chase up (not the rats, the problem).

Before Email, people phoned, wrote, or just turned up at reception and asked to speak to a reporter. Once, I answered a call from a reader who wanted to speak to the journalist who had recently interviewed him, as he had forgotten her name. I had my suspicions as to who it was, but as we had several female reporters at the time, I asked for a description – any clue. 'She was wearing barmy earrings,' he said. Yes, it was me.

Sometimes the problems were so huge, people came to us because they didn't know where else to turn. One time I was called down to reception to find a very anxious figure waiting for me. Simone had come straight from the job centre where she was listed on the computer as male, and as a transsexual, she wanted to tell her story to kick-start her campaign to get the law changed so that she could be acknowledged as a female. After I interviewed her she agreed to have her photograph taken. At these times, you just hoped that there was a photographer in the building and they weren't all out on jobs (we had three photographers then). If you had to arrange to take a picture at a later date, there was always the possibility of your subject changing their mind. A feature is nothing without a picture. Sometimes, where people were reluctant to be identified we had to blur the image or use models instead.

How things have changed now that we have the internet, where everyone thinks they are a journalist, and digital photography, where everyone is a snapper. Our togs (newspaper shorthand for photographers) would take care with their pics, framing them properly and so on, but now papers are happy to accept a quick phone camera image. It may be amateurish, even blurred, but it's instant and you would never have enough staff photographers to cover the areas that readers can. In the same way, television news relies on amateur photography and film to provide up-to-date pictures. Unfortunately, it has meant the end of staff work and permanent jobs for many talented photographers.

In the past, when organising photos on our patch, we were expected to help the photographer with a quick description of the story before they set off. I once forgot to do that and, on deadline, my editor was handed a picture of a smiling, leg-kicking group who were obviously celebrating something. Uh-oh. My story was about residents who were furious that a local public toilet was being closed. I was very, very unpopular when the photographer had to be sent out again to round up the group and take a gloomy replacement picture.

Simone's Story

Starting life as a boy called Kymberley, Simone later had a sex change operation in her early twenties. When I met her, she was still fighting for her personal privacy against unfairness, insensitivity and the law. At the time of our interview in 1991 she was aged 39 and had been living in Hayes for three years. Her formative years were spent in Greenford with her parents and brother.

'I played with dolls and put on girls' clothes in kindergarten. When I was nine, I had a test which proved I did not have the complete male chromosomes.' Simone told me how she was treated with hormone injections three times a year until she was eighteen. By the time she was twelve years old she was growing breasts. Secondary school was particularly difficult.

'I rejected my male organs from a very early age. I always went in a cubicle when I went to the toilet. I took girls' roles in drama. Most of the teachers were kind, but I was beaten up by some of the older girls who said, "What are you doing in our sex?" I never retaliated, but I felt hurt.' On Saturday afternoons, Simone went to the cinema, dressed as a girl. She wore a wig and let her own hair grow underneath.

Simone left school with seven GCE O-levels, passed three A-levels a few years later, and aged sixteen, she moved to Harrow with her family. At eighteen she started her first job as a travel agent at Co-Op Travel in Victoria. She took the post as a girl, but told the truth about herself to her manager. To her relief, he was very supportive.

In 1972, Simone finally had the sex change operation at a London hospital. The male organs were removed and female ones constructed. 'It was very easy; there were no problems. I returned three or four times for post-operative treatment,' she said.

In July 1989, the real problems began when she began working for a neighbouring council, dealing with rent arrears. This time Simone presented herself as an hermaphrodite – someone with both male and female characteristics – having discovered this was more acceptable to 'straight' people. There was no problem until she decided to join the company's superannuation scheme, which meant producing her birth certificate which would show her as male. Following a period of illness, she lost her job, being told she was 'too much trouble and too many questions were being asked'. It was then that Simone decided to campaign for transsexuals to have their gender changed on their birth certificates.

The final straw had come when she was signing on for income support at the local Job Centre. It proved be a harrowing and humiliating experience. 'When you sign on, you look at the VDU and it is turned around in front of you. It says clearly on the screen I am male – and everyone can see it,' said Simone. She asked for privacy at these interviews – pleaded to be allowed to have them conducted in private – but this was constantly refused.

Simone chose her local paper to publicise her quest to win the confidentiality she felt transsexuals deserved. Much harder would be the fight for birth certificates to be altered. She also hoped marriage rights would follow. Simone said she would never give up and we were happy to help.

Things have moved on since then. In April (2017) I was at the Oxford Literary Festival, during a talk by Radio 4's Jenni Murray who had recently upset the touchy transgender applecart by saying that transgender women would never be real women, and I thought of my interview with Simone all those years ago. As Jenni Murray spoke, a placard saying, 'Trans Women are Real Women', was unrolled in the gallery. It was all very English and polite, and the placard and the protesters were silently removed. Most people – including the speaker – pretended not to notice (although I of course had a sly gawp), and she explained herself afterwards, in response to a question from the audience.

Jenni Murray's comments (which had recently hit the headlines and had nothing to do with her talk that day), she said, were to do with the fact that transgender females wouldn't have gone through all the same stages, of girlhood, adolescence, womanhood, that the rest of us, born as girls, would have experienced.

Asked about the BBC, which had apologised on her behalf (she hadn't herself) she remained tight-lipped. 'I'm not going to answer that,' she said.

According to Citizens' Advice, since my interview a transgender person whose birth or adoption was registered in the UK – and who is granted a full Gender Recognition Certificate – can now get a new birth certificate. Registration is held at the General Register Office and someone looking at the new birth certificate will not be able to tell that a different gender has been legally acquired. The original birth certificate remains in existence but is not linked to the new entry.

***

Sometimes, as I mentioned earlier, people come to us when they feel helpless and are at the end of their tether. In 1993 one couple was clearly upset when I joined them in our interview room on the ground floor. 'How can I help?' I asked. They had come straight from the hospital where they had been told that their young daughter had terminal cancer and had only months to live.

Faced with a situation like this, the best you can do as a reporter is listen and offer practical support if possible. Inside I felt helpless until the distraught couple said they wanted to give Lucie a year to remember.

This led to a campaign by the *Gazette*. As a reporter, you take responsibility for your story and co-ordinate readers' offers of help, but it's a team effort. The editor manages and oversees the whole thing, including opening an account for readers' contributions, and appointing trustees; sub-editors design the pages; photographers cover the fundraising events.

Our story had an unprecedented response from readers who rallied round to make the final months for Lucie and her family as happy as possible.

Gazette readers looked at her wish list and didn't blink. Lucie wanted a tiered wedding cake – and got one. An early Christmas was arranged in the warmth of summer, complete with presents and a volunteer Santa, and there were numerous donations for trips and outings with her family – she had two siblings. The big toy company Hasbro, which had its headquarters in our area, provided games and toys thanks to its head of community affairs, Val Ross. Students at Uxbridge College raised money from their magazine and Lucie was a special guest at the Beck Theatre in Hayes. In London, she met her hero Jason Donovan after seeing him in *Joseph and His Amazing Technicolour Dreamcoat*.

When the news seems particularly bleak, it's good to be reminded of this fantastic story which started when Lucie and her parents walked into our offices. But it didn't end when she died ten months later, only nine years old. There are still many good-hearted people in Hillingdon who fundraise, care for others, or who are just community-minded or good neighbours. For proof, we only have to look at the Gazette and Uxbridge College's Local Heroes Awards, which ran for many years. The nominees, from carers to have-a-go heroes, were all put forward by local people.

Another case of people calling on their local paper when all else had failed, started with a phone call from the mother of a young woman with Down's Syndrome. Her daughter had recently married and desperately needed our help.

The couple both had special needs but did not think this should prevent them from having a home of their own; nor did their families, who pledged to give them support wherever they lived.

Paul and Samantha had had a wonderful wedding and wanted to start a new life together. They both worked part-time, but could never afford a mortgage on their wages.

Ironically, they met on an independent living course at Uxbridge College – but were finding it impossible to live independently. After the wedding, they had moved in with Sam's parents but, like any couple, wanted a place of their own.

Most private landlords didn't want tenants on housing benefit –

and those that did, had to have a total annual salary of 30 times the monthly rent or provide a guarantor.

After the story appeared in the paper, they were invited to Hillingdon Council for a fuller discussion of their needs. Eventually they moved into a flat of their own, while still being supported by both their families, who live nearby.

Happy endings are not guaranteed – but this couple's family were determined to do all they could, including contacting the *Gazette*, to highlight their story. If we do not protect our local newspapers, stories like this could fall by the wayside.

Schools

It was another gender change story – Sir becomes a Miss – that was the headline for one of the most unusual school stories I had to write. It was announced at the end of a summer term that a male teacher was to return to class after the summer holiday… as a woman. This unusual situation was handled impressively and sensitively by the secondary school, even to (cunningly) not informing us at the paper until the last day of term.

This was impeccably timed, as they had all left for the long summer break, which left us no chance to 'doorstep' him at the school. Doorstepping entails turning up without notice and hanging about in the hope of getting a quote. We had to be content with statements from the local authority and the headteacher. They both declared that this brave decision had their full support, and that the staff member would return to the same school in September with a new name.

Fellow teachers had already been briefed at a meeting attended by a specialist consultant with experience of working in organisations where gender reassignment had taken place. Students had been informed by their individual form teachers, and even offered the chance to ask questions. The news of the male teacher's sex change was broken to parents in a letter from the headteacher on the same day we received our press release by fax. He reminded parents that the school values were based on tolerance and understanding and the three Rs – Rights, Responsibilities and Respect.

This was a magnificent example of school managing news intelligently. Some schools were very good at this, even when things went wrong, but others stuck their head in the sand and hoped we'd go away. This never worked. If there was a story that everyone was talking about, readers would expect their local paper to cover it. I got to write the story. What they thought of the headline: 'High School Sir to Be a Miss', I never heard.

From Heinz to Hillingdon

This was the headline for a piece I wrote for the *Times Educational Supplement* in December 1991.

The marketing man who invented the phrase: 'I bet you can't eat three shredded wheat,' and linked it with cricketing hero Ian Botham, was taken on by an Uxbridge school, to look at ways to boost the school income.

This was a startling story at the time. The marketing of schools was very new, and to many in education it was regarded as the work of the devil. Some would have preferred to hang on to the ultimate power they had enjoyed for centuries, keeping their heads down, their schools remote from the community, and parents firmly at the school gate. But for others it was an exciting time in education with the chance to reach out to the world outside and even (gasp) 'sell' their schools using the dodgy tool of marketing. Schools were getting used to managing their own budgets and eventually (although none would admit it then) they would be competing for custom. This was the brutal truth. At St Andrews CE School in Uxbridge, though some governors were initially unsure, they didn't see using marketing as selling their souls. They rose to the challenge in a big way.

Charles Meyerstein had spent eighteen years in the fast-moving consumer goods industry, with companies like Heinz, Express Dairies and the Nabisco group. He relaunched Shredded Wheat, revitalised Smiths Crisps and launched the Hovis crackers and Digestive brands. Before he took on St Andrew's he handled a budget of £200m as head of marketing for the London borough of Enfield where he aimed to improve council services and show the borough as responsible and caring.

Mr Meyerstein's work for St Andrew's in 1991 was to be paid by results. At the time, he said he would certainly be breaking new ground 'but there's no reason why you can't market a school like a product. It should make Local Management of Schools (LMS) more viable.'

St Andrew's wasn't the only school to embrace the marketing explosion – over the years canny headteachers did it themselves rather than hire people. When Marie Stubbs took over the borough's only Catholic school she rang up the *Gazette* to introduce herself. Not only was this unprecedented, she also suggested a fun picture opportunity: she was willing to be photographed picking up rubbish around the school. We jumped at it.

When Lynn Gadd took over at the Harefield Academy she immediately gave reporters her mobile number. The more aware teachers in the twentieth century knew that they needed to tackle news – good or bad – head on. Get as many great stories in the public eye as you can, as often as you can, and it will cushion the bad when they come. And come they will. It may be pupils fighting on the way home, a case of meningitis at school, or a parent complaining about their child having to remove a nose stud. Heads used not to return our calls. Now, if they've got any sense, they get in first. It's called damage limitation and everyone does it. Schools have become savvy.

Marie Stubbs, now Lady Stubbs, who was pictured as a new

headteacher clearing the rubbish, eventually took over St George's school in Westminster following the death of headteacher Philip Lawrence who was stabbed outside the school gates. In a television drama about her time there, she was played by Julie Walters.

The ITV two-hour play *Ahead of the Class*, in 2005, was based on her book of the same name. It showed how she had eighteen months to save the school from closure due to poor pupil behaviour, low academic record and widespread truancy. Whether turning schools into businesses has ultimately been a good thing is still up for debate, but pupils' standards are still a hot potato.

***

When I was fourteen years old I was told that if I did not put a higher priority on school work I would be moved to a lower stream. I'm not sure what caused my intellectual decline at this point, but it couldn't have been a health problem.

We children of the 1950s and 60s obediently drank free school milk (warm in summer and frozen solid in winter), suffered compulsory exercise and, albeit by default, ate healthily from a menu which consisted of no choice at all.

Who could forget gristle pie or lumpy mash? Or the inevitable soggy cabbage? But we thrived, probably bolstered by the delicious puddings such as 'chocolate concrete' served with pink custard, and 'roast' which was never dignified by a specific name such as lamb or beef. Oh, and on Fridays there was great excitement as we were served fish with every child's favourite… chips! This was a real treat, as chips were only served once a week.

Strange creatures called vegetarians sat together on one table and, poor things, seemed to be given grated cheese and carrot every day. As someone who gave up meat much later, in 1989, I am glad that we have all become more imaginative about veggie food. Restaurant choices can still be pretty limited though, largely because they are disappearing under a glut of gluten-free dishes.

We hadn't quite got the hang of teenage pregnancies, and drink and drugs meant a bottle of Vimto and a Kwells travel tablet for coach journeys. The height of sophistication was graduating from junior aspirin to the grown-up version. I can only assume my grey matter was dumbed down by the time spent perfecting my backcombed beehive hairdo, and also daydreaming in lessons over my idol Billy Fury, the sixties singer I used to see performing at the Birmingham Hippodrome. I was in love with him, and intended to end up as Barbara Fury. It was the only time I ever joined a fan club – I still remember my membership number, 241. Being Mrs Fisher has proved to be a reasonable substitute to being Mrs Fury of course, but nothing could compete with the excitement, at 14-years-old, of standing outside the stage door waiting to see my idol. It was a real, but glorious, obsession. I never met him, but decades later, I went, out of curiosity, to see him at the Beck Theatre in Hayes. By then I was a middle-aged wife, mother and teacher and living in the London borough of Hillingdon. I was pleased he'd come to my neck o' the woods, but he looked an unhealthy yellow colour and was clearly unwell. Sadly, it was his last performance. It was the young Barbara Parsons who cried when she heard that Billy had died at the age of 42 in 1983, and I never regretted letting my school work slip, while concentrating on the one who I thought was my one true love.

However, after the shock of being pulled up for this at school, I knuckled down and did much better in exams. This proved I hadn't been working hard enough, so they put me down anyway. Not as in euthanasia thankfully, but to a lower stream. It shocked me into working again. I thought I ought to get some GCEs if I really wanted to be a teacher and a writer; both careers I was eventually lucky to experience. And school news was my route to eventually being (oh joy) paid to write… something I had always enjoyed doing.

I loved my sixth form years, and as a teenager studying A-level

English at school in Birmingham we were taken on visits to the theatre in Stratford-on-Avon.

I still have my first reviews, published in the school magazine. My disdain at the set for a performance of *The Tempest* was clear. Three black balloons attached to a cloud represented a stormy sky and I wrote rather pompously 'they bore more resemblance to a pawn-broker's sign'. I clearly hadn't discovered minimalism.

Later, while training to be a teacher, aged about nineteen or twenty, I managed to wangle an interview with the great 1960s writer Alan Sillitoe, author of *Saturday Night and Sunday Morning*, which made a two-page spread in the college magazine (see later).

As a ten-year-old, my plan had been to be a hairdresser or a missionary; later this changed to a backing singer with a Tamla Motown group. I always enjoyed writing, but my path to teaching was set in stone and I never considered veering off it. Journalism was not then an option.

Making contacts

I had clocked up fifteen years of teaching when I was first asked to write a schools' page for the *Hayes News*, a little paper which people still remember fondly, although it disappeared years ago. It was sold door-to-door by cute little boys earning a bit of pocket money. I've no idea why the sellers were gender-specific, but I know they wouldn't be allowed to knock cheerily on strangers' doors these days.

After the *Hayes News* folded, the *Gazette* (well, the editor Eddie Duller) was keen for me to start a schools' page for them, which I did for five years alongside teaching, never guessing this would lead to a new career.

It wasn't an easy decision – I enjoyed teaching – but I was eventually persuaded to give full-time journalism a go.

Newspapers were just changing over to modern technology

and on my first day I was greeted by an Apple Mac computer with a very tiny screen. I had no idea how to turn it on. When I did, and tentatively wrote a few lines, I was worried sick about deleting my words accidentally. Where and how was I to send these stories? Did they have to be printed out first? I looked around the newsroom for clues. Everyone was busy and in full command of their machines but I hated my computer and I was sure it hated me. Funny now, to think that I mourned the loss of Tippex and carbon paper, as technology has proved to be such a liberation. When it works.

Before I joined the staff as a full-time journo, I often popped in to the old building in Cricketfield Road to hand in my schools' copy, or to write a theatre review late at night. The place was buzzing with the clackety clack of typewriters. There were mountains of paper everywhere, from press releases and letters, to the actual copy which was typed in triplicate and laid out in trays. Used paper was speared on old-fashioned metal spikes. Everyone was smoking. Downstairs the presses rolled and I remember going home and telling my husband that I'd heard the printers talking about a 'scone'. How disappointing to eventually discover that this had nothing to do with light refreshments, but referred to a method of printing using a lithographic limestone or a metal plate with a smooth surface. Or something. By the time I joined the team, the works had all gone, so I never got to grips with the printing process.

Those early days were also pre-Google, Amazon or eBay, and the local paper was the best place to find a new job, house or car, or sell your child's outgrown pushchair or bike, never mind catch up on the latest news.

***

The *Gazette* and Hillingdon Council were recognised nationally in 1990 for having an excellent partnership when it came to relaying school news. The report from Tim Devlin Enterprises on the marketing of local authority schools described Hillingdon as a forward-looking education authority because of its good relations with the local paper. The *Gazette* was mentioned as being very helpful in promoting local schools with its dedicated schools' page.

The report said: 'Good relations with local papers were seen to be a priority by the more forward-looking authorities. The Gazette in Hillingdon runs a weekly schools page written by a reporter who is herself an ex-teacher (ahem – me).' The survey, which was carried out amongst all Local Education Authorities (LEAs) – 116 then – was not just interesting because we and the council came out of it well, but also because it threw up a few horror stories. Fourteen LEAs insisted that schools should have no direct contact with media in general, and the press in particular. Welsh authorities revealed a deep suspicion of the media, with one authority refusing to answer any questions, insisting that a list of written queries be sent to the director of education.

The headteacher was preferred as spokesperson by most authorities, but thirty-seven others were keen for schools to appoint their own press officer. Eighteen authorities had run courses for schools on how to deal with the media. Surrey County Council had published an advice pack with a cover made of dazzling silver foil described in the survey as a 'shining example'.

The best was Northamptonshire's guidelines which came in the form of a cheery red and black newspaper and contained excellent advice for heads:

- Don't ramble on in an interview
- Don't use your secretary to block access to you
- Don't attempt to write the story for the media.

I mentioned that my very first schools' page was in the *Hayes News* in 1983 – and it really put the cat among the pigeons. I was sent for, by Hillingdon Council Press Officer Roy Mills, to explain myself. An unknown person trying to extract news from schools for a dedicated page was an alien concept, but they eventually embraced it. Slowly, as heads started to trust me, they contacted me, rather than the other way around. Roy was often a much-needed bridge between the paper and those who were still suspicious of a journalist wanting to spread the good news about schools.

So, the schools' page had really taken off, and eventually the Hayes and Harlington MP, John McDonnell, invited me to meet Hilary Benn, who was then Special Adviser to the Secretary of State for Education and Employment, David Blunkett. Mr Benn was very interested in the idea of dedicated schools' pages in local papers which contained education news as well as school activities, and asked me to send him some examples at the education department in Westminster. He replied with a handwritten letter, saying 'Thanks very much for the School Talk Pages. They are excellent, and it would be wonderful if other local papers would follow the example. I am copying the material to the Head of News here at the Department for Education and Employment (DfEE) to see if there are ways we could promote the idea.'

In the eighteen years since, a lot has happened. Mr Benn has been an MP for Leeds Central, since winning a by-election in 1999. He was shadow foreign secretary from May 2015 to 2016, when he was dismissed by current leader Jeremy Corbyn.

John McDonnell is still MP for Hayes and Harlington, but now is Shadow Chancellor and tipped as a future leader. Our MP in Uxbridge is Boris Johnson.

Needless to say, nothing happened about schools' pages being established in every local paper in the country. The Head of News at the DfEE was clearly not impressed. He never contacted me, and I never heard any more.

When I became a full-time reporter, and had to write about education generally, including the newly launched – and dreaded – league tables, it was a different matter. My editor would require me to get a quote from the top and bottom schools in the table. Not surprisingly, the top school, usually an independent school in the north of the borough, would have their happy comment ready and waiting. But oh, how I felt for the school at the end of the table. It was often in a very disadvantaged area, where staff had their work cut out just getting pupils to attend lessons on a daily basis.

But neither I nor the paper had invented league tables, and as a paper of record we could not ignore them. The nationals produced huge spreads on the data with nationwide analysis, so the information was public anyway. It all meant that struggling schools found it even harder to attract the sort of pupils who would help their results improve. If it was a difficult time for me on the education writing front, then it was a devastating time for some schools, who felt publicly humiliated.

During the time I wrote the paper's schools' page there were huge changes in education, not only the new-fangled league tables, but before that, the introduction of the national curriculum and Local Management of Schools (LMS). It wasn't only the schools who had to tackle them – we journalists had to decipher it all too before dishing up the facts to readers in a palatable fashion.

In the 1990s, I was also doing occasional freelance work for the *Times Educational Supplement* (TES). Sometimes I 'sold on' stories I'd written for the *Gazette* – such as the advertising one at St Andrew's mentioned earlier. Reporters often do this but we were always expected to make sure that any local piece had first appeared in the *Gazette*. If not, there was trouble. I also wrote some bits and pieces for the governors' page in the *TES*. Occasionally I was commissioned to do a particular piece, and one of these was to go to a school in Bristol which was refusing to take on its own budget. It's incredible, now that we have academies and free schools, to remember how resistant the schools were then to go it alone and cut loose from local authorities.

This may sound naive, but having just changed careers, I was secretly thrilled to be asked to do this story by a national paper – particularly being sent first class on the train – and not even having to book the tickets myself. There were no such perks as a teacher and I must have spent the whole journey with a silly grin on my face.

It was great to see my by-line on a big story in the *TES* but, (in spite of the perks) it reinforced for me that I liked local papers best. Even first-class travel with a swanky breakfast and hot towels (I doubt if you'd get that now) didn't make me want to aspire to a national newspaper.

One of our biggest stories in Hillingdon was when the first school in our borough went Grant Maintained. Bishopshalt was probably one of the earliest in the country, and the first in the borough, and the day it broke I was off sick with a (genuine) upset stomach. I hadn't seen it coming.

I really didn't want to miss such a big school story, so I hauled myself out of bed. Later, I had a congratulations memo from the editor, not only for the story but because he knew I wasn't feeling up to par. Over the years I also had some memos that weren't so complimentary (putting it mildly), so I made sure I kept the good ones.

The changes in education continued to come in fast and furious, and many heads would confide in me about their unhappiness. Often, they felt it was a case of too much, too soon. The National Curriculum was generally praised, but the league tables were universally disliked, even by those who topped them. They knew that their colleagues in more difficult schools, maybe with pupils lacking books or parental support at home, did not get an easy ride, and hitting them with such a public stick was not going to help.

Mostly the comments from staff – heads and teachers – were off the record, although others were willing to voice their views publicly. One of these was Rod Stafford, then head of Mellow Lane School, who was known to be outspoken in public and was a great contact over many years.

Another headteacher decided when he was leaving the profession to be honest about why he was going, and promised me an interview. I knew that Derek Morris clearly loved the job, and he had always thought he would be a head until he retired. But in May 1998 he was off to become a full-time union official for the National Association of Headteachers (NAHT).

An unrealistic workload, mind-crushing responsibilities and league tables were all contributory factors, said Mr Morris, a dedicated teacher and a well-respected head in the borough.

'Since the introduction of LMS and the National Curriculum, the pressure on schools in general and headteachers in particular has been steadily increasing,' he told me. 'To hear that colleagues are working more than 60 hours a week is commonplace. That is not an efficient or effective way for anyone to work. We must find ways of allowing staff in schools to have a life outside education. I have seen teachers in my school who work equally as hard as I do, so I am not saying that it is only headteachers under this pressure. We must look after our teachers as well.'

One of the things that made him stop and think was a crucial moment during a training day at the school. He was speaking to staff when he got an urgent message.

'I had a phone call to say my mother was dying and I said to my brother, "I'll ring back and see when I can come". Then I thought, hang on, this is my mother.'

He left the conference and went quickly to his mother, who died the same day.

As he prepared to finally leave his school, and teaching, Mr Morris said, 'I thought I would have been a headteacher until I retired. The part of me that is the husband, father and so on, has been subjugated by this dominating part of me that demands more and more of my time and my physical, intellectual and emotional energy. I want to get some balance back in my life and rediscover some of the parts I have lost in recent years.'

He said being a head was an enjoyable and stimulating job and he would recommend it to anyone. 'But you must however have limitless energy and the potential to soak up pressure from all directions – children, parents, staff, the Local Education Authority

(LEA), Ofsted, an often-hostile press, and a government which talks about supporting schools, but does little in practice.

'When your school is doing well, you can ignore league tables or give yourselves a pat on the back. If you are in the middle you can breathe a sigh of relief and keep your head down. When you are near the relegation zone this can destroy your self-belief. I have no problem getting rid of lazy or incompetent staff, be they teachers or headteachers. But using public humiliation as a tool for school improvement is at best a blunt instrument and at worst enormously destructive. If the government wants to treat us as a football team – so be it.'

It is incredible to think this interview was 20 years ago.

5

Hair-raising Experiences – including jobs with the Old Bill

It must be clear by now that reporters never know what they may be asked to do in the course of duty. In 1989 we got wind that top stylist John Frieda, then married to singer Lulu, was in Uxbridge to demonstrate his products on passing shoppers. When I, and a photographer, arrived, there was no shortage of guinea pigs queuing up to have their hair styled by him and his team. We both looked round for likely culprits to interview and photograph.

Using his products, specially designed for photo sessions with models, John had set up shop in Boots, which then occupied the current Wilkinson's site. He aimed to show how a modern style could be achieved without washing or snipping the hair. Hearing it would only take five minutes for the consultation and 'make-over', to my horror, my photographer pushed me forward before I could say Kim Jong-Un. (OK, the dictator with the barmy barnet – the style that all men in North Korea must now copy hadn't even been born then – but I couldn't resist the hair link.)

So, there I was, hemmed in by curious shoppers waiting to see what John Scissorhands, whose clients included Jerry Hall, Brooke

Shields and Paula Yates, would do with me. Big hair was fashionable then, but he was about to make mine gigantic. I just wanted to shrink, or preferably disappear.

'Barbara has a perm which is growing out and her hair is now flat – a common problem,' he boomed over the microphone. I winced as he exposed my ends to the world, and I wished I was at the dentist.

But help was at hand. John – who made me watch what he was doing in a small mirror – convinced me that his magic ingredients would coax my untamed mane into a style that would turn heads. Soon the dreaded flat top disappeared and I certainly looked spikier, and (I hoped) more glamorous and sophisticated. Actually, I looked ridiculous.

Back at the office, I preened and waited for compliments. 'Oh, you're back,' said the editor. 'You really should have had your hair done. Just think what a challenge it would have been…'

Often the editor would summon reporters to a news meeting to tell them we were going to do a News Focus. This could be something to which we'd contribute as a team: a big subject shared between us to make an in-depth article over a couple or more pages. Occasionally one reporter would do a whole News Focus. This was a big job – organising interviews and photographs and writing copy.

The most interesting, and traumatic, one that I wrote was on the subject of rape. It included a series of interviews around a particular case, after speaking to police, victim support, medical people – and the victim. More on that later.

But there was lighter stuff too, and sometimes we would be asked (told) to get involved in a series of articles on a particular theme, each of us doing our own piece, dripped in week by week to (hopefully) keep readers' interest.

The morning I heard we were all to choose a sport to write about, after having had a go ourselves, my heart sank. Or more likely stopped. Like most people I have dabbled in gyms and aerobics over the years and I now walk a bit, and use an exercise bike (mostly to hang my clothes on), hoping to slow the descent into crumbledom. But serious exercise? I'd rather go to the theatre.

The young reporters studied the list of suggestions and signed up to their chosen torture enthusiastically. Eventually, just as I was about to suggest darts or clay pigeon shooting, I found I was left with golf.

I duly booked my lesson and arrived at Harefield Place Golf Club in perfect weather. The course looked brilliant, bathed in bright May sunshine as I set off for my first hurdle, lumbering behind the club professional to the beginners' area. I wondered if he knew what he was letting himself in for. Maybe he'd tried to get out of it? Fortunately for him, he said most of his pupils are not raw beginners like me but have at least had a go at pitch and putt. I considered mentioning Crazy Golf at Lyme Regis but decided against.

He told me he sported a handicap of four, whatever that meant. I was still wondering whether to sympathise with him or praise him, when we arrived at our spot.

Neil (for that was his name) was very patient. He showed me how to grip the club, thumbs at the front, fingers interlocking at the back. I learnt about alignment and posture which entailed looking like a drunk duck with bent knees and legs apart. I didn't catch him laughing.

My patient teacher said the next thing I would learn would be how to swing. This was still golf-related in case you were wondering. Shoulders pivoting, head down watching the ball, arms straight but not gripping too tight, I aimed the club. My brain had taken it all in, but sadly the rest of me didn't want to know. 'Strength, timing, control and co-ordination are most important,' explained Neil as I failed miserably on all counts.

Normally it is safe after three or four lessons to be set free on a golf course. As I attempted another swing I was pretty confident of being the exception to the rule. Maybe the golf balls were faulty. Some went all over the place but others didn't budge an inch.

'Youngsters learn the basics quickly because they look and copy, but adults tend to think of each thing individually,' said Neil.

By this time, this adult couldn't think of anything but her aching back, shaking arms and complete lack of co-ordination, but the best lesson was still to come. Neil took me to somewhere I was happy to sample and seriously shine – the 19th hole – the name for the bar at the back of the clubhouse. I have not been on the green since.

The Old Bill

The police/reporter relationship was never all one-way. We may have mercilessly quizzed them for information but they often needed our help too.

Every reporter had a contacts book, which started with blank pages and was then built up from day one on the newspaper. This was invaluable for quick access to emergency services, residents' associations, schools, council and church phone numbers. But the real challenge was to gather personal numbers of named contacts whom you could collar at short notice to help with a story or give you a quote. Building a relationship with these people was vital if you intended to keep their trust. This included honouring off the record comments.

In the 1990s BE (Before Email) we would get on our bikes, or in reality many used the bus to visit the local police station twice a week to get up to date with local crimes. I actually drove a car, but when I was teaching I'd ridden a moped, which inspired a lot of mirth. And not just from the pupils.

Once, staggering out of the pouring rain into a newsagent on my way home from school, I couldn't understand why the shopkeeper was laughing. He was so helpless, he could only point at me in my crash helmet and see-through plastic mac worn over a fur jacket before eventually spluttering: 'You look like a hamster in a polythene bag.'

Whichever mode of transport we used, visiting the police station was always a popular task amongst reporters. We were allowed to drive straight there for a 9.30am start, so we could have a bit of a lie-in. Punctuality was considered very important at the *Gazette* and a late arrival in the newsroom was dealt with anything from a frosty silence to verbal abuse. It was great therefore to have a bit of leeway if you were lucky enough to be chosen to go to police calls.

This may have involved the downside of life – a catalogue of crimes that had happened that week – but the occasion was actually very congenial. At West Drayton police station, the duty officer would make coffee for reporters from the local papers: The *Gazette* and *Leader* (now merged) and *The Informer* and *Recorder* (both now defunct), before getting down to business. First, we had to find somewhere to sit, as there weren't always enough chairs, particularly if we had work experience people with us. Something vaguely suitable was drummed up from another office – sometimes broken – or we just perched on a desk.

The officer thumbed through, and read from, a huge tome, rather like a Walt Disney book of spells. It contained crime reports on things like burglaries and street crime, which was mostly about nicking mobile phones then. Any serious crimes were reported separately, and a CID officer would be brought in to brief us on those.

We would take notes, and ask questions as we went along, but the funniest thing was trying to interpret the strange police-speak. Some reports said everything, but told us nothing: 'Victim A and B were proceeding in an easterly direction in a vehicle when they were alerted to an obstruction in the road'.

Were they men or women? Where were they actually heading? Was the vehicle a bus, car, lorry etc? How were they 'alerted'. Did they actually bump into it? What was the obstruction? A load of potatoes, a horse? A caravan? And so it went on. An endless game of catch-up, which I think the police rather enjoyed.

Sometimes an officer would have to phone whoever had dealt with a crime to find out more for us. Time, place and what was stolen were obviously vital, but in the case of robberies and muggings we hoped to get a name and phone number in order to interview the victim. We suspected that one police officer, who used to constantly answer our questions with 'sorry, it's sub judice', simply didn't want to follow anything up.

In my later days at the paper 'data protection' was the phrase that was repeatedly thrown at us. Fortunately, though, there were officers who were willing to contact a victim to ask them if they would speak to a reporter. Having a first-person account made a story – 'added colour' – and delighted editors. One of my stories, which came from Harefield police in 2008, resulted in a splash – a front page – with the wonderful headline 'Joan sticks it to a crook'. (You'll see where the stick comes in later.)

It was the sub-editors who placed stories on the pages and also created all the headlines. This is a tricky business as they have to sum up the story, be witty if appropriate, and fit everything into the available space. Not as easy as it sounds, and certainly not a skill that I have.

'Joan Sticks it to a Crook' was a fabulous, but frightening, story about a gutsy grandmother of nearly 90 who found a burglar in her bedroom. She was happy to talk, so I went to her cosy bungalow where she settled me down with a cup of tea and began to tell me her astonishing tale.

It began on an apparently ordinary Thursday morning when Joan was in her living room, resting while her washing machine finished its cycle. As she waited, she suddenly became aware that someone was trying to open her back door. She wasn't expecting anyone, so she moved quickly to see who the unexpected visitor was.

A shifty-looking man was there. He looked a bit startled but said he was selling carpets. Joan was at first puzzled as to how he got into her garden, as she always bolted her back gate, but then realised she must have forgotten to do it when she put the rubbish out that morning. After making it very clear that she had no need of carpets or carpet sellers, the intruder scarpered. Joan bolted the gate behind him, moved to the kitchen to put her washing in a basket, and happily continued with her day.

Her relief did not last long. As she moved around her bungalow, Joan thought she saw something move in her bedroom. Her mind raced. Had a second intruder slipped in unnoticed before she had spotted the man at her door? Peering cautiously around her bedroom door she was relieved to find there was no-one there. However, for peace of mind, she went to the conservatory where she had a different view of her bedroom, and took another look.

To her horror, she saw a man hiding behind the bedroom door. At this point, most of us would have run, but Joan saw red. This was her home and nothing was going to stop her defending it. Grabbing her walking stick, she thundered into the bedroom and whacked him hard while shouting 'What are you doing in my bungalow – get out!' The cowering intruder kept muttering: 'sorry, sorry' as he tried to shove her aside, but Joan continued to show she was no pushover and continued to whack him across his shoulders with her stick. Eventually the cowed burglar had had enough and got the message. He broke free and ran for his life.

Joan sat down to get her breath back and only then did she find she was shaking like a leaf. Eventually she summoned up the energy to ring her son and daughter-in-law who immediately alerted police. It was a brilliant victory but sadly marred when she found the strength to check her possessions. Joan found that the thief had got away with some cash and a lot of jewellery, much of it of sentimental value. Worst of all, his haul had included her mother's wedding ring.

Today, when so many people want to publicise their experiences, it seems almost strange that this brave woman shrugged it all off and refused to be applauded for her undoubted courage. It is typical of that generation that they are uncomfortable with praise or pity. Joan said the things he took were irreplaceable, but she definitely didn't feel like a hero. In fact, she felt foolish for leaving the back gate unbolted.

Local police acknowledged her courage but suggested we add a note of caution to our story and ask people to put their own safety first on these occasions. They knew Joan's story could easily not have had a happy ending. We couldn't let it pass, though. The Gazette and Uxbridge College Local Hero Awards honoured Joan in the then annual competition when she was overwhelmingly voted Citizen of Courage

The police/reporter relationship was never all one-way. We may have mercilessly quizzed them for information, but they often needed our help with appeals for witnesses. The paper would print CCTV images, photo-fits and details of a crime, with phone numbers including that of Crimestoppers, where callers could remain anonymous. This cooperation was important and it is great that over the years many criminals have been caught in this way.

We were always encouraged to make police contacts of our own, and I can remember enjoying drinks with our local officers in The Crown and Treaty pub, or the occasional coffee in town. I imagine there are too few reporters now to allow time for this (I have been freelancing since 2009, just emailing my column in each week, so am not involved in that side). Production these days is based in Guildford.

A closer relationship meant a build-up of trust, which led to good tip-offs and easier access at crime scenes, although (usually) not beyond the police tape. It is a shame that suspicion has clouded this kind of relationship since Leveson. It can be professional and above board and, to my knowledge, local papers have never paid police for information.

In 1993, I heard a disturbing story of the sexual abuse of young adults with severe learning difficulties, which came to us directly from police. They were frustrated that it couldn't be taken to court. Sexual abuse of this kind was a rare crime then (at least in news terms) and I was asked to attend a meeting of victims, police and social workers who wanted to be heard. This was highly unusual, but was arranged with the blessing of the appropriate authorities, so well done to them for sticking their necks out. If only those who knew about the Jimmy Savile crimes had had the guts to do the same.

I was sent to a secret venue where the group, who all had severe learning difficulties, was waiting. They were accompanied by their parents or carers, who said they intended to form a support group for the victims who had suffered sordid sexual abuse at the hands of a trusted volunteer. They told me that the man, who helped at a club in Hillingdon and even served on the committee, regularly molested them at their club. His name was known to the *Gazette* but couldn't be published for legal reasons.

He apparently abused them in the back of his car, at swimming, and on holidays, while their parents happily entrusted them to his care. Social services and police had interviewed the victims' families (many were Down's Syndrome aged from their teens to 40s), and compiled a gruesome dossier of abuse that spanned about ten years. It was therefore a kick in the teeth when the Crown Prosecution Service, having studied all the evidence, threw out the case. It decided the victims would not make good witnesses in court. Thankfully, since then, sexual assault has been taken much more seriously, and improvements have been made in the Criminal Justice system to accommodate victims of these kinds of crimes, including those with special needs.

At my meeting, one mother told me she accepted that they might have been ripped to pieces in court, but it was worse that they hadn't been given a chance. She asked 'How can we help them find a place in the community if they are treated as outsiders?' All the parents said they were struggling with their own guilt – blaming themselves for what happened.

They recalled remarks made by their sons and daughters over the years which they wished they had taken more seriously at the time. They also anguished over the trust they placed in a man who was thought to be a pillar of society, an uncle figure they thought above suspicion.

One said the awful truth was that she took her daughter to a club, left her there to be abused and picked her up later. That's how she saw it now.

All of the victims spoke clearly and confidently to me. One cried as she spoke. Another kept asking 'why did he do it?' I wished I could have helped more. The young female detective who interviewed the victims agreed to be named in the paper. She told me the descriptions were graphic and, in her opinion, could not have been made up. As she continued her investigations, the extent of the abuse shocked her.

My editor agreed to run the story but he confirmed that, for legal reasons, we couldn't name the alleged perpetrator. I kept in touch with some of the families for many years, and from time to time was able to write some positive stories about their lives, totally unconnected to this terrible time. As far as I know, the man has never been prosecuted.

There is often good cooperation with police, including reporters being asked to accompany them on early morning raids. These days they often aim to catch cannabis growers, but my most interesting experience was tagging along with police to check on possible canine criminals when the Dangerous Dogs Act came into force in 1991. Camera crews were also there to record it for Paul Ross's *Crime Monthly* programme on ITV. I will cover this story later in the book.

My story ended with indignant readers getting my editor to send a reporter to meet a Pitbull terrier which was being kept as a pet in a family with young children. This resulted in a picture of me taken by a mischievous snapper after the massive dog jumped up – the full length of me – and gave me a slobbery welcome. The story and picture was consequently headlined 'Kissed by a Pitbull!'

I fell for it again (me looking daft in a photograph for the amusement of readers) in 1991 when I went to catch a crew filming an episode of *Minder* in Hayes, which had inevitably drawn quite a crowd. Dennis Waterman had left the cast by then and new boy Gary Webster had taken on his new role. George Cole was busy in his caravan in the grounds of The Adam and Eve pub, apparently doing a crossword, and didn't want to come out to talk to us or be pictured, which was very disappointing.

Fortunately for me – it's never good to go back without a story – the new sidekick for Arthur Daley was game for a laugh. Gary, playing Ray, was still covered in fake blood after a filmed fight, so he suggested my photographer shot me pretending to punch him as it would look as though I'd really done him some damage. Unfortunately, he too thought this was a great idea, so… I took a deep breath, put on my best aggressive face and clenched my fist. Again, like the Frieda picture in 1989, the resulting photo took pride of place in the paper, and I looked a complete idiot. This time the headline was 'One in the Eye for New Minder Star'.

Twenty-six-year-old Gary told me his role would be very different to Waterman's rough and ready Terry, as his character Ray had O-level French and read *The Independent*. Our story was good publicity for Gary in his first big break and he went on to film the series until 1994 when it ended. Probably not my finest moment though.

I first heard the phrase 'papped' when I and a photographer door-stepped the home of *Big Brother* celebrity Nicki Grahame in Northwood. Door-stepping, you will remember, is calling on someone unannounced, usually at their home. I was amused when we were later phoned by the company responsible for the reality show, accusing us of 'papping' Nicki's mother. This means grabbing a quick shot in the style of the paparazzi. It was not so funny, however, in the story I mentioned earlier when I joined the press pack on the Sunday that Princess Diana's body was flown back to RAF Northolt. Although we were only doing a job we were all bundled together as killers and were shouted and sworn at by the huge crowd that had gathered.

Victim Support

Victim Support (VS) was a relatively new service when in 1992 I wrote a piece about its work in Hillingdon. The scheme, which was set up to help people affected by crime, began with a pilot project in Bristol in 1976 and took off in Uxbridge ten years later. I discovered that the volunteers were made up of a wide range of people, from students and working people to the retired and parents at home with young children.

In spite of dealing with some harrowing cases over a large area from Harrow to Hayes they were a cheerful bunch of people. At that time, there were twenty-three volunteers based at the Uxbridge office with fourteen more being trained. Sometimes they had been victims themselves.

I spoke to Alan (not his real name) who had been the victim of a violent attack that left him physically and mentally scarred. The pain he suffered from horrific injuries was followed by post-traumatic stress disorder. Because of the help he had from VS he was then counselling others suffering in a similar way.

Alan told me: 'I had to have more than 200 stitches in my face after I was attacked on my way home by a stranger with a knife. I was in hospital for two days and had micro-surgery. I thought, why me? There was no reason for the attack. I became withdrawn and wouldn't go out. I didn't want anyone to see me and only allowed two very close friends to call. I slept in the day and was awake at night. When I went to my GP I waited in my car until everyone had left the surgery before I'd go in. I was approached by VS but I thought who the hell are they? How can they help me?

'I was on the verge of a breakdown, and was offered help by a psychiatric nurse, who did me no good at all because he couldn't relate to me. The volunteer persevered and I realised I needed their help. They brought me out of it, along with my supportive wife and family. Over eight months I built up a relationship with my counsellor and eventually became a volunteer myself. I now usually deal with victims of violent crime. I used to be shy but the experience has helped me grow.'

So, how did volunteers find victims who needed help? VS co-ordinators visited Uxbridge police station three times a week where they were given the names of victims from police crime report books. For sufferers of rape, and relatives of murdered people, the names were not given out automatically – police would ask permission first. If they refused, the victims would be told the service was available, should they need it later.

At the office VS would look at the list of referrals, and they would decide how to deal with each case: a phone call, letter, or maybe a visit. Victims would be offered practical help and advice, as well as a listening ear.

Some victims were physically frightened to go out because they had been burgled, or because they were attacked or mugged while out. The counsellors might take them out – just a little way at a time – to rebuild their shattered confidence. Practical assistance could also include making insurance claims and getting windows or door frames replaced.

Anyone wanting to become a volunteer would find references strictly followed up because of the confidential nature of the task. There was also an interview with a senior police officer.

Training included all aspects of crime, and skills such as how to interview on the telephone. A visit to the police station to see how things operated was an essential part of training.

New volunteers were encouraged to start with less complicated cases such as burglary, theft or criminal damage, and there was plenty of support for them from experienced members.

Volunteers from Victim Support sometimes contacted the paper if they had worries about how people were being treated by us in our write-ups. Sometimes they would help us with a story. When a new suite at Hillingdon Hospital was to be opened for rape victims in 1992 I was invited to interview a VS volunteer, medical staff, police, and a recent victim of rape, which you can read about later.

It is the human interest stories that I have enjoyed writing the most, although 'enjoyed' wasn't always appropriate. It was hard to knock on the door of people who have lost a child, but it is surprising how many welcomed the chance of a sympathetic ear from outside the family. One story that has stayed with me (which appears later in the book) is the heart-breaking plight of an elderly lady who was wrongly accused of shoplifting, and how satisfying it was for us when we eventually got Tesco to acknowledge this.

It is always good when a local newspaper can be of help to individuals, or by highlighting concerns in the community. My time on the *Gazette* included plenty of these, but there have also been animal stories, celebrity interviews and some fascinating political anecdotes. These included the Uxbridge by-election of 1997, when all the big names descended on our borough, from the newly elected Tony Blair to Screaming Lord Sutch of the Monster Raving Loony Party.

Oh, and two incidents – a delightful interview with Sir John Mills and an awkward encounter with Alan Sugar – which taught me the value of good research before doing an interview. In this chapter I have just 'teased' some stories which I will expand on later. A bit like a film trailer.

But I hope the message has come over loud and clear that being on a local paper was never dull. We had no inkling about what the editor was going to throw at us, who was going to walk into reception and ask to see a reporter, or what the next telephone call would bring.

6

Lunch with the Queen and a Royal Garden Party

I've been lucky to have twice had lunch with the Queen. Bizarrely, the first time, we were the only two women on a table of nine. The Queen and Duke of Edinburgh were in Uxbridge to unveil a statue outside the Underground station as part of the Golden Jubilee celebrations in 2002 and my invitation came from the leader of Hillingdon Council, Councillor Ray Puddifoot, who'd phoned to say he'd like to nominate me for 'a special role for the Queen's Jubilee celebrations'.

The letter that followed was a real (pleasant) shock. It said I was to be part of a 'select civic group of eight to represent a cross-section of people who have contributed to the fabric of the Hillingdon community over the years'. This had a Shirley Bassey/ lifetime achievement ring to it, but I was more than happy to join the ranks of those who had hung around for ages. At this point I'd been a reporter at the *Gazette* for thirteen years and I'd discovered a real love for local papers.

Things moved pretty quickly after that. After providing my security details – passports and whatnot – the Royal Rules arrived through the post. This is what the blurb – standard notes for 'those seeking guidance on forms of address and protocol' – said:

- It is important that those meeting members of the Royal Family should feel relaxed rather than be flustered or worried by precise details of etiquette.
- Those presented to The Queen or The Duke of Edinburgh may wish to drop their head on to their chest (which counts as a bow for gentlemen) or curtsey (ladies).
- When addressing The Queen, it is usual, for the first time, to address her as Your Majesty and thereafter as Ma'am (rhyming with jam).

I briefly stressed about the curtsey which, to be honest, I'd had little use for since I had a dressing-up box and pranced about in my mother's high heels. Unlike Cherie Blair and others, I had no problem with giving it a go. I just regarded it as part of our history, sense of ceremony; thoughts of humiliating deference and peasantry did not come into it. And I love all things theatrical.

The day – June 25 – arrived and my group prepared for a strict 10am start by minibus from Uxbridge cricket ground. Officials wanted to make sure we got there before the Queen arrived. My fellow lunch guests were a mixture of local politicians and business people, and a headteacher: all men. One of them, Councillor Richard Barnes, a former GLA member for Ealing-Hillingdon, was then deputy to London mayor Boris Johnson.

As I boarded our minibus, I thought about my colleagues: the reporters and photographers who would be covering the Queen's programme in Uxbridge town, while I enjoyed my lunch. Though a weekly newspaper, this was a Tuesday – our deadline day – and I knew they'd be up against it. My boss had happily given me his blessing to go though – no editor will pass on the chance of an insider view of a Royal occasion. But I also knew they'd be a reporter short. I'd have to have my wits about me (not too much alcohol) and return promptly to the office in order to write up an account of the lunch. It wasn't only my experience which had to be put into words; there were also specially-invited residents from the West London boroughs who were having picnics in the grounds. The Hillingdon ones would need to be interviewed before I left.

As I left Uxbridge, reporters were getting ready to cover the Queen's walkabout in the town centre. After meeting the Mayor of Hillingdon Councillor Josephine Barrett, and members of Hillingdon Borough Council, the royal couple were to mingle with well-wishers and chat to pupils from local schools, who would show them their art projects. Photographers would capture the Queen unveiling a new bronze sculpture entitled 'Anticipation' following a fanfare from RAF Uxbridge trumpeters. Five hundred purple and yellow balloons were to be released from a net to reveal – hey presto – the sculpture of a young woman with two children and a dog. The bronze statue, called Anticipation, was commissioned by the Hillingdon Arts Association and is still, I'm glad to say, outside Uxbridge Underground station. Occasionally it is added to by passers-by, but these embellishments are hastily removed. Once, I saw the statue wearing a tatty pair of trainers and a baseball cap. These additions are good-humoured and the sculpture has become a popular meeting place and a respected addition to the town centre.

At Gunnersbury Park, where The Queen and The Duke of Edinburgh were due to join us, schoolchildren from the four boroughs of Ealing, Hammersmith & Fulham, Hillingdon and Hounslow were gathering in the grounds where they would celebrate with song and dance and picnics.

Many people think that because journalists have press cards we can automatically cover royal events. But it is not always possible to allow all media to be there for space and security reasons, so a pool system called the Royal Rota operates. Where several newspapers are being published for one area, there is an agreement that the one that gets permission to attend must supply prints – now electronic transfers – to their rivals. This is unimaginable under normal circumstances, where newspapers try to outdo each other by providing superior spreads.

But this time I was a guest, with no copy to be shared. And strictly no photographer, as it was a private lunch. Our group, the Hillingdon Eight – part of a 60-strong party from the four West London boroughs – were the first to arrive at Gunnersbury House. We happily sipped sparkling English wine on the terrace in hot sun while waiting for the others to appear. After a while I decided to slip into the cool darkness of the house, stepping straight into a room where several large, round tables, were laid out for lunch. Intriguingly there was no top table but, as there were place names, I decided to have a sneaky look at who was going to sit where.

That was when I discovered I was to be on a table of nine, seated bang opposite the Queen, with only a very large table decoration and a small handful of men either side of us.

Eventually we were joined by those invited from the other West London boroughs and were guided to our tables where we stood behind our chairs, as silent as the guardsmen outside Buckingham Palace, waiting for the Royals to join us. Prince Philip came in holding a glass of beer and went to his table while the Queen settled at ours.

Being directly opposite her, our eyes naturally met, but, as I had studied the rules I knew I shouldn't yell across the table, which was very frustrating. I followed her example and concentrated on chatting to the two men sitting on either side of me. To my left was Colonel Clark, who had a long involvement with West London YMCA and the Scouts, and David Parkin, manager of West London Waitrose, sat on my right. His staff – shop assistants, cashiers, and drivers – were working as waiters for the lunch. They were naturally very nervous, particularly when they served our table and I found myself unable to stop some seriously manic smiling, which I hoped showed solidarity.

By contrast the Queen was very relaxed, and was giving her attention to Lord Rothschild, and the Mayor of Ealing, Cllr Kieron

Gavan, who flanked her. She was surprisingly informal, eating and chatting, glancing up occasionally and very at ease. I started to relax. At times, odd bits of conversation floated over, and she made a remark to all of us about how impressed she was with her 'quite extraordinary' jubilee weekend when practically the whole country took over her garden at Buckingham Palace. Would you like to do it again someone asked? 'Not in my garden,' she joked. She was also amused when someone cheekily asked whether she worried about cutting someone when she knighted them, and she laughed as she did a little swish through the air with an imaginary sword.

The menu was delicious: vegetable terrine, salmon steak with a light herb sauce, ratatouille, salad nicoise and opera gateau. I felt the shape of the camera in my bag. Taking photographs at these informal events is strictly not allowed but oh, how I'd have loved to have got a shot. It wasn't worth getting evicted before I'd even eaten a mouthful, so I decided to tackle the cutlery problem instead. I know that at formal meals you start using cutlery from the outside, and work your way in. The snob value of using the right things in the correct order didn't bother me at all, but I was worried I might be left with a spoon to eat salad, or a fork to stir my coffee if I didn't pay attention.

Hovering casually over the outermost knife and fork, ready to eat the terrine, I watched the Queen closely to see what she did, and was delighted when she picked up her fork in her right hand, ready to eat it American style. I was particularly pleased that she didn't, as is generally thought, pick bird-like at her food and leave most of it on her plate. The Queen clearly enjoyed her meal and tucked in like the rest of us. While pretending to admire the leafy arrangement in the middle of the table, I took a few crafty looks at the Queen. Random thoughts jumped into my head such as, 'Why had she chosen that particular lipstick (pinkish) to go with her outfit (gold)?'.

It was then that 'the incident' happened. One of the nervous youngsters who were waiting on us knocked over an enormous, free-standing bucket of ice which crashed to the ground, right next to our table. The shock immediately silenced the room. Everyone stopped eating. Security men braced themselves, while those of us nearest to the disaster tried to pretend we were not disappearing under a tsunami of ice cubes.

The Queen, clearly unfazed and not a bit worried the big bang might herald a serious security incident, deliberately turned her attention away from the scene of the crime and, as if nothing had happened, continued chatting to the Mayor of Ealing. A big communal sigh went up, eating began again in earnest and, thank goodness, someone came to rescue my feet, and those of my nearest dining companions, from the icy flood.

The moment I raised my glass at the end of the meal is the one I'll always remember. Like many people I am used to doing this at formal dinners, but I couldn't quite get my head round the fact that as I said 'The Queen' and looked across the table, there she was in the flesh – and, head cocked on one side, cheerfully smiling back. After this the Royals left, with the Duke of Edinburgh moaning jovially that wherever they went he never ever got a coffee to finish his meal. The Loyal Toast, which always preceded it, was his cue to follow the Queen out, so the caffeine course was constantly out of his reach.

I learned later that after her lunch the Queen sent a message to the kitchen to tell the helpers not to worry about Ice Gate. She stressed it didn't matter and it didn't spoil anything. I wonder how many so-called celebrities would be that gracious.

***

People often ask me where I get ideas for my weekly column. They can be current affairs or family incidents, but frequently are from reading small snippets in newspapers, which I cut out and keep. For instance, I spotted a little gem that Windsor Castle had adopted duvets for its visitors and ditched the old-fashioned sheets and eiderdowns. The 'well-placed source' said our sovereign still prefers to be 'tucked in nice and comfy' and at 90, I thought, why shouldn't she? This led me to remembering my first experience of duvets, learning to do hospital corners as a Butlins chalet maid, then off at a complete tangent with patchwork quilts and early frozen food, resulting in this column:

Bm@il 11.05.2016

Her Majesty apparently likes the feel of a 'well-made bed', and I'd also like to think she is not averse to a hot water bottle when her toes get chilly. I couldn't wait to get rid of sheets and blankets. As a child I remember them sliding off as I slept or becoming so tangled up in them I was in danger of being mummified before I could kick myself free.

The day after I left school, I and two friends, Veronica and Jean, left for Skegness to work at Butlin's Holiday Camp for nine weeks – the whole of the summer holiday. We were chalet maids – as students, you got the unglamorous jobs – and on our first day, decked in droopy green overalls, we were taught how to do hospital corners with old-fashioned sheets. Our very strict supervisor Mrs Eyles (like Peggy's Miss Cathcart in *Hi-di-Hi*) must, I think, have been a hospital matron in a previous life.

My first experience of what were then called 'continental quilts' was on holiday in Austria with my parents in the 1960s, and we thought them exotic, on a par with eating rolls and jam for breakfast and venison for dinner. At home in England we were getting pretty daring, though. The new fish fingers had been invented and peas, out of their pods, were frozen in bags.

As we didn't have a fridge, and freezers were unheard of, they were put in the coldest room in the house – the bathroom – before being eaten pretty smartish.

We readily acknowledge the existence of comfort food (my favourite soother is still Heinz tomato soup), so we should understand the Queen's reluctance to leave her nest of blankets.

I am not a knitter or a sewer – I used to get sent out of needlework lessons for talking – but when Fisher Junior was born I proudly presented her with a patchwork blanket for her cot.

It was just a few knitted squares sewn together and far removed from the ancient art of quilting, but was a real labour of love.

Maybe I'll make one for a birthday present for Her Majesty… if she can hang on until her 100th.

Royal Garden Party, Buckingham Palace, May 23 2017

I had no inkling when I wrote the above column that I would be in the company of the Queen again, a year later. Well, that's a bit of an exaggeration, as this time I wasn't close up and personal with her, but I did chat briefly to other members of her family.

My friend Val Ross nominated Mike and I to attend a Royal Garden Party at Buckingham Palace. Of course, they get thousands – maybe millions – of names put forward for the three parties held in the grounds each year, so I never imagined we'd be chosen from all those nominations.

The letter from the Lord-Lieutenant of Greater London, Kenneth Olisa OBE, sent in December 2016 didn't sound too hopeful, saying 'As you may appreciate, there are a large number of worthy people considered for nomination and invitation from the population of over eight million, and as the quota for Greater London is relatively small, it is not always possible to grant everyone's request.'

We would not hear any more if we had not been chosen, so we were very surprised to hear shortly afterwards that we were. We had three dates to choose from in May and June 2017, and had to return our acceptance, along with a form filled in with our personal details. But then we would hear no more until three or four weeks before the date of our Garden Party.

Val and I met more than 20 years ago when she was covering community activities, and was at the time both Head of Community Affairs at Hasbro, the toy manufacturer based in Stockley Park, and Director of Hillingdon Partnership Trust whose aim was to persuade local companies to be more active in their community.

As Val told the *Gazette*, 'In these early days of our friendship we used to think that between us we knew all the movers and shakers in Hillingdon! When I went to Zambia for two years with Voluntary Service Overseas Barbara even wrote about my experiences there.'

In case you're wondering 'why me?' I don't blame you. I was aware that friends were itching to ask the same question, but didn't like to, and I know I was not doing much more than many people, who would also have qualified for a yummy tea at the palace.

This incidentally turned out to be a mixture of dainty, crustless sandwiches – cucumber and mint; gammon, mustard and vine tomatoes, and egg mayonnaise – as well as lemon tarts and fruit cake. And plenty of tea to drink of course.

Val had described my varied background in the local community from teaching to journalism. She mentioned good old Bm@il which has built up a loyal following over ten years, and added to the mix some (modest) voluntary work for children's centres in Hayes, Uxbridge College, and as a member of Hillingdon Hospital's Major Incident Casualty Support Team.

Maybe it was because she mentioned me being made an honorary fellow at Brunel University in 2005 and doing a Master's Degree in Creative and Professional Writing there in 2012 that swung it? Or perhaps the Lord-Lieutenant of Greater London (who decides who attends from our area) liked the fact that I'd helped Phyllis Whitsell with her best-selling memoir which was published in February 2016 and became a *Sunday Times* bestseller?

This was of course Phyllis's achievement, but they may have

thought that the fact that the idea for her book was hatched after we met, when she was a nurse looking after my mother who had Alzheimer's, was interesting and unusual.

So… I hadn't done anything earthshattering – I just got involved in the community like many other people. I've always enjoyed being embedded in Hillingdon, but let's face it, I hadn't tried to prevent disease with gene therapy, or made steps towards World Peace.

But it was nice to be put forward and eventually Mike agreed it was too, and, once we received a second letter to say we'd been chosen, we set about getting our outfits sorted.

A morning suit arrived a few days later. I could see it would do very nicely, although if I'm honest, Mike modelling it for me bare-chested, unshaved (well, beard untrimmed), and before breakfast, didn't really have the desired effect.

The day came – May 23 – and he looked grand, but any feeling of excitement went on hold when we woke up to the terrible news of the Manchester Arena bombing in which twenty-three adults and children were killed and 250 injured. Salman Abedi had planted the bomb, packed with nuts and bolts, to explode after an Ariana Grande concert. It was the worst attack in the UK since the July 7 London bombings in 2005.

Clearly the Queen was affected too, so our garden party began with a minute's silence for the victims and their families.

This was my write-up in the *Gazette*, with a few additions:

I decided against wearing a fascinator for the Royal Garden Party last week, but luckily, I'd also bought a hat. Rehearsing my outfit a few days before the big event, I rammed the grey organza on to my head and peered into the mirror.

I looked like a Spanish donkey, but without my ears sticking out of the top.

Trying out various jaunty angles, it was ages before I could get it right. This was not helped by Mike saying 'It will do' several times before realising a successful conclusion could only be reached by enthusiasm on his part.

It was spitting rain as we set off from Uxbridge. Neighbour Sue popped out to take a few snaps of us standing stiffly in our finery, including Mike trussed up in a morning suit and practising his best behaviour.

Arriving at the gardens at Buckingham Palace we found it was all very relaxed. After a glass of lemon barley water (no alcohol on offer!), we sat next to a couple from Durham, with whom we spent most of the afternoon. We enjoyed a good chat, then, at 4pm sharp, the Royal Family appeared.

We had been forewarned that there would immediately be a minute's silence led by the Queen and Duke of Edinburgh for the victims of the Manchester terrorist attack, which had only happened a few hours before, and it was moving to see people of so many different nationalities paying their respects. You could see from their body language that the Queen and Prince Phillip were very moved by the tragedy which had taken the lives of so many children and young people. It was a solemn start, but wholly appropriate as everyone there was talking about the terrorist attack.

The members of the Royal Family – The Queen, Duke of Edinburgh, Prince Charles and the Duchess of Cornwall, and Princess Eugenie – then made it clear that it was business as usual, as they talked to people in the crowd.

After the silence, as if on cue, the sun came out, giving us more chance to study the guests who had been invited to the garden party for contributing in some way to their community. Their outfits – from kimonos, saris and kilts, to all manner of uniforms and chains of office – were just as diverse as their reasons for being there. Our instructions for the day said that we were allowed to take photographs, unlike my lunch with the Queen fifteen years earlier, but at a respectful distance. No problem with that; in fact I was glad that they wouldn't have people clustering around for selfies, blocking everyone's view.

My new chum Diane and I moved around the crowds, while her husband John, a Durham councillor, and Mike, stayed rooted to their chairs and ate ice creams.

We got fairly close to Charles and Camilla, then to my surprise a member of palace staff in top hat and tails asked my and Diane's names, and why we were there, in order to introduce us to Princess Eugenie.

Suddenly Prince Andrew appeared from nowhere. (I later discovered he had just returned from China and joined the party late.) I was just about to get a sneaky picture of him when he spotted me.

He laughed and pointed at my camera and called, 'Now, I don't want to talk to a bank of cameras – put it down and come and talk to me.'

I said we were in line to meet his daughter (we had been asked not to move). He said: 'You don't want to talk to her,' and joked about speaking to him instead. He didn't seem bothered about waiting for formal introductions.

We were called over then to speak to Eugenie. She was fun and easy, and talked to Diane about her time at university up north. Asked if she enjoyed the nightlife, she said it was 'terrible' and rolled her eyes, clearly meaning the opposite.

The band of the Coldstream Guards were playing as we left, my hat still welded to my head, my feet killing me. As our new friends set off for the North we headed for home via a bar and a cold glass of wine in Victoria. Lovely.

7

A Right Carry On
– tales of Pinewood and Elstree

Good local contacts can lead to all sorts of things but I did pinch myself to the point of bruising when I found myself, in 1993, dining at Pinewood Studios. I had just missed Tom Cruise by a few days, but on the next table was film director David Puttnam, famous for classics like *Chariots of Fire*. Behind him sat Bryan Brown of *The Thorn Birds* fame. You may remember the TV series *Thorn Birds*, with Richard Chamberlain as a transgressing priest who had the hots (for a woman). This was in the days when we were so gullible we didn't realise that some clergy had their own rules of sexual behaviour. The flouting of celibacy was outrageous: so shocking in fact we were all glued to our screens.

My visit to Pinewood was thanks to Audrey Skinner, who was well known in amateur dramatic circles in the borough, but whose day job was at the famous studios, where she spent more than twenty years. At the time of my visit Audrey had worked for Peter Rogers, producer of 31 Carry On films, and Gerald Thomas, director of the Carry Ons, for at least a decade. Audrey told me that for many years she fondly referred to her bosses, who had become masters of the double entendre as 'my two gentlemen'. (I could almost hear Sid James haw-hawing at this.)

Audrey's first job however was at Pinewood in 1972, when she worked for the video company Zoom Television. 'I loved it here straight away,' she said, as we chatted over lunch. 'At first my eyes were everywhere. I was star-struck!' She remembered the heyday at the studios when stars like Sir Laurence Olivier, described as 'very unassuming', filled the restaurant.

However, there were often plenty of up-and-coming starlets – perhaps like some of today's reality stars – who were 'less than modest', said Audrey.

Carry On films were still being made regularly when Audrey arrived. She remembers seeing Joan Sims filming with Kenneth Williams on the set of *Carry on Dick*. Not arthouse maybe, but with characters like Reverend Flasher and Sergeant Jock Strapp, it was clearly great fun. Audrey said, 'I remember a scene where Joan Sims was about to walk down the stairs to Kenneth Williams, but they both kept bursting out laughing. They all knew each other so well, it was like a family. They would come into lunch laughing, laugh all through lunch, and leave laughing.'

Audrey, and her husband Michael, who were known locally for their appearances with amateur groups like the Phoenix Theatre Company and Theatre 7, couldn't have guessed that their love of acting would one day lead to them appearing in *The Great Gatsby* film with Robert Redford and Mia Farrow. It was shot at Pinewood in 1972 and their lucky break came as a result of a few bad hair days for the studios. Short styles were the Gatsby requirement, perfect for the elfin-faced Farrow, but it posed a problem when casting everybody else. Audrey explained, 'It was hard for them to get extras because big hair was in fashion. People didn't want to cut their locks for the film, so amateur companies were called in to help.'

After 12 years, Rank took over Zoom, staff were redundant and Audrey's time at Pinewood came to a sudden end. She filled her time doing temporary work, but said she 'pined for

Pinewood'. In 1984, she applied to work for the studios again, this time for the two Carry On giants who became her 'two gentlemen'. It was a bumper year for Pinewood, with a strange mixture of films on the boil: the James Bond film, *A View to a Kill*; *Steaming*; *Santa Claus*; and *Supergirl*. Actually, if you put them all together they sound like they could well have been a plot for a Carry On film.

During filming, Audrey would go on to the set in the morning to take director Gerald Thomas's mail to him. In between shots, he would dictate the answers to her. She would go back to her office, type up the replies, and then return with the letters in the afternoon to get them signed. Imagine, all in a day's work stumbling on a scene from a Carry On – seeing Hattie Jacques or Jim Dale doing their bit.

This letter-writing routine, which involved trotting backwards and forwards to the Carry On set, was a labour of love for Audrey, who revelled in seeing the action. She said: 'The novelty never wore off. Seeing how films were made could have taken away the illusion, but it never spoilt it for me. In the early days when they were setting up lights, I would day-dream and wish it was for me. I'd love to have been in a Carry On film.'

It is difficult to remember now, when more or less anything goes, how risqué these films were considered. With their nudge-nudge jokes and sexual shenanigans they were thought very daring, but watching them now, they seem so innocent. Particularly when compared to what children are exposed to every day on social media.

Our grown-up daughter says that she learnt much of her history from the Carry Ons: the French Revolution in *Carry On – Don't Lose Your Head*, the Roman Empire in *Carry on Cleo*, and the British Raj in *Carry On Up the Khyber*. A couple of years ago I found myself sitting next to Sid James's daughter, so I told her about our daughter's Carry On history lessons. Sue James, who was then working at Pinewood herself, laughed and said that her mother and the rest of the family would be most amused to hear that Sid had contributed to the education of the country's youth.

At the *Gazette*, we were lucky that Pinewood Studios were only ten minutes away from the Uxbridge office, and in 1994 I got another chance to cover a story there. I was to join a South Bank crew who were making a documentary about Kenneth Williams.

I arrived on a bright sunny carry-on sort of day where filming was beginning on a programme about the late star. The South Bank show was about to immortalise the man with the flared nostrils and camp voice who – like the films – became a British institution. Kenneth took part in 25 of the films, starting with *Carry on Sergeant*, and was one of the main figures associated with the comic cuts. The crew from South Bank wanted to dissect him for TV and they were on a tight schedule. Melvyn Bragg was due to arrive in the afternoon to interview Barbara Windsor, but the morning's business had to be wrapped up first.

I was led into the office of Peter Rogers, the producer of thirty-one Carry On films, who sat at his desk in his luxurious suite of offices at Pinewood, ready to be interviewed 'to camera' about the late star. Told to make myself scarce by sitting in the corner during filming, I was instructed not to move, or 'rustle' my notepad as they filmed. The big boss surprised me at first by saying said that he didn't miss Kenneth. However, he then explained that this was because he felt he was 'still there'. He had clearly been very fond of his star and Kenneth had called Mr Rogers 'the loveliest of all bosses'.

Barbara Windsor, Kenneth Williams and Kenneth Connor were the real professionals he said. 'They were line perfect. You didn't have to tell them anything.' Asked whether Kenneth Williams might have preferred a career as a serious actor, he replied: 'I don't think he would have wanted it. He loved fun. It was wonderful to see his ad libs.'

Did he feel there was a magic formula in the phenomenal success of the Carry On films? 'They're all alike, but there's no formula. It's 31 films out of one gag. The success is all in the script – give the writers their due,' he said. Was Kenneth Williams a comedian? 'I wouldn't call him that. I think of comedians being like Max Miller. He played camp, without being camp, as did Charles Hawtrey and Frankie Howerd,' said Mr Rogers. (Really? I was seriously in danger of rustling at this point.)

Mr Rogers revealed that after *Carry on Nurse* he had suggested pegging fees and giving performers a percentage of the profits, but they turned it down. With the huge success of the films how they must eventually have regretted it. It was only Kenneth Williams who said later they had made the wrong decision, admitted Mr Rogers.

He revealed he was shocked by the death of Williams, whom he described as 'a voice rather than a person', and to this day it still has a question mark hanging over it. Williams died on April 15 1988 from an overdose of barbiturates and an inquest recorded an open verdict as it was not possible to decide whether his death was suicide or an accident.

Clearly moved, Mr Rogers said he didn't think he took his own life. 'I didn't understand it. I think it was an accident. It's not the sort of thing he would do. He was an introspective, lovely person who wanted to be wanted.'

As the interview ended, Barbara Windsor came out of make-up, all set to totter on her high heels to the front of Pinewood's main building. Earlier, when I arrived, she had been sitting with her hair in giant rollers, but had flashed a bright greeting as we passed. She was tiny, but made up for this in speed; in fact, I had a job keeping up with her as she wiggled along on millions of little steps. She asked me anxiously 'Do you think me skirt's too short, darlin?'. They had wanted her to wear a shorter one but she had declined. 'It's naff, innit?' she laughed, with her familiar throaty giggle. As we wound our way through the corridors of Pinewood to the Rolls Royce where she was to be filmed with Peter Rogers for the South Bank documentary, she confided: 'Kenneth was very special. He chose you as a friend, rather than the other way around. I was one of four women friends whom he kept apart and we didn't all meet up until his funeral. He wined and dined on us,' she laughed.

In 1995, I paid a final visit to Pinewood Studios to a photo call with Norman Wisdom. It was 25 years since he had last filmed at the studios and was revelling in being the focus of press photographers and television cameras. The funny man of early British films was very happy to oblige the media pack, which had him climbing, running and squatting on the ground with the inevitable bunch of leggy young women. Goodness knows what they made of him. He took a child-like pleasure in the attention and was positively hyperactive, jumping about and pulling faces. The eighty-year old told me he had so many happy memories of filming at Pinewood, 'It is very exciting to be here. I've been here quite a few times before and have been back to say hello to a few people, but I'm really looking forward to starting the new film.'

The funny man in the ill-fitting suit had been a household name for more than 40 years. His first Royal Variety Performance was in 1952 and since then he had been chosen for eight more shows in front of royalty. It was at Pinewood that he made films such as *A Stitch in Time*, *The Square Peg* and *The Bulldog Breed*. His new film was an adaptation of JB Priestley's Adam And Evil. I'd never been a fan of slapstick, or of Norman's frenetic brand of comedy, but his enthusiasm was so infectious I found myself warming to him. Rather like a Labrador winning over someone with a preference for cats. He told me: 'In the film I play an elderly man who has no friends and lives in one room by himself. He has never had a lady friend and wants one before he dies. He finds a way, through Chinese mythology. There is drama, pathos and a lot of comedy.' (Really?)

In the same year that I met him, the popular comedian had been awarded an OBE and the freedom of the City of London. 'Apparently it means I can park anywhere I like but knowing my luck, I'll be clamped!' he said. The diminutive Londoner – he was only 4ft 10ins – who ended his days in the Isle of Man in 2010 aged 95, told me he had been amused to find he was a big star in Albania. His films were the only ones with western actors that dictator Enver Hoxha allowed to be shown. Norman told me that thanks to 'the universal language of music and comedy' he had no problems communicating with the children when he visited a local hospital there. 'I sang I'm Forever Blowing Bubbles, and they all blew bubbles back to me,' he laughed. Better than raspberries, I suppose.

Through another local contact – a BBC journalist – I once visited Elstree Studios, which were then home to an unlikely mixture of BBC programmes and projects. In the 1990s, you could find suited men and women on BBC management courses rubbing shoulders with hard-pressed journalists writing and editing stories for Newsroom South East (NSE). In the centre was Albert Square, home to long-running soap, *EastEnders*.

I arrived in time to join the busy Newsroom South East team, who were wrapping their items for the 6.35pm bulletin. Tim Ewart, who went on to become Royal Correspondent for ITV News, was then writing links for the stories which he would be reading to camera later with Gargy Patel. Broadcasting regularly to viewers had made him a familiar face; many would recognise him from his days at ITN where he was foreign correspondent for three years.

After jobs on local papers in Bury and Leicester, he moved to an enviable position at the *Bermuda Sun*. The World Service at Bush House followed, then a stint as a BBC television reporter in Leeds. A year with Thames TV, then a spell at ITN led him to being in the hot seat at Newsroom South East.

He said: 'When they hired me, they wanted someone who had done the writing as well as presenting. When you are a reporter you think presenting is easy, that you don't have to get wet, messy or in dangerous situations. I thought it would be a doddle, but presenting is not as easy as it looks. Live interviews can be difficult as they are rarely longer than two minutes. I have worked out that one and a half minutes is only one hundred and eighty words. Not very long for a politician to answer a question!'

Instructions from the gallery in your ear while you are interviewing and keeping your eye on the autocue would unnerve most of us. To add to this pressure, he said there were always eagle-eyed viewers ready to pounce on the slightest lapses of grammar or pronunciation.

Touring the news area, I met graphic artists and reporters putting finishing touches to filmed reports – that night it was a football clash and a sale of costumes from the Royal Opera House. A Ruislip man (and *Gazette* reader) was in charge of the gallery as the seconds were counted down to the beginning of NSE. Fascinated, I watched as the programme went out live to around a million homes.

Leaving the huge Elstree complex, I spotted enormous crates marked with labels like 'David and Cindy's house' or 'Queen Vic attic'. What appeared to be old collections of wood and pieces of wallpaper were parts of the different sets for the cockney soap. I'd stumbled on a bit, or bits, of *EastEnders*.

***

Finding extraordinary people in unexpected places gives you a huge buzz, and one of my favourite discoveries was found at our local Uxbridge Further Education college. Hugh Stewart had worked as an editor and producer with directors like Alexander Korda and Robert Boulting, and in his eighties, he was still teaching.

Hugh invited me to his home in Denham where he told me how much he enjoyed occasionally taking English classes at the college. Lucky students, I thought, to be taught by someone from the film world. Actually, we did have a tutor at my college in the Midlands who was the sister of the famous actor Donald Sinden.

She taught drama and was always addressed by her surname as grown-ups didn't have first names in those days. Starting an MA at Brunel in 2009, I discovered that all tutors – including icons like Fay Weldon who taught on our creative writing course – are now always addressed by students in chummy first-name terms. Miss Sinden would never have stood for that!

Hugh (why not take liberties now, though he was still 'Mr Stewart' in 1997) had a degree in English literature from Cambridge. He had seen real drama, filming scenes from World War Two for the War Office. Taking film of a real war was naturally fraught with problems, including personal safety. 'We just had a couple of photographers, cameras which were not very good, "stills men" (usually from newspapers) and cine men. We needed long shots to establish where we were, and then close-ups were needed, followed by the main shots in the heat of battle.'

'In battle, you can't say "take two". It's easy, of course, to fake something, but I took the view you can't. You have to get the real stuff to make sense. However, you can't think of your own safety; you are not protected by a camera.'

Hugh was in the War Office for a while, and then he worked at Pinewood Studios where he was in the RAF film unit. He filmed war scenes in France and North Africa, and he was very proud of the stills used on stamps to commemorate the Normandy Landings, which were taken by Mr Stewart's crew. 'I could look at all the stamps and say which of my blokes shot them,' he told me, absolutely bursting with pride.

His film career was soon established, working for MGM, then Rank, at Pinewood, where he stayed until 1967. Married with four children, he got most of his work after being an editor for Alfred Hitchcock. He said he was 'wonderful' to work with. 'Everything was perfect. You knew exactly what to do. I got my jobs on the basis that I had cut for Hitchcock. He was such a master.'

As the film industry slumped Hugh turned to teaching, but he still had a link with showbiz – Sir John Mills was a near neighbour and he helped him with his scripts. The famous actor was having trouble with failing sight so Hugh helped him learn his lines. He told me he had recently joined a Mills family play-reading.

'Sir John's wife, Mary, wrote a play Duet for Two Hands which they planned to be directed by Sir John, with his older daughter Juliet, and her daughter Melissa, playing parts in it. They were doing a reading but were short of one part, a surgeon, so I went along and read it,' he said.

Hugh died in 2011 aged 100, outliving Sir John by six years.

8

Airport Tales

There was great excitement when a potentially massive story filtered in, just as we were putting the finishing touches to the *Gazette* for the week. It was one of those moments you plan for in theory but you know is unlikely to happen in practice – an aeroplane crash would be unusual enough, but on deadline…

It may sound a leisurely life working for a weekly paper but there are still daily deadlines, fewer staff, and a smaller pool from which to find our stories, and in all of my 20 years I found the job pretty full-on. Local people feel very passionately about their area so everything that concerned them, from dog poo on the pavement to the future of the borough's schools, needed close attention. Reporters covered most council meetings, numerous residents' gatherings and yes, summer fetes, which often meant evening and weekend work.

We were also expected to add colour to our stories by fitting in interviews with the people involved, as well as arranging for our photographers to call. For this we had to fill in forms and liaise with the snappers' huge diary which was kept next to the darkroom.

Sometimes a serious road accident or other drama would divert them from a planned job and we reporters would panic about finding a replacement picture for one of our pages. There was no email and no digital photography then, so everything by today's standards was ridiculously time-consuming.

When it came to deadline – midday on Tuesdays for reporters – we started to breathe a sigh of relief as the last pages (which were the front pages for four editions!) were done. Even though the sub-editors would be working into the afternoon to place our stories and write the headlines, we could start on the 'early' pages for the following week's paper. They were the pages at the back of the paper which contained the 'softer stuff' like leisure, theatre, Memory Lane and the Schools' Page.

But on this day, August 14 1996, something very big seemed to be breaking. We had several calls from local people about massive traffic jams in the area which led us to believe that there could be a big pile-up on the busy road into London. The A40 is an extension of the M40 from Birmingham. It soon became clear, after phoning police and listening to radio reports (there was no TV in the newsroom then, never mind the internet), that it was a plane crash, so it really was a case of 'Hold the Front Page'. The editor, Anthony Longden, cleared two other pages inside too, in case the stories were to extend to a big spread (it did).

The team at the office began feverishly ringing contacts and emergency services and I was dispatched by news editor Claire Bushell (now Moreton), to find the plane. This was not as easy as it sounds. I set off – we were then based in Ruislip – with scant information, just that a plane had landed on the A40. I didn't even know which end of the very long road to start, so I parked my car at the Polish War Memorial (which turned out to be the wrong end), slipped under the security tape and started the long trek down the ghostly, totally empty A40. With no plane in sight for miles, I was gradually joined by daily newspaper reporters and TV crews, many of them cutting across fields with their heavy camera equipment, none of them having any idea where the crash had actually happened.

The A40, or Western Avenue as it is also known, stretched for miles, and as it was a swelteringly hot day with no shade in sight, we were sweating and panting in unison. I remember the *Sun* reporter playing to type by saying 'Why don't you hitch up your skirt love, and tuck it in your knickers?' I demurred and continued to stride manfully on to … goodness knows where.

When we spotted the Learjet in the distance it really was an incredible sight. The plane had landed on top of a van and looked like a giant bird that had broken its neck as it landed.

Luckily mobile phones were by then in general use so we all rushed off with our notebooks to get briefings from the emergency services, phone in a description of the scene to our bosses, and to try and get a few eye-witness accounts from the crowds of residents who had gathered behind the police tape.

It turned out that the privately chartered plane from Palma, Majorca, carrying an actress Lisa Hogan (currently Jeremy Clarkson's girlfriend), was on its final approach to RAF Northolt when it overshot the runway and tore through the perimeter fence. Ms Hogan was on her way to Pinewood Studios where she was working on the film *Fierce Creatures*, with John Cleese.

The plane had crashed on to the road at about 9am, before breaking into pieces and starting to leak its fuel. If it had happened in the height of the rush hour the casualties could have been catastrophic.

A tipper truck driver saw the plane coming and got out of its way so was able to call 999, but the van behind him was not so fortunate. The driver, with the plane on his roof, was trapped for forty minutes while emergency crews fought to stabilise him before rushing him to Ealing Hospital. The pilot, who had bruising and cuts, the co-pilot, who suffered a fractured skull, and Ms Hogan, who was only slightly scratched, were all taken to Hillingdon Hospital. None had life-threatening injuries, to the astonishment of fire crews and police who repeatedly said it was a miracle no-one was killed.

We all often witness accidents – too many on motorways – but that day I realised more than ever how lucky we are to have such calm, capable emergency services. Everything clicks into place, from police, fire and medics, to – on this occasion – a pollution team from the Environment Agency. They arrived to mop up the fuel, oil and foam, before it leaked into nearby Yeading Brook, which runs to west of the airport and under the A40.

Wreckage from the crash was taken to Farnborough in Hampshire to the Aircraft Investigation Bureau for a full Inquiry.

There were many heroes that day, but we had our own: chief photographer Chris Berry, who got to the scene even before the emergency services arrived and was able to get fairly close to the plane. He remembers feeling nervous in case it should explode, but only three minutes after the crash he had taken dozens of pictures.

In many of the national paper stories there will obviously be stories which are of local interest too. Murderers, lottery winners, errant politicians, mothers of multiple births, Crufts champions, even reality stars, had to come from somewhere, and our readers expected to find more about them in their local paper.

When I started at the *Gazette* in 1989 quick reference websites were just a gleam in Mr Google's eye, so a reporter was assigned each morning to leaf through the broadsheets and tabloids to find the neighbourhood news. The main challenge was to discover these before the editor did. There was hell to pay if he or she leafed through the papers later and any had been missed.

Our West London borough of Hillingdon covers three parliamentary constituencies and 22 council wards so if we spotted a story about anyone from our area in the national papers, it would get the old pulse racing.

Local reporters had to complete a university degree before doing their training, which included being indentured at a local paper (a two-year programme followed by exams), so they came from all over the country and were not necessarily familiar with the area they were writing about. Those who were from the newspaper's catchment area would obviously have a big advantage. The rest of us – I was born, bred and educated in Birmingham but have now lived in Uxbridge for more than 30 years, and in Hillingdon borough for more than 40 years – had to learn quickly. I, of course, was also trying to catch up with the young trainees. They may have been novices but they were well ahead of me. Writing a schools' page for five years did not compare with being a real reporter. I soon realised how much the subs had improved my weekly offerings, including adjusting my copy to newspaper style.

Every paper had a style guide which included how people had to be addressed in our stories. At the *Gazette*, we used first (Christian) and surnames the first time they appeared, then Mr, Mrs or Miss was used for every other mention. So, for instance, I would be 'Barbara Fisher' the first time and 'Mrs Fisher' thereafter. It was practically a hanging offence not to get this right and although it was easy when it was a man's name, some women were a bit miffed to be questioned on their marital status. How outdated – and intrusive – it seems now. There were many heated discussions with readers when 'Ms' came into general use, as the editor would not bend the rules. The paper eventually conceded, and allowed its use, but adults wishing to be referred to by their first name throughout a story were not so lucky. One feisty contact (Noeline Ambrose) insisted, though – and eventually we had special permission to call her Noeline at all times.

One of my favourite stories, which was plucked from a national headline and proved to have enormous local interest, was that of the unlikely-sounding plane-spotting 'spies' held in Greece in November 2001.

The eleven men and one woman were arrested for allegedly taking photographs at an air show at a military base near Kalamata in southern Greece. They denied snapping planes inside a restricted military zone – a very serious offence in Greece because of past fisticuffs with Turkey, just over the border.

At first our diplomats expected that the court would view the affair as a cultural idiosyncrasy, a misunderstanding, as plane-spotting is virtually unheard of in Greece. Some people at first thought this all sounded rather amusing – plane spotters, anoraks etc – but it was definitely not. The whole matter was to spiral seriously out of control.

In the newsroom, we scoured the papers and discovered we had a serious stake in the story. One of the men, Peter Norris, was from Uxbridge. We set out to find more about him and, as the Government was closely involved, contact our MP John Randall to see what he was doing to help. Things had to happen fast because if found guilty, the group were looking at a 20-year stay – bed and board without swimming pool or themed nights – in a Greek jail.

Peter Norris, though only one of the many accused mentioned on TV and in newspapers, was a big story for us. This is the great advantage of local papers. We are able to concentrate on just our man, and other regional papers up and down the country would be doing the same for their residents caught up in the drama. Sometimes in these cases we need to share with other papers. For instance if our local man or woman awaiting trial had been born and bred in a different region in the UK. They may have only recently moved to our area. Or vice versa.

The aviation club members were travelling with an organisation called Touchdown Tours, and its owner Paul Coppin was one of those held. The company organised regular overseas trips for military aviation enthusiasts, including a similar trip to Greece the previous year.

Their website said that in 2000 a group had visited 18 bases in five days, logging more than 700 military aircraft at bases including Kalamata. All their photos and notebooks were seized, to be examined by Greek security services, so that a report could be sent to a magistrate.

Though the group was remanded in custody we knew that relatives were in touch and we managed to track down Peter's wife Perdita, who had flown to Greece to visit her husband. She was horrified to find the group held in a prison wing along with criminals, including murderers.

She told me, after several daily 30-minute visits, 'They think it's hopeless and don't believe a release will ever come. Their hopes get built up only to be dashed. Hopelessness has gripped them all. They can try to keep each other's spirits up, but the whole thing is so depressing.' Peter even doubted whether they would ever be released, and, as he kissed her goodbye he whispered in her ear: 'It's never going to happen.'

Perdita was able to tell us what life was like for her husband in the Nafplio prison. 'Prisoners are let out of their cells at 8am, return at noon until 2.30pm and are released again until 8pm, when they are locked up for the night.

'Peter exercises out in the yard. There is a TV in the cell, but there are no English programmes and they just keep flicking channels. Food follows the same monotonous pattern, starting with soup at midday – there is no breakfast – and the main meal of the day is usually just potatoes and onions.

'Peter has lost weight and is gaunt, but the members of the group are all on good terms, and try to keep each other's spirits up.

'However, I am trying to impress on everyone (back home) that their mental state is really worrying. They don't believe anything anymore.'

He was allowed to phone from prison, but had to queue up to take his three-minute turn. On the previous night he had only been speaking to her for 30 seconds before it was time to go back to his cell. 'It was a bit fraught,' she said.

Meanwhile the then Uxbridge MP John Randall was working behind the scenes to help his constituent get home. He had also written to the Greek embassy and was in constant touch with the Foreign and Commonwealth Office in London. Raising the matter in parliament, he told the House: 'All 12 tourists are bona fide aviation enthusiasts who have followed their hobby in many places around the world without problems for many years.

'As a fellow resident of Uxbridge, I know that Mr Norris is a locally known expert on that subject and has written articles in the *Uxbridge Gazette*.'

Others rallied round, including his local paper (us) which sent copies of articles written by Peter, which we found in our bound volumes, to his wife. The Chiltern Aviation Society, which met in Ruislip, also confirmed he was a serious aviation historian and not a spy. The then chairman Keith Hayward wrote a book, *A Short History of the RAF*, jointly with Peter, whom he had known for twenty-five years.

The prisoners were eventually freed on £9,000 bail before a trial the following year, and when Peter returned for Christmas I was waiting outside his front door and later filed this report:

The weather was cold but the welcome could not have been warmer for plane spotter Peter Norris as he returned from a Greek jail to his family for Christmas.

As Peter and his wife Perdita arrived at their house the couple clung to each other, broad smiles etched on their faces. Their happiness was tangible, and in marked contrast to the previous grim weeks when he languished behind bars, while his worried wife faced the national media to campaign for his release.

Neighbours called out and waved their welcome while a tinsel-framed notice was hurriedly erected between the houses opposite declaring: 'Welcome Home Peter – Free at Last'.

He said: 'It's a great relief to be back. I was beginning to think we wouldn't be back for Christmas.

'We never gave up hope. We were confident we had right on our side, and could prove it. One of the low points was when we arrived at the prison, but we have no complaints about the guards.

'Before that, we spent ten days in the police cells, which are not designed for long stays, had high ceilings and lights on 24 hours a day. There was no sense of whether it was day or night. But we were able to keep our mobile phones, which kept us sane. They would even take them away, charge them up then hand them back through the bars.'

Mr Norris was surprisingly fit after his ordeal, calling it 'a complete detox'. He also made sure he exercised, doing press-ups and squats in his cell. He was looking forward to a cup of Co-Op 99 tea, a curry, some non-salty fresh vegetables, and most of all, any hot food rather than lukewarm.

His wife had made him a cake for Christmas which she couldn't face completing until he had returned home to her, his five children and eight grandchildren.

'As soon as I heard the news it was the icing on the cake – literally – and then I finished it,' she said.

His daughter Estelle said, 'The last few weeks have been surreal, particularly seeing Dad in handcuffs. But he kept his sense of humour. If it had gone on over Christmas it would have been cruel. We were worried both about Dad in prison, and also about mum being on her own. But he looks so happy and it is going to be a good Christmas now.'

His MP John Randall shared in their delight. He said, 'I am obviously delighted part of the episode is over, and Mr Norris is home for Christmas.

'I still find the whole thing unbelievable, and in the New Year we will do everything we can to clear his name.' In April 2002 Mr Norris returned to Greece with the 12 others and two from Holland to face trial on lesser charges and were confident of being cleared. Instead eight were found guilty of espionage and sentenced to three years in jail. The other six were convicted of aiding and abetting and received a one-year suspended sentence. Those who received prison sentences were allowed to leave Greece while their appeals were heard.

In November 2002, thirteen of the plane spotters returned to

Greece and succeeded in overturning their convictions. All were cleared of spying.

Most amusing was this line from one of the group's defence team. During the summing up, Nikos Salavrakos said, 'We are lucky in Greece, we do not have this as a hobby. Here we have the sun.'

As far as we were concerned we also breathed a sigh of relief when Mr Norris laughed at something we had done in the paper. You will remember I mentioned that sub-editors write the headlines? Well, they thought up a brilliant one for this story when it first broke.

'Just Plane Daft' summed up the daftness of the accusations, the intransigence of the Greek authorities and the keenness of the plane spotters.

Unfortunately, just above it – and quite legitimately – was a smaller strap line, a quote from Mrs Norris saying 'My husband is No Spy'. That was fine, until you read the two together: 'My husband is no spy. Just plane daft'. Luckily, when he returned Mr Norris saw the funny side.

9

Tales of the Unexpected

As a ten-year-old I discovered the word 'meander' and included it in any piece of creative writing I could, including my 11-plus exam. It may even have contributed to my getting to grammar school. My very first published work (long before I discovered meander) was a story called 'Tassel-Shine-Star'. Though it was lost long ago, I still remember my infant effort, written in pencil in a big loopy hand and taped together by my dad to resemble a tiny book. It started with a big fight in Fairyland but I don't think any weapons of mass destruction were involved. It ended in love and peace, after the fairies saw off the wizards.

As a child, this was how I hoped life would roll out, with the good guys always winning like they did in the films that my parents took me to on a regular basis. When I played cowboys and Indians in the street with my friends – which involved a lot of running around and yelling 'bang bang' – no-one wanted to be what we now call Native Americans. We knew they were the baddies and they had to be tied up, shot or shouted at. It never occurred to us that they could actually be the victims. I always secretly wanted to be Pocahontas so I hope that redresses the balance a bit. In real life, of course the goodies and baddies sometimes get mixed up, and there can be a fine line between the two. As I discovered when I went to meet some rough sleepers in London.

Homeless and Hippies

One day, in September 1992, I found myself shoehorned out of a warm office to help feed people sleeping on the London streets. Homeless people begging in the streets or huddled in doorways is a familiar sight in cities but it's hard for those of us with a roof over our heads to understand what it's like. The nearest I'd got was listening to Ralph McTell's song 'Streets of London', which I used in drama lessons, but this was clearly not high on the street-cred meter. Here was a chance to find the real story.

I, and fellow reporter Ian Gilbert – together we covered Hayes and Harlington – were invited to join a group from the Immaculate Heart of Mary RC Church in Hayes Town, which fed the homeless in Lincoln's Inn Fields and Kingsway areas of London every Friday night. The volunteers had been doing the food run for a year, and had built up trust and friendship with those living on the streets and in the parks.

We were crammed into the minibus next to mountains of sandwiches which had been made that day by church regulars, and were apparently preferred to soup, as that was what most charities offered them. As we bumped along, surrounded by Catholics, I thanked God I'd taken a travel tablet. Throwing up as I stepped out of the van would not have endeared me to the hungry homeless.

When the minibus came to a halt at Temple, Ian and I were surprised not to be surrounded by a jostling crowd; instead a queue of patient people waited for the weekly delivery. They were unkempt, unwashed, and the worse for wear, but tired faces lit up as we jumped on to the pavement, loaded with flasks of hot tea and coffee. Some shuffled away with their drinks; others queued for a sandwich or a piece of cake. Ian spoke to a man in his twenties who, since leaving his home in Wolverhampton, had lost touch with his family. He was finding it impossible to move on because of the age-old Catch-22 problem: he wanted a job to get money (the benefit cheque didn't go far) but first he needed an address in order to apply for jobs.

It was no secret that many spent their benefit cheques on alcohol which helped them blur the present and forget whatever they had left behind. I spoke to a 23-year-old man who'd been homeless for two years. He was evicted from his flat owing £600 in rent following a spell in prison. He'd given up living in hostels after his possessions were stolen, and was then sleeping rough.

The helpers from Hayes were compassionate and caring; hugging and chatting to the homeless people, shaking their hands; listening to their stories. At Lincoln's Inn Fields, a middle-aged man told me he'd forgotten how long he'd been homeless. He said he was too proud to beg for money and he tried hard to look decent.

One particular conversation stayed with me long after we had left the area. At Kingsway, some of our 'customers' were settling down for the night under thin blankets in shop doorways. A man stood up as we arrived, clearly pleased that he was going to get a hot drink. As I poured him a coffee I noticed his hand was injured and asked him what had happened. He said he'd been knocked down by a car. I asked if the driver had stopped. 'Yes,' he said, 'he got out of the car. Then he came back and kicked me.'

***

Homeless people come in all shapes and forms, and one of my earliest jobs at the *Gazette* saw me trying to pin down a tribe of New Age Travellers – the locals were calling them hippies – who had descended on Hayes and were squatting in an old warehouse. A few days earlier they'd been visited by police, who'd asked them to leave. They had refused, saying they were on the dole and this was now their home.

The New Age Travellers, or 'electrical aborigines' as one later told me they preferred to be called, were told an application for a court order to evict would follow. Having been dispatched to get the story and hopefully an interview with the squatters, I drove to the deserted warehouse which they were making their home.

When I arrived, my heart sank. They'd made sure they were securely fenced off from prying people like me, the council and the law. It was clear this scoop wasn't going to fall into my lap. To get any information might even, heaven forbid, involve a bit of fence climbing.

Playing for time, I circled the vast fenced warehouse several times like a demented wagon train. I mean what do you do in this situation – shout? I couldn't tackle the fence on my own and anyway I'd probably have ended up in an undignified heap on the ground. I've always been a bit accident prone and was one of those children who often had a big bandage on her knee. Later you will hear how I got a black eye from being knocked over by a man on a push bike as I crossed the road – in too much of a hurry to get home from the park for my tea.

These thoughts did not help at all and I tried to push down the terrible thought of returning to the newsroom with an empty notebook. This could not be contemplated. I started to feel desperate.

Thankfully a couple of squatters emerged then, probably thinking I was an official person and they might as well take a look at me. I was often mistaken for an authority figure – a social worker or council person – when I visited disadvantaged areas; the teacher in me I suppose.

It was sometimes an advantage. People were so relieved I wasn't official; they were then all too happy to chat.

The two squatters however were very wary and would only speak to me through the fence. They told me their 'family' came from all over the country and the present group had been together since the beginning of the year. They insisted they were not taking homes from the homeless but that they were the homeless and at that time they couldn't get bed and breakfast unless they were 'twenty-six, pregnant or insane'. One pointed out that the warehouse which provided them with shelter was derelict, unused and due to be demolished, so they didn't see there was a problem.

The hippies, as everyone else seemed to prefer to call them, fetched water from nearby petrol stations and bought food locally. They had found people friendly, sympathetic and helpful. Some were on benefits, while others found casual work wherever they set up home.

I was fascinated by the group, who didn't seem at all threatening. They told me there had been no trouble on the previous Saturday when they'd had a 300-strong party (were they called raves then?) and had cleared up after themselves. When I later contacted the police, they backed this up and said there had been no disorder and they'd had 'zero complaints'. However, they added, they would be 'concerned' if there was another party. It wasn't clear whether this was because of health and safety fears, fire hazards, possible drugs use – or simply illegal squatting.

By this time the borough's newest residents had decided I might be OK and asked if I'd like to take a look inside. A young man with a green Mohican leapt over the fence and kindly found me a broken bit that he thought might be an easy-ish entry into the squat and didn't involve too much climbing. Luckily, I was wearing trousers.

Safely inside, and without obvious injury, I was greeted by a peaceful, unwashed, friendly lot; the grime brightened by colourful hair and piercings. They accepted that I was an official intruder and relaxed enough to tell me about their way of life, which appeared impressively democratic. All domestic chores were shared and each night a big pot of rice was cooked. They were all vegetarians apart from one carnivore. I felt rather sorry for him as he grumbled gloomily in my ear that he never got any meat.

If you've ever considered relocating the family to a warehouse, a definite plus is that you have lots of spaces to park your car. Gary, who was the family's driver, showed me around their big coach, which was parked at the back of the warehouse. The battered old bus doubled as sleeping quarters at night. It was warm and cosy inside, heated by a large wood burner with a chimney that poked out of the roof like a periscope from a submarine. Old carpet lined the floor, giving the mobile bedroom a homely feel.

Outside again in the vast, chillier, warehouse, several New Age Travellers were sitting on old sofas which they had picked up on their travels. One or two were eating a delicious-smelling concoction – apparently a combination of potato, tomato, cheese and vinegar – while another totally uninhibited member danced to bongo drums. If this sounds like I was watching a movie about New Age Travellers, well I have to tell you, that's exactly how it felt.

I was surprised to hear that their dog, which was called Mischief, was not fed on muesli and chickpeas, but had conventional canine slop from tins. I bet the one human meat-eating electrical aborigine was jealous. Mischief wagged her tail and scampered around, dodging between several paintings which had been created on cloth that was stretched on the ground. Some of the artists were still at work.

Gary accepted that many people found their way of life 'abnormal' but said they tried to stick within the law and avoided confrontation. He had been squatting for four years but had never taken a home from anyone else, and didn't intend to.

Knowing that all the 18 to 40-year-olds slept together on the coach I had to ask the obvious question: didn't the family unit just end up being couples and wasn't that a problem sometimes? Privacy? Jealousy? He was adamant that they had high morals 'in fact very high morals' and said it was easier, particularly with the sleeping arrangements, just to remain friends. If this was really the case, I couldn't help thinking it was very different to the flower power and free love ethos of the 1960s. What they did have in common with the old hippies, however, was that in the summer

85

the 'wider family' met up at festivals. Sadly, they told me, this was not at Stonehenge, as at that time it had a five-mile exclusion zone around it.

Feeling very at home by this time, I could see the attraction of 'dropping out'. Gary said that sometimes as they watched the sun set, they wondered how many of those still trapped in the rat race saw it too.

Later, heading for home, stuck in a traffic jam, the deadline for my story niggling away, I realised that, like many others in the 'real', responsible world, I hadn't that night, like most nights, seen the sun setting.

Dangerous dogs

MORE than 20 years ago I and a TV crew joined a police raid to three houses where it was thought that particular breeds had not been registered under the newly enforced Dangerous Dogs Act. In spite of the DDA the problem continues – in an eight-year period alone, eight children and six adults had lost their lives in dog attacks – leading to Environment Secretary Owen Paterson ruling that pet owners must have all dogs microchipped by 2016 or be fined up to £500. As I write this, in 2017, another child has suffered a horrific attack. However, the raid in 1992 reinforced for me that it is owners that need educating, not the dogs.

Pitbull – the name conjures up pictures of vicious dogs foaming at the mouth, ready to launch themselves at human flesh. I therefore questioned my sanity when I accompanied a police raid to three houses in Hayes, Middlesex, which they suspected held unregistered dogs.

Bred in America for dog fighting, pitbulls can leap 12ft into the air from standing. They can cling on for an amazing length of time – one was known to grip a hanging tyre with his teeth for an hour and a half and then just walk away.

In 1992, it was an offence to have a pitbull, Japanese Tosa, Dogo Argentino or Filo Brasileiro without an exemption certificate – in fact time had run out on November 30 the previous year. The owners who did register in time would have paid £12.50 plus VAT and had their dogs neutered and tattooed with an ID number. A microchip implanted in one ear and third-party insurance completed the package.

Rules state that pitbulls, whose life span is only about ten years, must not be bred, sold, exchanged, given away or allowed to stray from the owner or person in charge. Police hoped that this would eventually lead to the breed becoming extinct in this country.

As a TV crew gathered to join the raid I watched police dog handlers don protective gear: helmet, gloves and titanium arm and leg protectors. In their back pockets they carried release pegs, a thick stick to prise the dog's jaws open, should it attack.

At 7am the operation began. At the first house, a woman burst into tears when police told her they were removing her dog. She pleaded that the dog was her only protection. Tonka was certainly a friendly animal, well fed and wagging his tail deliriously, but this quickly changed. As he was taken away in a cage from his distressed family, he too started wailing.

It was now 7.25am, and on to the next address where a notice 'Beware of the Dog', with pictures of snarling pitbulls, greeted us at the front door. Not a good start. We were led up the stairs to be greeted by Sykes who bounded out to greet us, singling me out for special interest. He failed – or passed – the dangerous dogs test, depending on how you look at it, being described as a 'bad Staffordshire' by the sergeant whose role it was to identify dodgy breeds. Owners sometimes think they have a pedigree pet, but the disappointing news for them that it isn't after all, can be a life-saver for the dog. So, Sykes was reprieved – he was legal after all. We moved on to the final address.

At the third house, there was the biggest surprise. The owner told police that she had had her Pitbull destroyed. What had once been a sweet little pup had grown alarmingly big and was turning against the baby. My blood ran cold when she said it had started to sit and stare at the baby, and more recently had bared its teeth at it. The dog had to go, she said.

At 8.10am it was all over and Tonka was back at the station. There it was discovered that he had actually been tattooed and castrated, but, as he had not been registered in time, the owner would still be summoned to court and the dog would probably be destroyed.

For me, this was not the end of the story though. The piece appeared on London Weekend Television's *Crime Monthly*, which was presented by Paul Ross, but the reaction to our story in print was totally unexpected. We received a storm of protest from readers, not just dog lovers, about how not all pitbulls are bad and that it is usually owners who are to blame.

One family even threw down the gauntlet and invited the paper to send a reporter along to see their pet. 'Come and see my pitbull and I know you will have a different outlook on this breed of dog' was something the editor was never going to refuse. I was duly dispatched to meet the pet face to face (or nose to nose, as it happened).

Driving to meet what I hoped was a friendly pitbull (really?), I remembered the protective clothing which the police had worn to round up illegal pitbulls. It didn't compare with my leather jacket and flimsy skirt.

I arrived at their home, took a deep breath, knocked nervously, and waited for what seemed like hours. My palms were sweaty, my heart was banging in my chest – could the dog hear it from wherever he was waiting for me? I hoped they had all gone out for a long walk in the park and forgotten about the challenge.

The door opened, Spike (as it happens, son of Tonka), a 50lb canine whirlwind, exploded down the hall and almost knocked me over. A huge tongue, toothy grin and barking bonanza preceded a slobbery smacker, and I sincerely hoped that Spike and I had bonded.

When I came up for air it was clear that this was indeed a much-loved pet and not the doggy devil incarnate. The family's three children aged ten, seven and six, played happily with him in their living room. He paused briefly to sit and offer his paw for a biscuit. His owner, who had correctly registered his dog said: 'My dog is one of the most placid I have ever known. We know the law is the law but please tell me you can't say that all these dogs are the same. That is like saying every young girl will go off the rails or every young man will be a criminal. The last thing I want with three children is a dog that snarls and snaps. Spike even sleeps with the children. All he would ever do is kiss you to death.'

I had to give in. I kept to my word and wrote a follow-up article officially declaring that pitbulls are not all bad, and that Spike in particular was a real softie.

But the whole business continues to make news. Microchipping all dogs is a start, but the Government needs to focus on educating dog owners and there should be harsher sentences for cruelty, not just fines. Cruelty should include breeding dogs for undercover dog fights, or using them as weapons to terrorise the neighbourhood. And allowing children in their care to tease (or torture?) pets. A dog that has its tail pulled constantly is going to fight back. Wouldn't you?

In 2006 – 14 years later – I got a call at the newspaper to tell me that Spike had reached the ripe old age of 16 but had to be put down because of ill health. Apparently, he had a good Christmas first, eating half a turkey and wearing a paper hat. After a long and trouble-free life, he'd certainly proved his point. And I wrote Spike's final story.

When our family pet died my editor asked me to write about it. He was convinced that personal accounts were the thing for the future in journalism; stories that people could empathise with. I hadn't been sure I could do it at the time he asked me, but he put no pressure on me, and in the end, I found it remarkably cathartic. How right he proved to be.

We had the biggest mail bag at that time, in response to that article, with readers saying how much it had touched them, and relating their own stories.

The popularity in first-hand columns, 'confessionals' and memoirs has grown enormously in the 16 years since I wrote about losing our Cairn terrier. And here I am again, adding to the market (I hope).

Ben

(This appeared in the *Uxbridge Gazette* on August 29 2001.)

Ben would have been 16 years old tomorrow and until recently was still the family pet we had brought home as a puppy from the breeder, Susan Weinberger in Moor Park, in 1986.

Our family was living in Hayes at the time and we joked he had more pedigree than us – in fact one of his relatives had been a Crufts winner.

But we didn't have him to be a dog show star – we just wanted a Cairn to raise from a puppy and join our family: Fizzy, the cat, Sam, a Shetland sheepdog, and Fisher Junior who was a real animal lover (still is).

I had always wanted pets too but as a child lived in flats and had to be content with a passing selection of mice and budgies or borrowed cats. And looking after my grandpa's bull terrier, a gentle but fierce-looking dog called Battle.

It was clear from the start that our little terrier, Ben, was a real character, confident, and very intelligent. Wrapped in a blanket, the tiny puppy was immediately at ease on FJ's lap as he headed for home, leaving his mother and siblings behind.

Unlike Sam, he loved going in the car, and as he grew older

would happily sniff at the windows and get very excited about the changing scenery.

At that time, we had a caravan in Dorset where we took FJ and her friends during the long summer holidays, and no one was more enthusiastic than Ben on these occasions.

After sitting quietly on the journey, he would know when we were near to the site, and would jump up and down, race around, jump out of the car, and fling himself into the caravan.

Enthusiastic about any new experience, Ben particularly enjoyed the snow. After sliding his face along the ground, he would return, panting, to the warm house, his white whiskery face a picture of contentment.

Sam and Fizzy grew older – both coincidentally living to sixteen, the same age as Ben when he died, but the sadness of losing them was always tempered by the constant company provided by Ben. At first, he was so tiny he would walk under Sam's legs, but as he matured, the older dog was no match for the cunning Cairn.

Ben had many funny quirks, and was particularly good at narrowing his eyes and ... peering. He would look through the crack in the kitchen door at his food dish, rather than waste time going in to see if we had filled it. If it was empty, he would do a dog equivalent of shrugging his shoulders and tutting. And then walk away.

Ben would also peer from the top of the stairs, like an annoyed parent, if he had thought we were going to bed and had become fed up with waiting. He had his own little bed upstairs and we often fell asleep to the sound of Ben's peaceful snoring, or woke to his urgent request to be let into the garden.

Ben became a real member of the family, moving house with us to Uxbridge, having presents at Christmas, loved by everyone, particularly for his propeller-like tail wagging.

In June 2001, we took him to the vet to get his teeth fixed, an operation under general anaesthetic.

Even though we were warned of the dangers of this at his age, he bounced back.

Then he started getting very badly infected lumps, which were first thought to be sebaceous cysts, but could have been cancer.

But he kept recovering, and we began to think he would live for many more years.

When it became clear to us that he was dying, we still desperately didn't want to accept it.

However, one evening when Mike tried to take him for a walk, I looked up the road and saw Ben being carried home.

It was obvious everything was failing. He could not stand, eat or drink, apart from out of my hand, and as he lay down and began to fade away we knew we had to do what we had dreaded so much.

Sadly, at that time FJ was in Italy on holiday, but had been phoning regularly for a progress report. However, she sensed what had happened, and having given us strict instructions to do the best for Ben if the time came, stopped asking – as she later explained – to spare us the agony of relaying the news by phone.

The vet was marvellous. He and a nurse came to the house. If, stupidly, we had hoped for a miracle cure, it was not forthcoming.

We were told there was no choice.

The sun was shining and it was peaceful as we stood in the garden where we had taken Ben.

I was next to him, stroking his warm body and giving him water which he lapped from my hand. When the vet asked if we would like it to be done there we did not hesitate.

This was where Ben had sat with us through many summers, where he had drooled at barbecues, barked at squirrels, and mischievously eaten the bread put out for the birds.

I carried him to the table where the vet let him lie gently on his brown, shabby, corduroy beanbag which had grown old with Ben, and which held wonderfully funny memories of his pounding it into shape before snuggling down.

As we said our goodbyes, Mike and I stroked him. We both

cried as Ben slowly stopped breathing and finally left us. I felt a strange mix of emotions – desolate, bleak and joyless, a bit angry and also slightly relieved that Ben was not suffering any longer.

As we watched the vet go, I was almost unaware of clutching Ben's yellow collar with the identity disc we would no longer hear jingle through the house.

'Have a cry and a cup of tea and then think about all the happy times,' the vet said as he finally left us.

I took Mike to the train, but before going to work myself, I drove around for a while. I couldn't go home and clear Ben's food bowls, his bed and other things just then, and I knew I couldn't cope with the new, unwelcome silence that would greet me.

We still miss him – but the vet was right. We have wonderful memories of a little life that made such a difference to ours.

We truly will never forget little Ben, the faithful friend who shared so much with us – good and bad, happy and sad – and who was so brave and uncomplaining at the end.

***

It must be weird having your mother working on the local paper doing embarrassing things like turning up at your school with a photographer, but our grown-up daughter was pleased when the editor of the *Oxfordshire Guardian* allowed me to write a piece about her cat that went missing on the hard shoulder of the M40. I also wrote about it in my column.

Bm@il May 2017

Pets really do become part of the family, so you'll understand how upset we are that Jangles, our daughter's cat has gone missing.

Fisher Junior (FJ) had collected the ten-year-old ginger tom from us, as we had been looking after him while she packed her things to return to her house in Wales. He had journeyed many times before between Surrey, Wales and Uxbridge, with no problem. She and her dad had checked his cat box was secure before she set off, but when she was nearly at Junction 10 (Cherwell Valley) on the M40, Jangles, whom she had had for ten years since he was a kitten, somehow escaped from it.

Knowing it would be dangerous to continue driving with him loose in the van, she pulled over and prepared to secure him again, quickly sliding the door open a fraction so that she could scramble in the back, and calm him more easily.

To her horror – and it only took a split second – he shot out of the door. Maybe he thought he had arrived home, but, sitting at the top of a steep, grassy bank, Jangles was clearly as shocked as FJ, and was getting freaked out by the noise of the traffic.

She kept calling him, but he was frozen to the spot and wouldn't budge. Highway Patrol men soon arrived to help, alerted the traffic ('Animal in Road' flashed above the motorway!) and then tried to coax Jangles back into the van, but he became more frightened and eventually bolted in the direction of some woodland.

We, and SiL (son-in-law)'s family who live in Chalgrove, Oxfordshire, as well as friends from Amersham, have spent several days scouring the countryside, particularly the village of Fritwell where he was most likely to have scarpered. Everyone in the area and beyond has been brilliant and helpful, and alerts about the Great Escape have gone out on Facebook, in the Oxfordshire area, and through vets and catteries.

Jangles loves people, and is very trusting and friendly. He does not have a collar but is microchipped so he can easily be traced back to FJ.

We really, desperately want him home.

Just in case you are in Oxfordshire – he could be anywhere now though – and see a wandering ginger tom, do contact me.

Who knows – he might even have hitched a lift back to Uxbridge and be spotted in the cat food section of Sainsbury's.

This piece (above) appeared on May 31 2017. Thankfully Jangles was found ten days later, thanks to a response to the appeal and posters around Fritwell. He turned up in the village, malnourished and with a head injury and was recognised by a resident who phoned us. We were there that day with FJ having a last search so were able to rush over and collect him. Thank goodness we didn't give up.

Fatal Fire 1994

Another unexpected, but totally different story, came when I was chief reporter and attended an inquest in January 1994.

A fatal fire which took the lives of two young children was a tragic start to the New Year for a Hayes family. A four-year-old girl and her three-year-old brother had been playing with matches in the back bedroom of a bungalow in Hayes. The station officer from the Red Watch team at Hayes told me, 'We saw the glow from the station as we set out. An inrush of air had caused the fire to flare up quickly. Three of us went around the back and the fire was coming out of the windows at this stage. Firemen who went in by the front door at the side of the bungalow found the hall alight. This was put out and the rest of the house was searched.' The two children were found, one on the bed and the other by the window. Both were already dead. One of the officers who attended the fire at Kings Cross station, which he said was terrible, added, 'when it's children it hits a little bit harder.'

I know what he meant. The following month I was sent to cover the inquest at the coroner's court in Uxbridge. It was one of the most distressing I have ever attended. The mother, who had been in hiding since the fire, collapsed while giving evidence and had to be taken out for a while. I had had strict instructions to try and speak to her, but

I dreaded it. We reporters are often accused of intruding, of being insensitive, but we are a paper of record and it had to be done. After the inquest I tentatively introduced myself, said the name of my paper and asked for an interview. I then waited for a browbeating from her friends and relatives. I wouldn't have blamed them but I hoped they would understand I was just doing my job. I was sure Jane (not her real name) would say no, at which point I would retire gracefully.

To my surprise I heard her repeat my name. She must have remembered it from my coverage of the tragedy which had been a front-page story (headline 'Tots Die as Fire Rages'). 'Oh, you're Barbara Fisher?' she said. 'I wanted to speak to you.'

Journalists do get a bashing these days but sometimes, even in the very worst circumstances, people want – need – our help. She wanted to put the record straight. She could hardly stand up, never mind speak, so we arranged to meet and chat at a later date. It resulted in her story with the headline, 'My Lovely Children', appearing next to the formal inquest– both on the front page. 'Nothing Anyone Could Do To Save them – Coroner' was the headline for the news piece.

Jane, white-faced and drawn, wanted, through the *Gazette*, to scotch rumours that had haunted and hurt her since the tragedy a month before, when she had done all she could to try and save her children. She said: 'Some people said I was out when the fire happened, but if I was out how could I have tried to rescue my children?' Malicious tongue-wagging and the burden of her double tragedy had not dimmed her faith in human nature though – she had been overwhelmed by a wealth of kindness and support. She asked me to thank neighbours, fire and police officers, as well as family and friends who had supported her. She praised staff at the accident and emergency department of Hillingdon Hospital, in particular a nurse who did not go off duty but stayed with her on the night of the fire. She was touched by the number of cards and messages of sympathy she had received. One man had sent flowers addressed simply to 'The Little Boy and The Little Girl'.

Jane had hardly eaten or slept since the fire and suffered nightmares. 'Sometimes,' she said, 'I don't want to live. I just want to be with my kids.' Both youngsters had been 'happy, lively children' she said.

Her son had previously cheated death several times. Born with jaundice, he suffered several serious conditions such as salmonella, septicaemia and rickets, but had survived them all.

Some time later Jane phoned to tell me that she had had another child. It was so good to hear that life was at last looking up again for her, and very touching that she felt she'd like to share her good news.

Mandy Rice-Davies and meringues

I have covered many tales of spectacular weight loss, and we all love reading them, particularly if they have accompanying before and after photos. At the paper, reporters were grateful to be alerted to such success stories from local slimming clubs, as they were particularly useful for our 'neighbourhood news' pages.

We all try to eat healthily these days, as childhood obesity is on the increase, but when I was young it seemed to be the aim to fatten us up. Born a month early, the health service in its wisdom decided I should be built up, most agreeably with yummy sugary welfare orange juice and spoonfuls of malt.

In the post-war years, reconstituted orange juice was provided for young children to improve nutrition, while malt extract, a lovely treacly sugar and yeast concoction, was supposed to ward off colds and winter illness while building up our little bodies.

Now the experts would line up to tell us that it can lead to a slump in energy levels, a craving for more sugar and, in the long term, an increased risk of type 2 diabetes. Ho hum.

Money was scarce, but we ate healthily at home: rabbit stews and lamb chops, scrambled egg, cheese. We had fruit and veg in season – oh the excitement when strawberries were ripe for picking or new potatoes were in the shops – and chicken at Christmas (it was a luxury then).

But my slim, glamorous mother loved sweet things too, so there were also homemade bread and butter puddings, drinking chocolate, Penguin biscuits and Kit Kats. For Dad, there was tooth-pulling toffee you smashed with a little hammer. Nana, whom we often visited for Sunday tea in Great Barr, made delicious sugar-sprinkled Victoria sponges and custard tarts.

I loved going to the City Centre with Mum where we might have a 'coffee dash' (today's latte – I would hate it now; I like to taste the coffee) at Lyons (not as upmarket as the London Corner Houses), or as a special treat, a pot of tea in the big swanky department store, Marshall and Snelgrove. There, real live, beautifully made-up models paraded between the tables, showing the latest fashions.

Later, one of these unbelievably glamorous creatures was a young Mandy Rice-Davies, famous for her part in the Profumo affair in the 1960s, who modelled there as a teenager. Interestingly, her 'partner in crime' Christine Keeler came from Uxbridge, where we now live.

Those times with my mother were usually topped off by a fluffy meringue, sandwiched together with cream that melted in your mouth, or a slice of Battenberg or angel cake. These treats were very special; not just the food – the whole occasion, and it cost very little.

I feel sad when I see young kids eating their burgers silently while their mothers concentrate on their mobiles. Eventually we may discover that the lack of communication proves more damaging than the fast food.

Mind the Gap

Have gap years always existed? If so, most of my generation missed out on them. We spread our wings between A-levels and college by taking a holiday job which we hoped would include the same things as youngsters enjoy today – earning our own money, meeting new people and, let's be honest, plenty of booze and partying on the side. I sometimes think today's hype on the problems of so-called binge drinking in the young has been made worse by giving it far too much attention. It was always so – certainly when I was a student, although we didn't tend to beat each other up.

However, in those days people did drink and drive and seat belts were not compulsory. In my early twenties, I did find myself at our local hospital A&E department in the early hours of the morning after a very nasty accident. It later prompted another column, mainly about Clunk Click, but ending with a very strange tale.

Bm@il 11.12.2013

ARE you old enough to remember the public information films on TV that promoted wearing seatbelts in cars? If so, you'll know there was strong opposition at the time to this law.

Some thought wearing a seatbelt was an infringement of their liberties, others worried about creasing their clothes. Pregnant women thought wearing a seatbelt would damage their unborn.

Car manufacturers had been legally obliged to fit them in front seats since the late 1960s, but most people didn't bother to use them. These adverts did provoke us into belting up by combining a catchy phrase 'Clunk Click Every Trip', with pictures of bad car accidents.

In 1983 it did become law and thirty-five years on we can't imagine travelling without them.

It's shocking too, to recall that over decades of motoring, driving under the influence of alcohol wasn't always considered a problem either. The Bright Young Things of the 1920s thought it a hoot, and waved their champagne bottles about as they danced on the roofs of their cars.

As a young woman, I learned the dangers of irresponsible driving when I had a lift home in the early hours of one morning. We'd been drinking with friends and three of us were squashed into a two-seater sports car. We weren't belted in, and the driver suddenly revved up, along a straight, wet road and skidded.

I don't remember much about the crash but the car demolished a lamppost. I had three months' hospital treatment on my arm and the wounds around my stitches went gangrenous. It was thought that I might lose my arm, so I value the scars that remain.

How things have changed – we belt up and we take away the keys from drivers who've drunk too much. I wish I'd done both of these things all those years ago.

The other passenger in the sports car (who was not hurt) was soon in another accident, but this was very different. Thelma was at a bus stop when a lorry plunged into the queue of shoppers. At A&E her head was oozing a pink substance and she was alarmed to hear a brain injury being mentioned. However, as they cleaned her up, they discovered her hair was matted with something from her shopping. It was strawberry yoghurt!

***

I mentioned earlier that it was great fun working at Butlin's with my friends Veronica and Jean. It was an experience we'll never forget, mainly because we met lots of lads and danced to live music. I've still got the photos. The three of us were going to Colleges of Education in the September to train for three years as teachers, but until then we were just teenagers who intended to live it up for the nine weeks we were there.

Being chalet maids didn't sound very promising... until we heard which chalets we'd be cleaning. Yes, Butlin's decided in their wisdom to assign us – teenage girls – to clean the boys' rows (they kept the sexes apart in those days). We never looked back.

After dark, we were allowed to mix with the punters, where

there was live music and pubs packed with young people. Everyone grouped according to their towns and we all belted out our home songs. For us it was the Birmingham City FC song: 'Keep Right on to the End of the Road'. Strangely, although much alcohol was consumed, no-one thought to punch anybody's lights out. Not even when the Manchester and Birmingham 'tribes' got a bit rattled about which was the second city (Brum is).

Less exciting was getting up at the crack of dawn next day with a throbbing head; bucket, mop, dusters and smelly cleaning fluids at the ready.

The next year we returned as coffee bar assistants, which we preferred to cleaning chalets, and this time, after three terms of noses to the grindstone it was good to forget about essays and teaching practices for a few weeks. Being in a responsible job as proper teachers would come all too soon.

Story of a postcard, 2003

One of my favourite *Gazette* stories was about the discovery of a wartime postcard written in Belgium in 1944, which turned up 60 years later in a Welsh antique shop. It eventually landed in Ickenham, its original destination.

Kenneth Fenn, who was 80 when I met him in 2003, was astounded to be sent the card by Sylvia Davis, who discovered it for sale while surfing the internet for any links with Ickenham, where she had lived.

She bought it for £1 in the hope of giving it to the family who had never received it, and could not believe her luck when she found their son living there.

The poignant postcard, sent to Kenneth's parents in Almond Avenue, gave a fascinating glimpse of the times, including fears for their loved ones fighting abroad in WW2.

It also revealed the jubilation of the newly liberated Belgians.

Dated December 10 1944, the card, from a Mr and Mrs Verbeke, who ran Hotel du Comet d'Or in Bruges, said: 'Dear Sir and Madam, we had twice the pleasure of seeing your dear son. He looks happy and is in the best of health. We hope you are well. We are so happy now we are living with the English. We appreciate so much that we are free again. What a nice change this is for us.

We wish you a Happy Christmas and New Year. May the war soon be over and we wish that your boy come safe home' (sic).

Mr Fenn, who was in the Royal Artillery, was the 'boy' in question. He had moved back into the family home with his wife Lillian, whom he married in 1949, after his parents died.

He told me he was 'astounded and overwhelmed' to get the card. He couldn't speak at first as a mixture of feelings flooded through him – sad and happy.

How he came to connect with the Verbekes during the war was interesting. As a soldier passing through Bruges, he spotted the hotel and remembered going there on holiday as a child. So he called in. How comforting that warm reception must have been to a young lad away from home at such a difficult time.

He was very moved by the couple's wish for his safe return and for letting his parents know that, at that point in the war, he was alive and well. Typical of his generation, he was stoic about his time during the war and said he never thought about dying or not getting home.

He told me: 'It was a great relief to be back but you never worried about surviving. You had to think positively.'

Bros and Hard News, 1989

One of the most surprising stories came to us after a schoolgirl joined us for work experience. It ended up with us both appearing on TV.

I was looking after Julie Allday, who was only fifteen and keen to do a stint on her local paper. While we were driving to a job she told me she was a huge fan of Matt and Luke Goss who made up the hugely popular pop duo Bros.

She had recently had an asthma attack outside Matt Goss's flat in Maida Vale and he had come out to give her a glass of water. A good little yarn for our paper I thought – and she agreed that I could write her story. I arranged for a photo to be taken of her proudly showing her Goss memorabilia and it went on the front page of the *Uxbridge Gazette*.

After her story appeared in our paper Julie and her mother were furious to see it pop up in a national paper in which her hero was supposed to have given her the kiss of life. To turn a kind act into a life-threatening situation was just not on. They thought we might be responsible. We weren't. It was re-written by a freelance and sold on, undoubtedly for a generous fee.

Julie's mum complained to *Hard News*, the award-winning Channel 4 programme which aimed to find the real truth behind newspaper stories. It seemed unlikely they would follow it up (their most recent episode had been about the wife of the Yorkshire Ripper) but to their credit, they did. They thought such a big inaccuracy was the sort of thing that gave journalism a bad name. (How would they tackle today's 'fake news', I wonder?)

Julie and I were both interviewed by presenter Raymond Snoddy before Julie was taken back to Maida Vale to film at the scene of her asthma attack.

I was miked up ready to be interviewed at my desk. Reporters were removed from some desks and background talking was kept to a minimum. We couldn't move for lights and equipment.

As the interview began, I wanted to laugh, as everyone around me was pretending to work and trying not to look at the camera. I was desperately hoping I wouldn't make an idiot of myself. Thankfully the tension broke when reporter Kristian Foden, who was leaning over a desk behind me, was asked by the producer to remove his bottom from the picture!

The episode was shown in September 1989.

World cruise, 2012

If you enjoy writing it's something you can take with you on holiday. When Mike and I set off for nearly four months at sea on a World Cruise, I bought my first journal, and have kept up these daily accounts ever since. I wish I'd done it much earlier, particularly in my youth! When we got home from our World Cruise I had plenty of detailed information to draw on and wrote the following piece.

It includes many tales of the unexpected (which is obviously why it has popped up here uninvited). As well as the fun bits, I have written about the drug smugglers on our ship who were arrested in Sydney; also the very real threat of terrorism on land, and pirates at sea.

This will lead you nicely into the next chapter which contains first-hand accounts of terrorism in the 1990s which were closer to home. (I'm also giving you the chance to skip this 'what I did on my holidays' section.)

***

Many of us never sampled backpacking in our youth with just a Rough Guide and a change of underwear, but it's never too late to try a long-distance trip. Older travellers are using redundancy payments, inheritances or pension lump sums to go on World Cruises. Mike and I boarded P&O's Aurora on a cold January day in 2012, and, although this was an adventure, it wasn't always the soft option one might have imagined.

'Laydeez and gentlemen. I hope you hear me OK – particularly in the backsides' says our guide. We are in Nha Trang, Vietnam, drinking green tea and eating slices of fresh ginger, and sweet potatoes that taste like hot chestnuts. I feel very content and hope my parents would have approved of our decision made twelve months earlier, to spend some of our inheritance money on a world cruise.

Planning our three-and-a-half-month trip had been much the same as it would be for gap year students – visas, vaccinations, anti-malaria and travel tablets, insect repellent, Imodium – but travelling in later life also means spare specs, four months of pills and disposable contact lenses, as well as indigestion tablets and painkillers for bad backs and creaky hips.

At Southampton, we were handed letters from P&O telling us that norovirus had been a problem on our ship but Aurora had had a 'complete disinfection'. Also, we wouldn't be calling at Mexico because of 'security worries'.

The sea was very rough for the first two days – gale force 10-12 at its worst. All I could do was lie down with my travel bands and sea sickness pills, while Mike remained annoyingly unaffected. Shortly after the unsettling news that the Costa Concordia had sunk, we were both confined to our cabins with norovirus. Sanitation squads wearing masks and gloves squirted us regularly with disinfectant, cleaned our room and did our washing. Spartan food was served on cardboard plates.

However, things started to look up when we had stops at Madeira, St Lucia and Curaçao, San Francisco, Hawaii, Samoa and Fiji, and we will always remember leaning over our balcony as the crew squeezed our massive (76 000 tons) vessel through the Panama Canal with only about a foot to spare on either side. Luckily, we were breathing in.

Other highlights included passing under San Francisco's Golden Gate Bridge at dawn, and later seeing scores of noisy, smelly, sea lions at Pier 39; being drenched in a tropical rain storm in Samoa; and in Fiji watching traditional dancing and fire walking. Then we were whizzing along to New Zealand, the captain having made a vital detour to avoid tropical cyclone 'Jasmine'. We loved being at sea but at one point I did get cabin fever when we didn't see anything but water for a week and was glad to get to Auckland.

Our second call in New Zealand was the Bay of Islands, where we visited friends, who had emigrated there ten years ago. Three days later we arrived in Sydney where the Opera House and the Bridge slowly came into view as it got light. In the evening, we went to see *The Magic Flute* at The Opera House and at midnight, again in the dark, we moved on. This time accompanied by sheet lightning.

Two sea days later in a hot and humid Brisbane we paid a visit to the Lone Pine Koala Sanctuary to see the obligatory koalas, kangaroos and other Oz wildlife.

For several days we had no mobile, text, email or internet connection from the ship because of a 'fault with the satellite which is used for non-emergency communication purposes' (ie passengers). This would be 'mended' when the spare part arrived in Darwin, we were told.

Conspiracy theories abounded because we were being so closely scrutinized by the Australian authorities after three passengers had been arrested in Auckland and in Sydney, for possessing big amounts of serious drugs. In Sydney, we were made to walk in single file, and then stood against a wall while immigration officers and sniffer dogs marched up and down. Cabins were searched, seemingly at random, and we were all told we must cooperate

We headed optimistically for our next port, Yorkey's Knob, where we had booked a trip through the rainforest in a jungle train and an army 'duck' (DUKW – an amphibious vehicle). Some on the ship planned to snorkel in the Barrier Reef; others had arranged to meet relatives.

The ship was refused entry. We would be allowed to dock at Cairns, where serious screening could again be carried out, but it was too narrow for the ship to pass through safely. Unsurprisingly, communication was restored when we left the country and we remain convinced we were deliberately cut off.

Next stop was Bali, where the shuttle bus drivers immediately went on strike. However, we couldn't get back to the ship because the pontoon was swaying and crashing and bits kept falling off it as the tenders tried to 'park' (moor) alongside. After three hours standing in the blazing sun, and lots of angst and chain clanging and rope-tying from some of the ship's crew (who were sent to sort it out with the locals), we eventually returned to Aurora, apart from one woman who collapsed in the heat and was taken to hospital.

In Vietnam, we travelled two hours to Ho Chi Minh City on a shabby motorway, where our coach was lost in a sea of bikes ridden by young men carrying everything from fridges to goldfish, and young women wearing surgical masks to protect their complexions.

M and I shot into the Rex Hotel (where the Americans gave daily bulletins during the Vietnam War) and had lunch in a shady courtyard. I bought a fan from a street seller which became a crucial part of my tourist backpack, along with travel pills, toilet paper, insect repellent – and a damp flannel.

On the way back, the coach's air conditioning stopped working. Our driver unloaded us into a handy military cemetery, which surprisingly had a bar, and while we wandered hotly among the gravestones he changed the fan belt. Travelling back to the ship a little late, again flanked by thousands of mopeds and motorbikes, we had a more peaceful glimpse of people gathering for the evening, including families flying multi-coloured kites.

Along with the world seeming very small – on a ship you don't suffer jet lag so are not really conscious of the distances covered – we became very aware of the high risk of terrorism practically everywhere. At several ports 'travel advisories' were delivered to our rooms the night before we disembarked, outlining threats, and giving the number for the British Embassy. Just in case.

Thailand was one. Our trip to Bangkok took two and a half hours past mango trees and rice fields and it was a vibrant, noisy, happy place. We saw Chinatown and a flower market, the Suthat and Marble temples – both with gigantic Buddhas. Next stop Penang in Malaysia, then Singapore: more temples and lots of orchids. Our ship's reputation must have gone before us as we had a reminder in our passports that the penalty there for being in possession of drugs is death.

At Colombo, we were welcomed on the dockside by male dancers dressed in white 'skirts' with metallic vests and red pom poms at their waists. Stalls were set up and we shopped until the stifling humidity made us slope back to the ship's air conditioning. Sadly, our all-day trip to an elephant orphanage was cancelled as our ship was unable to dock for long enough.

We had some fascinating speakers on board, including Mark Lewis, the lawyer acting for the Millie Dowler family, journalist Martin Bell, and later a commander from the Royal Navy who was on board with armed guards. He was there to explain what might happen if pirates got near enough. They travel in skiffs and pretend to be fishermen, then fire at the bridge with their AK47s and RPGs to persuade it to slow down or stop.

After dark, we had to shut our balcony doors, turn off outside lights, and be locked out of the promenade deck. One day we had a piracy drill, which saw us passengers weedily sitting in corridors while the crew manfully strode about doing goodness knows what with fire hoses and anti-cutlass devices. Our cabin steward Suneesh, clearly relishing his new responsibility, counted our heads and ticked us off on his register.

On to India and a visit to a fascinating, but still very nervous, Mumbai, following the terrorist attacks in 2008. We had gone though many hoops to get visas before we left, but still had to have individual meetings on board with immigration officials, fill in yet more forms and show our yellow cards many times during the day. We saw the famous Gateway to India and the fabulous Taj Mahal Hotel which had taken the brunt of the terrorist attack. A display at the National Centre for Performing Arts – five dances, each representing a different Indian state – was a real highlight.

In Muscat, Oman, we took a trip on a dhow, a traditional wooden Arabian boat. Clear air, creaking wood, sea slurping gently against the sides while we were served tiny cups of coffee, boiled sweets and dates. When we docked in Abu Dhabi, Mike and I stayed on board Aurora. There had been a sandstorm the previous night and we couldn't see a thing from our window but heavy 'fog'. We also needed a rest from being tourists. The last leg of the World Cruise began at Dubai, which we thought a rather soulless place, and we were glad to set sail the following day for the Suez Canal.

At Sharm-el-Sheikh it felt very cool after the baking heat of the tropics. We watched a young local family on the beach – a man, woman and their two children. He was bare-footed, bare-chested and wore shorts, while she had her head covered with a hijab, top tightly wrapped, full length sleeves and legs modestly encased in trousers. However (hurrah) she was smoking a hookah.

On March 29, we opened the curtains to find the noisy open sea had been replaced by a gently swishing Suez Canal. Spookily, the sun had cast a giant shadow of Aurora on the bank, so it looked as though we were being accompanied by a ghost ship. Lining the canal were square-roofed houses, blocks of flats, palm trees and occasionally people waving, some of them military men guarding the canal.

We were sixth in a convoy of 39 ships, with a strict two-mile gap between each one. Speed police along the banks made sure we did not exceed nine knots but the canal is only 230 metres across, so there was no chance of overtaking. The canal opened out into Little Bitter Lake, then into Great Bitter Lake where we met the southbound convoy. Here, passing was allowed.

At Port Said we docked and waited for people to return from the pyramids (they were dropped off at the beginning of the canal and picked up at the end) and were startled, as it got dark, to see blow-up figures being inflated... to line the main streets. We counted about 60 and there were probably more beyond our vantage point on the ship. No explanation. They just kept popping up one after another like a cartoon army. Bizarre.

Next stop was Limassol, Cyprus, and a trip to Paphos, then on to Israel. Galilee was not all sand and mountain goats – it's green, particularly the Golan Heights – and Nazareth is all built up. Kibbutzim are now big businesses. We saw people being baptised in the River Jordan, visited a church built on a rock which was supposed to have held the loaves and fishes, and a shop in Canaan selling 'wedding wine' after the nuptials where Jesus turned water into wine.

On to Turkey and Izmir, where, off the tourist trail, we had Turkish coffee – thick, dark, treacly sweet, which was served with salted popcorn. Nearby a man was selling huge lemons off the back of a truck.

Next day at 5am we rushed up to the top deck to snap the sun rising over Istanbul. The city sits on two continents and later we travelled by coach from the European side to the Asian side via the Bosphorus Bridge. No pedestrians are currently allowed on it because of so many suicides. Sadly, they still happen occasionally – people just jump out of taxis now.

The Roman aqueduct and the ancient Theodosian walls which go from the Sea of Marmara to the Golden Horn were impressive, as was the famous Grand Bazaar, which dates back to the 15th century. Four thousand shops, many housed in sophisticated arcades were such a contrast to the ramshackle souks of many of the countries we'd visited. Carpets, spices, gold, silver, copper, suede and leather didn't tempt us but we used our new haggling skills to buy a couple of cashmere silk pashminas.

We should also have spent the following morning in Istanbul but the captain made a crack-of-dawn announcement that we were leaving early, and immediately, because of bombs in the capital during the night which police said were 'indicative of fundamentalist terrorist activity'. Could be Kurds, Islamists or leftist extremists, he said. It followed bombs on the two days before we arrived when there was minor damage to buildings and two passers-by were slightly injured.

On April 5 we woke, in what we hoped was going to be a peaceful Athens, only to hear that a man had committed suicide outside a government building during the night, sparking riots in the city. After the ship left that evening there was more rioting, but we had managed to spend a peaceful day traipsing round the Parthenon on the Acropolis. From there to Lisbon and home after visiting more than twenty-four countries over nearly four months.

Would we recommend a World Cruise? Absolutely. The staff are great, the food is wonderful, but some things are out of the company's control so don't expect it all to be plain sailing.

Meeting a Famous Author

Part of my course, at West Midlands College of Education in Walsall, involved studying a main subject at post-A level standard and I chose English. For my final thesis, I had decided to do 'The Change to Realism in Contemporary English Literature' so I wrote to all the famous authors of the day to ask for an interview. To my amazement the writer of the classic novel, *Saturday Night and Sunday Morning*, invited me to London. I was only too happy to accept the invitation to trundle up from the Midlands to Alan Sillitoe's home.

As a young student, I wanted to know his views on contemporary literature and his general approach to writing, in order to flavour my thesis with a few original quotes. Two letters and a few weeks later, I arrived on his doorstep in Clapham armed with pencil, pad and another English student, my good friend Marg – still a great pal and a big part of our family's life, including being godmother to Fisher Junior.

So, there we were, at the home of the author of the cult book/ film *Saturday Night and Sunday Morning*. A short man with longish hair and big grey eyes, Sillitoe smoked a pipe as he showed us into his ground floor flat where I was naively impressed by bookshelves that covered an entire wall. I was surprised to find he had no trace of a Nottingham accent and that, although one of the biggest authors of the day, he had a quiet modesty about him. By contrast, as we drank tea, and I nervously started on my questions, his four-year-old son David tore around the room, ate the sugar, then lay under the sofa.

The great man soon changed my idea of realism. 'Everything that is written is embellished, and stops being true. The only truth is the actual thing itself,' he said.

When suffering from tuberculosis for two years at the age of 20, he felt he must write everything down because death seemed so near. Novel writing is not a soft option though, according to Sillitoe, who once wrote two hundred pages of a book and stopped because he felt it to be a failure. He also revised *Saturday Night and Sunday Morning* eight times before he was satisfied and, after cutting *The Death of William Posters* mercilessly, still felt that book was too long.

He told me to forget the writing 'rule' that you should only use what you know, as you don't have to have done something yourself in order to write a novel in the realist genre. Instead he said: 'You can learn from others who have experienced it.'

Nevertheless, for his bestseller Sillitoe used his own knowledge of working in a Nottingham factory, and agreed that there first-hand experience was necessary. Of the film version of *Saturday Night and Sunday Morning*, he said: 'The screen characters lived more or less, but the best medium of course is the novel.' Albert Finney, he thought, was the best available actor for the part of Arthur Seaton in the film of the book, released in 1960.

As I quizzed him, he was very relaxed, continually lighting his pipe and talking to his son David, who continued to run around the room, in between quieter moments when he stood on his head. (I believe David Sillitoe is now a very grown-up photographer.)

Sillitoe believed that self-expression was not enough for creating a book, as that usually meant writing down what has been said before. 'Every book you pick up is stuck in a rut. It is always about someone's relationship to society. Inspiration is what is needed; authors must make changes in society by writing them.'

He was never concerned with the impression he created of himself through his novels. In fact, in 'The Rats', his long poem, he attempted to show that one becomes inhuman when faced with all the rules of life.

Once he finished a novel, Sillitoe said he distanced himself completely from his work. For me, this was the feeling he created when he talked about his books: it was as if he was discussing the novels of another writer in whom he had a profound interest.

He certainly inspired me to have a long career in journalism and I always hoped that as an adult I would get to interview him again. Sadly, I left it too long to approach him, as he died in 2010.

My first ever 'scoop' eventually appeared over two pages in the West Midlands College of Education (now Wolverhampton University) magazine. I think my youth and enthusiasm saved me from making a fool of myself in my first ever interview. Sillitoe, at the height of his fame, was brilliant to take on a student, and I'll never forget our meeting.

Marg and I returned starry-eyed and unscathed, apart from a flasher sitting opposite us on the tube who chose to display his wares before he got off at Belsize Park.

It was the second time my friend and I had seen a man expose himself. The first time, we were shown mugshots by police – a gruesome gallery – but they gave up when none of these men looked familiar and anyway we couldn't agree on details like whether our flasher was wearing a hat. How times have changed. Everyone seems to be deliberately exposing themselves all the time on reality shows and social media, and no-one 'cares a kipper' as my mum used to say.

We didn't report the flasher on the Underground. We had met a famous author.

We were now women of the world.

10

Terrorism

Never underestimate the importance of reporting suspicious packages. We had two instances in Hillingdon where suspect bags were seen and reported. The quick-thinking of passers-by probably saved hundreds, maybe thousands of lives. Mind you, I once spent about half an hour in WHSmith telling anyone who would listen that there was an abandoned rucksack in the post office section. I reported it, but as time ticked (!) away I was torn between losing my place in the queue and not getting my stamps – or making a run for it. A manager eventually turned up and took the offending item away (aren't you supposed to leave them there?). As I left the shop, he found me to say a red-faced youth had eventually returned to the store to collect the rucksack. He'd forgotten to take it with him. Hmm.

We have to be more vigilant don't we? Even as I write this, there has been an explosion at Parsons Green Underground station. There were no fatalities following the explosion on September 15 (2017), but 29 people were injured. The homemade bomb was on the floor of a carriage, in a carrier bag. How long was it there? Did anyone notice it?

It is of course very unusual to have terrorist attacks in the suburbs, as it is the big towns and cities that are normally targeted. A denser population means a bigger bang, and more publicity. Who could forget the terrible attack on Westminster Bridge in March last year (2017), in which eight people lost their lives, and many more were injured?

Or Manchester Arena in May when twenty-two people died, including a number of children, after a suicide bomber struck following a concert by Ariana Grande.

In Hillingdon borough, even at the height of the Irish troubles, we felt pretty safe. This was in spite of the fact that the RAF base in Uxbridge had been attacked in January 1981. An IRA bomb exploded, but no-one was hurt thanks to the prompt action of an airman who spotted the discarded satchel. The collective thinking of the rest of us was that, although we sympathised, this was an isolated incident on a military base. Not so.

In June 1991, curious readers rang to ask why our local theatre, the Beck, had been cordoned off, so I was sent with a photographer to see what was going on. Outside the theatre, staff told us they had arrived for work to find early morning cleaners evacuated, their theatre closed off, and the place over-run with police. Standing behind the taped entrance, they were as shocked as the rest of us as they watched the frenzied activity in the grounds.

The previous night when the bomb was placed, a packed house was enjoying a concert by a 27-strong military band. Police believe they were the target, as a bomb – bigger than the one which killed 11 Royal Marines at Deal in 1989 – was left outside the building beside a back wall only fifty yards from the stage. The Blues and Royals mainly performed on ceremonial occasions, but they also had an active role in the British Army. Four of their bandsmen had been killed in an IRA attack in Hyde Park.

By 10.30am police cars and ambulances were lining the road, while sniffer dogs and their handlers searched the grounds. Experts defused the 20lb bomb and Britain was immediately put on full terrorist alert. About 15 members of the Territorial Support Group (TSG) in full protective gear then combed the area on all fours, looking for forensic evidence.

The bomb was later found to be the work of the IRA and, as it contained the biggest amount of Semtex up to that time, we would have been writing a very different story if it had detonated. Thank God for another alert resident; this time it was a canny woman who had alerted police after spotting the brown canvas bag about 9am as she walked her dog.

A spokesman from the anti-terrorist squad said, 'The bomb contained a substantial explosive device which, had it exploded, would have caused multiple deaths and serious injuries to both bandsmen and members of the audience.'

We were fortunate that one of our photographers who was in the audience that night had taken a photo of the band. It was of course even more fortunate that the bomb didn't go off, as he would have been one of the many casualties. As it was, we had a bit of a scoop with his picture.

Three years later the IRA took us by surprise again when it launched a mortar attack on Heathrow Airport. It was March 1994 when the call came into the newsroom at about 6.30pm, with first reports describing a car bomb at the Excelsior Hotel. The last people in our office had gone and I was just about to put my coat on, turn out the lights and go home. I lived closest to the Gazette offices and I was also then chief reporter, so there was nothing for it but to phone my editor and head over there myself. I phoned my husband to tell him I was chasing an IRA bomb, and he told me to make sure I was careful… with his car. Honestly! I'd borrowed Mike's beloved BMW that day, as mine was out of action.

When I got near the airport, the roads were so jammed that I had to leave his car in a side street and continue on foot. I passed two schoolgirls who told me they'd heard that two bombs had landed on the runway. I was sceptical but they were to be proved remarkably close to the truth.

At the Excelsior Hotel (strictly out of bounds to the press – I was soon to discover why) I hitched a lift from an ITN reporter to Heathrow police station, where we expected to get a statement. A press pack of more than 50 reporters, cameramen, technicians, photographers and radio journalists were all hungry for information. What we heard was like something from a James Bond film: mortars had been fired from a Nissan Micra car parked at the Excelsior at Heathrow's northern runway.

A police press officer chose a small group to photograph the car which had been set alight by one of the mortars. We were lucky: Reuters, the Press Association, the BBC – and the local paper (us) were selected and our then chief photographer Chris Saville snapped the remains of the blasted car for the *Gazette*.

A friend Jenny, whom I had known since we were teenagers, and who was then living on the Isle of Man, later told me how she switched on the TV news and not only saw the images of a blown-up car, but also her old friend Barb… in a corner, scribbling in my notebook as we were briefed by a member of the anti-terrorist squad. Mike also switched on, and was so taken aback he thrust in a video tape (remember those?), so I now have a memento of that night. I can't play it now of course, as we no longer have a video player.

The journalists I admired that night were the ones who had been dispatched to Heathrow to speak live to camera. I could see the panic on their faces, because at that point we had not been briefed. They had nothing to report but, as soon as Trevor McDonald spoke to them through their earpieces, they filled the space admirably. What a skill.

A second attack at Heathrow followed twenty-four hours later, from the Hatton Cross side, and a third a couple of days after that, from the Bedfont area. None reached their targets.

Because of the vulnerability of Heathrow there were calls from politicians and local residents to abandon the plans for Terminal 5. We know where that went, don't we? The same environmental arguments are raging as I write; this time about plans for a third runway.

In 2001, it wasn't our area that was under attack, but because of our closeness to the airport we were affected by 9/11, since at Heathrow there were crowds of Americans waiting for flights home when news broke of the attacks in New York and Washington.

Four coordinated terrorist attacks were launched by the Islamic terrorist group Al-Qaeda on the United States in downtown Manhattan and in Washington, DC on Tuesday, September 11, 2001. Americans, who could no longer get flights home, were taken from Heathrow Airport and given food and beds in Uxbridge Civic Centre, and I was sent to interview them. A nearby fitness centre offered them use of the showers.

Many were concerned about relatives; some were naturally anxious about getting home. But it was a lovely moment of camaraderie at a truly devastating time, and the travellers were all very grateful for the help given by Hillingdon.

Unfortunately, London's turn was to come four years later: the 7/7 attacks in 2005 which killed 52 and injured 700. I remember the day vividly. A puzzled Mike, who, terrifyingly, was on the Underground at the time – he commuted daily to Westminster – texted me from West Hampstead to say there was some problem with the trains. An electrical fault, they were being told. As the truth of the Al-Qaeda attack filtered in I, like thousands of others, was desperate to know their loved ones were safe.

Mike then texted to let me know they had been herded off the train and on to a bus. Phew. I got on with my day but – would you believe it – while at Northwood doing an interview for the paper, someone came in to tell us a bus had been blown up. I was petrified.

For us it ended happily – he wasn't on that particular bus – but

I've never forgotten the terrible feeling which for many others, of course, sadly turned into a permanent tragedy.

It may seem a trivial point, but it also made me so grateful to be living in a world which has mobile phones for instant communication.

11

Family/ancestors

We often feel sated with miserable news, but all media, including local newspapers, have to reflect what's actually going on in the community, whether good or bad. With the increase in rumour-fuelled blogs and tweets it's even more important for future generations to have a paper of record. Hillingdon residents have always referred to the archives of the *Gazette*, which is more than a hundred and thirty years old, to check stories from long ago.

This is increasing with the growing interest in researching family history. We may look at old copies or search the internet. If going a long way back, copies can be viewed on microfiche at Uxbridge Library.

After writing a feature on the Hillingdon Family History Society, which helps people trace their ancestors, I wrote a piece on my own family which was also published in the *Birmingham Post*. It is a sister paper in the Trinity Mirror group and serves my home town, dear old Brum. This was the article:

My own interest in finding out about my ancestors was not sparked by the clutch of television programmes which have recently prodded the pasts of celebrities but by a series of more personal events. My mother, a sociable and lively woman who died in 2009, had often told me snippets about interesting relatives and unusual episodes in her life, but there were several blanks which I always thought I would fill in later. Then living in a nursing home, with her Alzheimer's worsening rapidly, and no short-term or long-term memory left, I realised I was not only shut off from my mum, but from my past too.

My grandparents on both sides came from very large families (though not large for the times) and when a cousin, Anita, contacted me, because she was researching the family tree, I was just the accomplice she needed. Anita, who lives in Cornwall, was very excited by discoveries she had made about her Birmingham roots and in particular because she had found some new relatives neither of us knew existed. So it was that I found myself in a party of six women (only blood relations allowed, so no partners this time) in a restaurant in Birmingham. All six of us were descended from Oliver and Clara Roberts, who married in Birmingham cathedral in 1866. Two of Oliver and Clara's five children, sisters Tamar and Martha who were born in 1871 and 1877 respectively, were of most interest to us as they were our grandmothers. Anita (Tamar's granddaughter) and Lisa (Martha's great-granddaughter) had 'met' on the internet through the Genes Reunited site while researching family trees, and were particularly keen to share the wad of information they had uncovered. Tamar Elizabeth Dunn, nee Roberts (my great-grandmother) has always been a fascinating figure to me, partly because of her beautiful name but also because I knew she died dramatically in a fire. She was a singer – opera, my mum told me – and perhaps most startling of all she gave birth to my granddad in 1897 out of wedlock, and kept him at home. This was unusual then, as adoption, or being brought up as a sibling, was the usual way of coping with the 'shame' of being a single parent. This was something my mother did not tell me about (I'm not even sure she knew), but Anita has since got a copy of his birth certificate, and we found them on the 1901 census.

Three-year-old Joe was living with his unmarried mum Tamar, her sister Martha, and Martha's two children at their granddad Oliver's home, a back-to-back house in the centre of Birmingham. Anita had been puzzled about the whereabouts of Martha's husband when the census was taken, but the new relatives were able to tell us he was a sailor, so presumably he was at sea when the information was recorded. The six of us shared some remarkable photos, birth and death certificates and many anecdotes were produced. Tamar, who in later life looked like a very serious old lady (even though she was only 62 when she died), was a regular performer in the Birmingham music halls, and even appeared with Vesta Tilley. Her sad end came in 1933 when her long dress caught alight while leaning over a coal fire. My mum had told me she had run into the garden and a neighbour rushed round to wrap her in a rug, but she died later at the general hospital. To see her death certificate for the first time was a chilling reminder that looking back into family history is definitely no soap opera. The reality of the grim past was also drummed in when, two days later, Anita and I visited a workhouse – still standing but boarded up – where two of our relatives had ended their days.

The day after our family meal, the six of us new rellies met up again to visit the last standing back-to-backs in the centre of Birmingham. Court 15 has been restored by the National Trust and it was very moving to be taken on a conducted tour of houses identical, and geographically very close, to those our relatives had lived in. For much of the 19th century, and some of the 20th century too, the back-to-back courts were home for the majority of people in the Midlands and the North. In Birmingham alone there were 20,000 such courts and it seems our family lived in several of them, as they moved around a lot. People apparently moved frequently for work, to better themselves, or to avoid paying the rent. These houses were one room deep and shared a back wall with another row of houses facing into an inner court or courtyard. Tamar, my great grandmother, was born in Back 70 Lower Pershore Street and her mother Clara Roberts died in Back 24 Claybrook Street, aged only 42. In 1901 my great great grandfather Oliver Roberts, then a widower, was recorded living with Tamar and her three-year-old son Joseph, my granddad, Martha and her two children, William and Alice at 2 House, 24 Court, Cheapside.

Although the houses were cheaply built, over-crowded and badly maintained, these addresses represented a real sense of community. Everyone joined in the highs and lows of life, assisting with the many births and sharing the trauma of too many early deaths. On our tour of the National Trust back to backs we noted the old brewhouse where they did the washing, brewed beer and boiled Christmas puddings, ancient pushchairs for the toddlers and dolls' prams for the children, old toilets in the yard – three serving up to 60 people – and most poignant, the tiny rooms, some lit with candles, others seen by gas light, where our families would have lived. It was good to hear Brummie words familiar from my youth; the NT guide showed us an old sweetshop which sold kali (lemonade powder to you soft southerners, and pronounced 'kay-lye'); troach (a sort of cough candy); and the gap between houses he correctly called an entry, (not a passageway or alley).

Anita and I also visited a cathedral and an old workhouse where past relatives had wed or worked. We saw the house where Tamar died on my mother's (her granddaughter) 13th birthday. Very moving.

After Herbert Dunn, who was from London and living in nearby lodgings, married Tamar he took on her illegitimate son (my granddad) too and together they produced another seven brothers and sisters for him. One of them was the mother of Anita Ballin, my first cousin once removed, who has done so much of the family history research. After their mother's tragic death in a fire three of my great grandmother's daughters, Lilian, Mollie and Olive moved to London where they married and produced families of their own. They were always referred to as my 'London relatives' and for many years I had no idea they started life in Birmingham, like me. Little did I know when I was at school in Birmingham I would also marry a southerner, Mike, and we, and eventually our daughter, would make our home in West London – a bit of a family trait.

***

Birmingham was the home town of both my parents and their families (way back) as well as Prime Minister Neville Chamberlain, author JRR Tolkien, Black Sabbath singer Ozzy Osbourne and comic Tony Hancock. Sadly, not all at the same time. That would have been an interesting crowd to hang around with.

My mother went to King Edward's School, which only took the brightest pupils. It even had a special entrance exam on top of the 11-plus. Because of her home circumstances, and then WW2, she never really had a career. This made her keen that I should carve out a proper career path. Being a teacher would be good, she thought; a particularly convenient job if I ever intended to have children myself. It's a wonder we did eventually have our daughter Zoë, as Mum always told me (without the gory details, I'm glad to say) how terrible her experience of childbirth had been.

Employees were not paid too well after the war, and people were just happy to get a job. So, because of my unplanned appearance, and the need to supplement my hardworking father's income – even office staff worked Saturday mornings then – Mum always worked too.

I was influenced by each of her jobs in different ways.

When I was very little it was just odd days at the weekend at Birmingham Repertory Theatre which, as I would sometimes go with her, started my love of plays, shows and musicals.

The earliest production I remember at the Rep (a brilliant theatre where many famous actors, from Laurence Olivier to

Derek Jacobi, started their careers) was *The Bluebird* by Maurice Maeterlinck, in which a boy and girl are searching for happiness.

Sitting in the dark, I can remember being thrilled by real people up there on the stage acting out stories, sometimes accompanied by music, and always under lights that made everything more magical. I couldn't imagine a better place to be and I wanted to be part of it in some way.

I was never actor material – and still can't for the life of me remember lines – but I got my fix putting on shows in the garden with my friends. We hitched up a sheet between two trees for a curtain which we zipped open and closed at an alarming rate, not having yet learned about the more dignified Theatre in the Round. We made props and programmes and my dad, Gordon, would perch upstairs on the kitchen window sill to play the old wind-up gramophone on cue.

Our favourite thing was marching along in our shorts to 'The Happy Wanderer' which began, 'I love to go a-wandering along the mountain track' and had a brilliant chorus: 'Val-Deri, Val-dera, Val-Deri, Val-der-ha-ha-ha-ha-ha Val-Deri, Val-dera My knapsack on my back.' Hmm.

Another favourite was 'Rudolf the Red-nosed Reindeer', which was a bit odd in the heat of summer, although our kind audience and critics thankfully never pointed this out.

Dad loved digging, growing things and tending plants; but apparently this garden, shared with the downstairs tenants, was unmanageable because it was 'full of ants'. Well, that was what I picked up as a child, in the same way that I thought that King George VI died because he didn't wear a hat. Old newsreels I've seen since do show him (while still recovering from a lung operation) waving his daughter off at a cold, blowy airport HATLESS. The general consensus at the time seems to have been that he should have covered his head. This took hold in my impressionable mind, and I remained grateful for the rest of my childhood that I had my trusty Fair Isle beret to see me through.

In later years, I belonged to school choirs and, while training to be a teacher, was in college productions playing a Puritan, a handmaiden to Cleopatra, and a prostitute (all non-speaking roles apart from the Puritan.) As our daughter said dryly of my less than auspicious stage career: 'Well, at least you weren't type-cast.'

In case you're interested, this was my speech, which surprisingly is still fixed in my memory, which has seen better days:

'Look but upon the common plays in London and see the multitudes that flocketh to them and followeth them. Behold! (big breath and lots of pointing) the sumptuous theatre houses; a continual monument to London's prodigality and folly.' (big sigh of relief).

It was such a mouthful that I was never sure each time I opened my mouth that it would come out properly – or at all. Luckily it did, but I suspect it was a bit garbled as I couldn't wait to get it off my chest and go back to posing. There was of course more scope for simple showing off when I played the prostitute as there were no lines to remember. I was even allowed to wear a short, black, PVC mac and smoke on stage.

Even later, I inveigled my way into teaching drama at a primary school (I had done a 12-month course as part of my three-year teacher training!) and in the 1980s I was part of a steering group that set up the Beck Youth Theatre in Hayes, which is still flourishing. And, oh joy! when I went to work for my local paper I was able to write theatre reviews for productions – local and national – which also meant complimentary tickets.

Contentment for me though at three years old was actually a pantomime. Cinderella was my first; most likely at the Birmingham Hippodrome, and it was a real spectacle with fountains and real ponies on stage. This heady experience probably also spawned my love of tiaras.

I finally got to wear one in 2016 at our street party in Uxbridge to celebrate the Queen's 90th birthday. Mr F had bought it for me from Claire's, as a joke, after I wrote a piece about wanting to be

Princess Anita. My idol featured in the *School Friend* comic which I adored when I was a child. As a result of that column I was also presented with an old 1950s *School Friend* album by a regular reader (thank you Sue), which I will always treasure.

When I was at secondary school, Mum worked part-time for many years at Boots the Chemist where she was able to bring home free samples and testers. I honed my make-up skills from those mini potions and still love experimenting with the old slap.

Although she enjoyed all her jobs, Mum's final working years were spent at Aston University in the registrar's office, which were probably the most intellectually satisfying.

Her first job when she left school had been at Bucklands, a refined shop in a Victorian arcade which sold embroidery silks and linens, and which conjures up pictures of old black and white movies. There she met Irene, who became her best friend and eventually my godmother. Irene married a Canadian officer and moved to Canada after the war, but the devoted pair always kept in touch until my mother's Alzheimer's meant she remembered no-one, including me.

Dad, hoping to be a journalist, went to what was called a commercial secondary school. He learned Pitman's shorthand and typing, but again the war years got in the way of this ambition – he was in the Middle East with the RAF – and he spent his whole working life as an office manager for Wimpey. That's the builders, not the burger company – home of the pork 'bender' (I can't believe they still call it that).

Dad was very pleased when I later started a 20-year stint in journalism, a second career after being a teacher for roughly the same amount of time. He kept a file of all my cuttings and became an expert on the London Borough of Hillingdon, even though the stories were about West London, not Birmingham. I suppose a pot-hole problem is the same anywhere.

Sadly, he died suddenly and unexpectedly from a heart attack in 1990, too soon to hear about the best moments of being a reporter, which I'd love to have shared with him. It's such a shame that he was not able to do the job himself. He would have been good at it. He was a very bright, patient man, fascinated by the world in general, and people loved him.

Amongst my happiest memories are the Saturday mornings I accompanied Dad to his office in Wimpey's head office in Castle Bromwich. I was allowed to play with a typewriter, a huge treat in those days, unlike today when every child can use a keyboard.

Dad was a great story-teller and could spin a yarn using any three words I chose – such as a lump of coal, an umbrella and a rabbit. He 'published' my first book, stapling together the pencil-written 'Tassel-Shine-Star', mentioned earlier.

My parents worked hard all their lives, without the help of any benefits. It was a matter of pride never to be in debt; the only concession being buying 'on the never-never'. This was hire purchase, which required a deposit and endless further payments to pay off interest, and there was great excitement when we had delivery of a new three-piece suite – or a sideboard complete with a sliding-topped cabinet to hold the sherry and the best glasses.

Too many buildings where I lived in Birmingham have been bulldozed in the name of progress, but scenes from those days – my other life – still play on a loop in my head like the old cinemas where you could stay all day and watch films over and over again.

Recently, while shopping in West London, my home now for more than four decades, I saw a small child pulled back from busy traffic and – click – I was back in time, the young me tearing across the road, anxious to get home for tea, but instead crashing into a startled man in a pullover riding a push bike.

When we moved to our flat in Edward Road, I was told to learn my address parrot fashion in case I got lost. I can still remember clearly reciting it to my parents' friends: 'Two five six Edward Road. Flat two. I'm three.'

I was the smallest and youngest of a group of girls who lived in my road. They taught me a new vocabulary to shout across the park and, although I had no idea what the four-letter words meant, I was happy to do as they asked, as, mysteriously, it made them nudge, giggle or fall helpless to the ground. I never heard my parents swear, and my mother, who prized respectability like a crown jewel, would have had a fit had she known. But the girls looked as though butter wouldn't melt in their mouths. And I was in awe of them.

At the time of my near-death experience (as I thought) with the push bike, I was a bit older, not so easily bossed about, and allowed to return home on my own. We – the girlie gang –– had climbed over the fence to play in the park as usual, mostly on the witch's hat, a pointy, rusty roundabout.

When I realised I wasn't dead, there was only one thing to do: stagger home and face the music. I was hugely embarrassed, not only because of grazed knees and the beginnings of an evil-looking black eye. I had a limping cyclist in tow (he insisted) – a man! – and I wasn't even allowed to talk to strangers, never mind take them home. Also, crossing a road without looking was surely going to mean big trouble.

But my startled mum quickly summed up the situation, and was kind, realising I had learned my lesson, albeit the hard way. She also sympathised with the man who, felled by a running child, was clearly the innocent party. Thank goodness he hadn't been riding a motor bike. I still fall over a lot – in fact I've recently returned from a cruise where I tripped on the stairs and ended up looking like I'd done ten rounds with Mike Tyson.

At three years old, I had moved with my parents from living in rooms (we were not welcome at my grandad's house, which was now a love nest for him and his new bride) into a flat, the top floor of an old house. Sadly, it has gone – yes, all bulldozed – and, visiting my home town again as an adult, I am sad that I can no longer look at the skylight where I would stand with Mum to listen to the rain, or watch the light change as heavy snow melted away from that magical window.

We played in the streets – Sandra Webb, Joyce Keenan, Meryl

Tarpy and me (my peers, not the older girls who led me astray) – happily unaware of any health and safety rules, but always under the watchful eye of friendly neighbours. Brummies are the warmest, friendliest people you can meet and they should give courses in being open and approachable. I have met many friendly and lovely people in the Deep South too, but it doesn't always come naturally when they are confronted by strangers. When I moved down to London – a very young newly married teacher – I soon learnt that as well as remembering to stand on the right on escalators, I must never, ever, try and speak to people on the London Underground.

But long before I became a teacher, I had to be a pupil myself. When I arrived for my first day at primary school I was a Rising Five who'd just got over whooping cough. I was sick in the drain before I even got to a classroom.

Moseley Church of England was a very old school, founded in 1827 by the Rev Walter Hook as a day school for the children of 'estate servants and labourers'.

There were still outside toilets and coal fires, and on the iciest days the little bottles of school milk would be put next to the flames to thaw. In the darkness of an old air raid shelter we breathed in the damp, musty air and watched black and white films about hot cocoa-producing countries. We never gave a thought to the children who lived there, or even those nearer to home who must have spent long frightening hours in these very buildings, not long before we filled their space. The war was just never mentioned.

The bespectacled and grey-suited headteacher Mr Grail was very strict, and corporal punishment was the norm, but he was ambitious for us and we were well-taught.

In later years I was amused to hear that in teaching circles he was known as the 'Holy Grail'. I loved writing stories, singing in the choir and, after playing the part of a cook in 'Sing a Song of Sixpence', my love affair with play-acting grew.

At home, my dressing-up box included costumes from my

mother's brief theatrical career during the war, when she was part of a cabaret troupe called the Kynoch Follies. I was impressed to learn she sang, danced and acted in sketches. I've already mentioned that my great-grandmother had an operatic voice and sang in the music halls in Birmingham, sometimes on the same bill as male impersonator Vesta Tilley.

My friends and I acted out stories from our comics, mainly fighting to be tiara-topped Princess Anita of Sylvanberg, the character I mentioned earlier, who featured in *School Friend*. Or maybe we'd become The Silent Three (also in the comic), fighting against bullying head prefects. In those days, little girls wanted to look angelic rather than raunchy, but I did promise myself I would wear red lipstick, smoke, pierce my ears and dye my hair as soon as possible. Which I did.

Also in the dressing-up box was a yarmulke, an embroidered Jewish skull cap which my father brought back from his time in the Middle East where he served with the RAF in WW2. We didn't have a television until I was twelve, but my parents wangled a seat in the front row of Nancy Partridge's house to watch the Coronation, along with an eager crowd of neighbours.

Nancy and Albert had a son Michael whom they had adopted. I was always impressed by this and used to tell 'Auntie Nancy' (all grown-ups were addressed as aunties and uncles then) that I also wanted to adopt a baby when I was old enough. She just smiled and said 'wait and see'.

Michael, a good friend and star footballer, was made to feel proud of being adopted, something I find particularly interesting now, having been involved with helping Phyllis Whitsell with her book (see later chapter) in which she describes how she was made to feel ashamed of being adopted from an orphanage. She was told that her mother was dead (not true) and that she should never tell anyone she was adopted.

Phyllis's book, published in February 2016, has been a huge success, featuring on *The Times* and *Sunday Times* bestseller lists.

There have been many TV and radio interviews, wide newspaper coverage and the film rights were sold.

But, back to Nancy and Albert's house where we were watching the Coronation. I remember the hoo-hah involved: curtains shut fast and the ritual of warming up the TV before the picture came on. Sitting in that small back room, close together and squinting in the dark, we must have looked like a family of moles.

Before that, all our home entertainment, apart from the odd game of draughts or Ludo, was from the wireless (radio). A programme for under-fives, *Listen with Mother*, meant just that. Mum and I would tune in, then sing along with the instrumental introduction, which I have now discovered is actually 'La Berceuse' from Faure's *Dolly Suite*.

Journey into Space, which came a little later, was something I listened to with Dad. It could probably be described as a forerunner to TV's *Dr Who*. I can still recall characters like Jet Morgan and Lemmy, and the thrilling excitement of a serial drama where you had to use your own imagination.

If Mum got a sniff of confetti or spotted a bride while we were out shopping, she'd nip into the church, me in tow, and we'd sit at the back of the congregation, total strangers joining heartily in the hymns. My education also included stage door trips to see legends like Ingrid Bergman whenever she found they were performing in this country. Mum regarded such stars as theatrical royalty, and my favourite memory is staring at a little girl about the same age as me while my mum chatted to Judy Garland. The girl I locked eyes with was, of course, Liza Minnelli.

Judy was appearing in Birmingham, and my mum had spotted her leaving her hotel. I remember her saying, 'Are you feeling better now, Judy?' Much later, I realised she was referring to one of the star's suicide attempts. Oops.

In our old albums, my favourite snapshots include birthday bashes as a child. The biggest excitement was waiting to see if the blancmange or jelly emerged whole from its metal mould. Once, when the biggest part of the animal remained firmly in the mould, my mother swiftly mashed it all up with a fork and assured us it was the new way to serve jelly.

She was very resourceful: another trick was adding cochineal – red food dye – to tinned pink salmon to make the sandwiches look as though they were filled with the more expensive red variety.

Birthday parties were all about iced gems, love hearts, fairy cakes, party dresses, Alice bands and hair ribbons. I positively glowed in my fluffy pink bolero and a taffeta dress which rustled as I moved.

We drank pop, which stained our mouths red, and ate only one variety of crisps: potato flavour. Our going-home treat was a single piece of birthday cake. The icing invariably stuck to the napkin so you ended up eating bits of pink paper with your sponge.

My parents generally used the wireless to accompany the party games. Unfortunately, radio stations didn't then play continuous daytime pop, so in games like musical bumps we invariably ended up dancing awkwardly to the weather forecast.

I recently went back to visit the old library, which was opened in 1895 and is still next door to the swimming baths I used as a child. Both buildings in Moseley Road are still standing – and historically interesting. The baths, which opened in 1907, described as 'grandiose Gothic Renaissance' is only guaranteed to stay open for swimming until 2018, but campaigners are working hard to ensure it is still used beyond that.

I had been hoping to feel again the excitement of borrowing a new Enid Blyton book, or at the pool experiencing the chlorine smell, knowing that a soothing hot chocolate drink would follow a swim. But I couldn't conjure up sensations from so long ago.

What did feel the same, though, was the church I had attended for eight years. Edward Road Baptist Church was just down the road from the swimming baths and library, and the minister kindly let me have a quick look inside (he was just locking up on his way to a wedding reception after conducting the service).

Standing amongst the same pews, I clearly remembered my time there from the age of three, wearing a white dress at church anniversary services and attending Sunday School where we coloured in Bible story pictures and sang songs like 'Jesus bids us Shine with a Pure, Clear light', and 'Zacchaeus Was a Very Little Man'. Oh, and being a shepherd in a nativity play.

During that time, I sang with the Band of Hope, and signed 'The Pledge' in which I promised never to drink alcohol. And all before I was eleven years old.

I took all this in my stride; in fact, I enjoyed my activities at Sunday School, particularly as Mum and Dad would collect me afterwards to go to Cannon Hill Park. The only thing that did scare me – spooked me out actually – were the full immersion baptisms.

Many decades later, standing in the empty church which had just hosted a wedding, I looked anxiously around for the great bath (or baptistery to give it its proper name). No sign of it. Phew. I was very relieved to find that it wasn't there.

'Oh yes, we still do them,' said the minister, and lifted up the carpet.

I was instantly a child again, staring at what was basically a font for grown-ups. I remembered the stirring music on the organ and the high emotions that saturated the church, even before the vicar donned his big boots and accompanied his first candidate down the steps to the water. Were they frightened? Might they drown? Would they be different creatures when they emerged?

I thanked the vicar and made for the door, glad to get out into the sunshine and, for once, away from my past.

When I was 11 years old we moved to one of the first multi-storey blocks of council flats in Longbridge, on the outskirts of Birmingham. I now know we were part of a social experiment. We were described as 'selected tenants' – that is, people who had paid their rent and kept within the law. My parents would never have dreamt of doing anything else.

As they were both white collar workers, in Longbridge,

Birmingham – the heart of the car manufacturing industry – I suppose we were looked upon as a lower middle-class family.

Birmingham City Council at that time had a generous programme of what we now call social housing, and I was never aware of any stigma attached to living in a council flat. In fact, people who are not from the area, think that I'm joking when I say the civic centre is called The Council House!

The excitement of a lift, a chute for rubbish, a balcony and – for the first time – my own bedroom, decorated in lilac, is still vivid. I remember watching the sun go down over the Clent hills in summer, but also the harsh winter of 1962-63, when several feet of snow fell and hung around for two months.

I have a distinct memory of that February because that was the year that Beauty the budgie died. As everyone else in our neighbourhood huddled together indoors, we prepared for the budgie burial: me solemnly holding a torch while Dad shivered, sweated and shovelled the frozen earth. Beauty lay snug in her scented coffin, a little box which had once been home to a trio of soaps. Mum watched sadly (and warmly) from our flat five floors up. Never mind that the canals had iced up, or the hills had turned into a ski slope. We were wrapped up in our own tiny tragedy in the big freeze of 1963.

These were happy times too, of course, and the best thing that happened when we lived in Aylesbury House was meeting our neighbours Margaret and Dave. They were a very modern young couple with a baby, Christopher, the first of their three children, and they were also the first grown-ups that I, a mere 11-year-old, was allowed to call by their Christian names. They were brilliant friends to my parents (and now to Mike and me), and they stood by Mum, still visiting her when she was in a nursing home with severe Alzheimer's. She may not have known who they were, but they never deserted her, and I'll always be grateful to them.

The move to Longbridge coincided with my starting at grammar school in Bournville, not far from the Cadbury's factory. Whenever it was about to rain, the delicious smell of chocolate wafted over the playground. We were brought up to know about the philanthropic Cadbury family who had created a whole village for their workers, and we took enormous pride in it. Never mind Willy Wonka and his weird lottery; in Birmingham we all had golden tickets. Everyone visited the chocolate factory (some of us several times) and we came away with tins of chocolates, which we turned into boxes for our pencils.

I can forgive it turning into the commercial monster/ theme park Cadbury World in 1990 with its 'animatronics, video presentations and multi-sensory cinema' as I suppose it had to move with the times. I doubt today's children would anyway be satisfied with the simple factory tours that we enjoyed: the noise of the machines, the wonderful aroma of the chocolate, the hair-netted workers putting squiggles on the Milk Tray selection. Being so close to the machines is probably banned by Health and Safety now.

However, I felt very sad when I heard that Cadbury's had been taken over by US company Kraft in 2010, a view shared by many in Birmingham (and those who complain on social media about the change in creme eggs). Having just researched the history of Cadbury's products, I wondered who on earth thought it was a good idea to replace the Turkish delight in the Milk Tray box with something called an Apple Crunch? If it was Cadbury's nod to healthy eating, Jamie Oliver has a lot to answer for.

Travelling home from secondary school, I loved the camaraderie of the Austin factory car workers on the buses, and the heady mix of oil and sweat and cigarette smoke that surrounded them. Lights burned day and night at the rows of factory buildings on Bristol Road, but I knew the real power came from the human production line that filled up the number 62 and 63 buses. I now realise that those Austin men with their Woodies, Daily Mirrors, cheeky jokes and steady jobs were like the miners, secure and content with their lot, little knowing that it was all to disappear.

By the late 1960s Longbridge was employing around 25,000 workers, but by 2014 there were only 400 working there. In September 2016 MG announced that all car production had ceased at Longbridge and in future cars would be imported into the UK.

Mike and I stayed at a Premier Inn Hotel in Longbridge recently, and it was as if the Austin factory had never existed. The shops, restaurants, offices, and technology park are now part of a rather soulless site which is 'an international beacon for creativity and commerce'. Or so the publicity goes.

My school friend Veronica's father worked at the Austin as a sheet metal worker. (Brummies always pronounced it 'Orstin', not 'Ostin' as they do elsewhere. And it was always simply 'The Orstin' not Austin Factory or anything fancy like that.).

Von's mother Doris was a local councillor and eventually MP for Ladywood (1970-1974), the constituency later held by Brian Walden, and then by Clare Short from 1983. It is still a safe seat for Labour, and is currently held by Shabana Mahmood.

Doris, who remained active in politics until she died in 2005 aged 86, spent her last years in the House of Lords as Baroness Fisher of Rednal. I was fascinated by her career in politics, and joined the young socialists when I was old enough. My parents voted Tory but it was never a problem and I always enjoyed discussing politics with my dad.

From about the age of 16, Von and I would go to the hops (dances) at Birmingham University on a Saturday night. It was great to meet blokes who were intelligent and from all over the country, but rather embarrassing when they asked what we were 'reading'. I was into historical fiction at the time, but fortunately I didn't say *The Captive Queen of Scots* by Jean Plaidy! We had to confess we were schoolgirls doing our A-levels.

We had an agreement that if one of us was offered a lift home we would insist the other came too. Once we were given a lift home by a whole jazz band, who took us for a coffee first. Yes, coffee. In town.

If we didn't strike lucky (not in the way youngsters mean it now) Von and I would hitch home. From 11pm onwards we would stand on the Bristol Road, thumbing a lift. My mother would (yet again) have had a fit. Because we were savvy, always stuck together and didn't get drunk, we never ran into any trouble, apart from when a bubble car stopped and we had to cram ourselves into the equivalent of a giant egg.

Our school, Bournville Grammar-Technical School for Girls, had a boys' school on the same site and one of the pupils was Ian Lavender, famous as Pike in *Dad's Army*. As I had kept an old programme of him appearing as Professor Higgins in a school production, Mike and I presented it to him for signing at the stage door when he was appearing in the West End many years ago. He was amused! I can't say I was a friend of his, unfortunately, although Von's husband John knew him. Timetables were arranged so that we weren't allowed to mix with the boys, including lunchtimes, but I remember seeing 'Pike' at the bus stop. The school is now comprehensive, co-ed, and most recently had a pupil in the cult TV programme *Peaky Blinders*.

12

Meeting Mandela…
and other name-dropping

The day I met Nelson Mandela was one of the best moments of my life. Unfortunately, as a reporter, it was possibly one of my most embarrassing too.

Mandela was the one person I had always hoped to meet, so when I took a call in the newsroom from RAF Northolt, asking if we'd like to send a photographer to snap him on his way home from London, I said a very definite 'yes'.

'And, er, could a reporter come too?' I asked.

'Absolutely not,' said the Royal Air Force (RAF) press officer. 'We were told no-one is to speak to him.'

'But he's my hero,' I pleaded, as the phone went down.

Shortly afterwards the phone rang again.

'OK, we've got permission. You can come, but just to see him. No conversation.'

I was ecstatic. Just to breathe the same air would be enough.

Mandela had been to the South Africa Freedom Day concert in Trafalgar Square to celebrate seven years of democratic government in his country. The ticket-only free concert, organised by the then London mayor Ken Livingstone, also recognised the role that British campaigners had played in the anti-apartheid struggle.

Twenty thousand people had gathered for a glimpse of the great man but, if all went according to plan, I would be standing only yards away from him on the following day. I couldn't wait.

We arrived at the base in good time and my photographer was all set to snap Mandela as he walked to his plane. After going through strict security, we gathered with RAF officials for coffee and small talk, and there was real excitement in the air.

Everyone who works at RAF Northolt sees celebrities and Royalty passing through on a regular basis, but this visitor was clearly something special.

Who could fail to be touched by a man who'd fought for his beliefs and been imprisoned for 27 years simply because he wanted a fair society? Now he was in power and multi-racial democracy had been established in South Africa. Most impressive of all was that he had forgiven his enemies and was working with them.

Word filtered through to Northolt that Mandela was on his way, although he was running late.

Then we heard (hurrah) he was nearly at the base.

Finally (oh joy), he'd arrived.

While trying to appear cool, I actually felt like a teenager at a rock concert, as we were ushered out to line up by his plane. We stood and waited in reverent silence.

A big shiny car coasted into view. It stopped not far from the plane and several of Mandela's staff got out, all looking rather fierce. Finally, (deep breaths) the man himself.

He was taller than he looks in pictures but was dignified, smiling and had a magnificent aura, just as I imagined him.

To everyone's surprise, particularly the astonished RAF press officer who'd ensured that the duo from the *Gazette* were gagged and glued to the spot, Mandela strode over to us, instead of heading straight for his plane.

Ignoring his staff's diktat, that no-one was to speak to him or approach him, the great man proceeded to shake hands with our small group. I waited my turn, dizzy with anticipation and trying not to grin stupidly.

As a reporter you meet famous people, often interview them, but this was different. Here, at last, was the one I most wanted to see.

So, did I seize the moment?

Did I say 'thank you Mr Mandela, for all you've done to try and make the world a better place; to unite different cultures; to demonstrate tolerance?'

Er, no, actually.

I'm embarrassed to say I was totally overawed, and, as he took my hand, and locked his kind eyes on mine, my Brummie accent chose to return, as I said: 'Did you have a noice toime?'

***

Someone who made a better job of meeting the great man was the then Mayor of Hillingdon, Councillor Albert Kanjee.

Mr Kanjee had himself fled from the cruel apartheid regime in South Africa when he was only a teenager. Born into a well-off middle-class family, he was fiercely opposed to the government. Mr Mandela was the guest of honour at the South Africa Freedom Day concert I mentioned earlier. It was a gift from his government to the British people for their role in overthrowing apartheid.

The 82-year-old watched performers, including The Corrs and R.E.M at the 20,000-strong free concert in Trafalgar Square, after praising Britain's part in the battle to end racial segregation in his country. Daily vigils had been held outside the South African High Commission which overlooks the square.

The meeting was a defining moment for our mayor, who was greeted by the former president at South Africa House. They talked about Pretoria, and Mandela said it had changed so much that he should go back and see it for himself. But Mr Kanjee said he was afraid to, and asked whether he would be able to go into buildings without seeing notices to stop non-whites. Mr Mandela laughed and said everything was very different.

There was more nostalgia when Cllr Kanjee discovered one of Mr Mandela's aides was at school with him and remembered his father's general store.

The mayor had been unable to return to South Africa after his marriage to his wife Margaret, as under apartheid mixed marriages were not allowed. He would have been tried under the country's very strict Immorality Act.

The Nave

One of the most exciting and unexpected spin-offs from my new career as a reporter was a career, albeit short-lived, as a talk show host. Well, that's a grand way to describe it. A public interviewer anyway. Not a TV chat thing – but much, much scarier.

Sitting on a platform, quizzing my 'victims' from a Michael Parkinson-type chair and knowing that the audiences had paid to see it, was so bizarre. I expected someone to stand up and say 'Barbara Parsons – what do you think you're doing?' and send me home.

The Nave arts centre in Uxbridge was opened in 1989 by Prime Minister Margaret Thatcher. Based in St Margaret's Church, the then Rector of Uxbridge, the Rev Michael Colclough said the town had been described as a 'soulless gold rush town with no heart'. This description was just slightly better than the jurist William Arabin, who said of Uxbridge residents in the early 19th century: 'They will steal the very teeth out of your mouth as you walk through the streets.'

The Rev Colclough promised that the new arts base would 'put the beat back into the heart of Uxbridge', the town that has been our home (Mike, Zoë and me, not the Rev and me) since 1987.

He was true to his word. The Nave attracted big names in the news, showbiz and politics like Terry Waite, Kate Adie, Jeremy Paxman and Nick Park (the man behind Wallace and Grommit).

A full programme was already in full swing when I became involved. Alastair Cutting masterminded it in the early days and did many of the interviews, although others were also invited to quiz some of the guests. Such as, to my surprise... me.

When John Bird, the editor of *The Big Issue* was signed up, my newspaper was asked if they could provide an interviewer. Our editor couldn't make it, so I was dispatched.

Over the next few weeks I collected every press cutting I could find on John Bird. No internet searches available then. He was a fascinating character, having been inspired to help people on the street to help themselves because of his own experiences.

As this was my first attempt at doing a live interview in front of a paying audience, I was determined to arrive early and be well-prepared and look confident. Being obviously spooked quickly transmits itself to an audience and makes them feel uncomfortable too. Don't you cringe when a public speaker announces they are nervous before they start their talk/speech/best man offering? I want to shout 'no!' – pretend you're OK; that you're in charge. We don't want to worry about whether you're going to make it to the end of the session without fluffing your lines or drying up. I suppose having had a first career as a teacher helped me, as standing in front of a class is two thirds acting. However, I still have memories of catastrophes on teaching practice when I hadn't taken control. On one particular occasion, my mask of confidence looked more like Munch's painting *The Scream*.

At 19, a college tutor came to observe me teach my first ever drama lesson. My plan was clear: the eight-year-olds, helped by my sound effects record, would pretend they were sitting on a beach, experiencing sand and sea through their imaginations; they would mime making a sandcastle, fish in a rock pool, eat an ice cream. But my nerves got the better of me, I lost control and, as the pupils mutated into manic beach bums, whizzing round the school hall, screaming and knocking each other flying, a frosty-faced tutor took over my lesson.

I vowed never to teach again, but fortunately this turned out to be a temporary hitch; I qualified and enjoyed 15 years in primary schools before later changing to journalism. The sweetest irony was eventually having special responsibility for my favourite subject – drama – and also later becoming a tutor at the Beck Youth Theatre in Hayes. So – youngsters – never give up!

Back to The Nave, and the day of my first public interview arrived. I was rigged up with a microphone (microphone! Oh no, this really was serious), and was led into the hall where rows of empty seats scared me even more. What if no-one came? What if John never came? (Actually, that might be a good thing. Simple matter of refunds and I'd be off the hook.)

As I was doing the interview I obviously couldn't take notes – so a fellow reporter Jo Francis was sent along to do the write-up. When I spotted her in the audience and also our own Uxbridge Big Issue Seller, Scottish Mick, I relaxed a little, feeling I was amongst friends.

I clung tightly to my clipboard (did this make me look official?) while resisting the sanctuary of the toilet for the umpteenth time. I was scared of being locked in anyway and interrupting a gathering audience with my cries for help.

Deposited backstage, as the audience started to file in I did a bit of deep breathing, but stopped when I thought I was in danger of passing out. John was late (oh no, had I willed him not to turn up) so I was shut in a cupboard-like room where, when I was sure no-one was looking, I grimaced and gurned to myself, which made me feel better. Still no John.

I peered through the door. The restless audience was rapidly running out of small talk, some were looking at their watches, and the lure of the loo was getting to me. Again.

Then – hallelujah, he arrived. As we walked on to the stage to applause (oh no, a full hall and applause, they must have high expectations), I ushered him to his seat opposite me, sank into mine and, to my surprise immediately started to enjoy the experience. With all my 'victims' it was the same. They were all so willing to talk and had led such interesting lives, I just had to fire the starting pistol, make the odd comment, curb prevarication and steer them to a natural conclusion within the allotted time.

John Bird revealed he knew exactly what it is like to be on the wrong side of the tracks. One of six children in an 'aggressive family' with money problems, he learned about living on the streets from the age of ten; he frequently ran away from home. He and his four brothers were put in an orphanage, run by the Sisters of Charity, for three years. He recalled nothing charitable about the nuns who ran it saying they were 'incredibly vicious and took pleasure in taking their frustrations out on the children in their care.' He said that they were some of the most damaged people he had ever met.

He got into trouble with the law so went to France where he became involved with a Marxist group, mainly because 'all the good-looking girls were on the Left'. Some years later he had a chance conversation with Gordon Roddick, husband of Anita, the founder of The Body Shop.

They spoke about *Street News*, an American paper for the homeless, and their conversation led to the most important decision of his life, the launch of *The Big Issue*. He said he hated the class system and didn't much like politicians. 'There are so many people who need our help but there is only one way to do anything in the world – get up and do it yourself.'

He said his advice to anyone is 'get involved or shut up and stop moaning.'

Dora Bryan, November 1996

One of the easiest public interviews I ever did at The Nave was with a popular actress who seemed to have been around for ever; certainly for all of my childhood.

Having been brought up with cinema and theatre from the minute I could squeak, I jumped at the chance to quiz Dora Bryan. I've already said that knowing people had to pay for tickets for these events always made me slightly anxious, but I was to discover that the great lady could have just been left to chat to the audience on her own. I'd done my research and carried the obligatory clipboard with my list of topics, but none of this was necessary. All I had to do was fire the occasional question – and she was off. Brilliant!

The live interview was a sell-out and Dora, who was then in her seventies, had the audience eating out of her hand. She was still in demand to perform, in between demonstrating against the exportation of live calves, teaching tap-dancing and updating her autobiography. Her performance as Mrs Candour in *The School for Scandal*, at Chichester Festival Theatre, had been described by the late theatre critic Jack Tinker as 'a comic creation which has few equals on the stage today'.

Dora talked about her two appearances on *This is Your Life*, a popular series which ran from 1955 to 2003, in which details of a celebrity's life were read out from a big red book and real people from their past turned up to regale viewers with their anecdotes.

It was sprung on them live, and was meant to be a great honour, although Noel Gallagher is reported to have said: 'Stuff your red book.'

One guest that Dora could have done without was an unhelpful sleeping car attendant she met on the way to her wedding in Manchester in 1950. 'He told me I couldn't take my dog on board and he would have to go in the luggage van. I couldn't bear to be parted from him so I accompanied him in the luggage van. So, who did they bring on for *This is Your Life?* The sleeping car attendant!' she laughed.

She gave brief glimpses of an exciting film career. In a film with Robert Donat, the pair of them laughed so much, one scene went to 26 takes before they were told to go back to their trailers and pull themselves together. When playing a mermaid in *Mad about Men*, with Glynis Johns, they had to perform in a tank filled with water, about the size of a big room. 'We were covered in Vaseline and wheeled in, wearing our tails, made by Dunlop.

'Glynis was the star so she said "Dora will go first". They tipped me in and we discovered the tails were buoyant. The tail went up – and I went down.'

Dora also spoke about her depression and breakdown two years previously when she says she had 'a lot going on' in her private and professional life.

'I was carted off for a couple of weeks and sedated, but I got through pantomime afterwards. Work puts me right,' she said.

Her most famous part was in the film *A Taste of Honey*, which I saw resurrected on the stage of The National Theatre in 2014 with Lesley Sharpe playing her role. Dora won the BAFTA for Best Actress in 1961 against stiff opposition from Deborah Kerr and Hayley Mills. But there was one mistake, the result of bad advice. She chose to take £1,500 rather than a percentage of the profits, which would have been huge.

In 1999, she made an appearance in the Victoria Wood sitcom *Dinner Ladies*, and in 2000 she joined the cast of the long-running BBC comedy series *Last of the Summer Wine* as Aunt Roz Utterthwaite. In 2001, she was a guest star on *Absolutely Fabulous* as June Whitfield's on-screen friend Dolly (originally called Milly). She received a BAFTA nomination in 2002 for this role. In her 90s she stopped taking on roles because of difficulties memorising lines and died in 2014, aged 91.

Cliff Richard, September 1990

I wasn't the on-stage interviewer when Cliff Richard came to The Nave, but I was given the chance to meet him before taking my seat in the audience, from where I was to watch and take notes. When I entered the room set aside for those of us allowed to mingle, I felt really sorry for the man. I don't have a problem talking to famous people – in fact I always wish I could spend longer with them as there's never enough time to ask them everything I'd like to. But people were standing in a semi-circle around Cliff and no-one was making conversation. They were clearly overawed and speechless.

Unfortunately, my reaction to this kind of situation is to make up for the silence by gabbling at top speed to fill the gaps – or on this occasion the GREAT VOID.

This is not to be confused with the Mandela moment I described earlier, when I was told I could not speak to him at Northolt airport, then he came and shook my hand and I missed my chance to say something memorable.

I can't remember what nonsense I was talking to Cliff to spare him making all the running but he was clearly relieved when I asked him how he kept so fit and trim. This is very clear in my mind, simply because he then proceeded to lie on the floor and demonstrate his daily exercises for me. I think this may have broken the ice.

Our photographer Alison Holman took a picture of the moment I was first introduced to Cliff, just as I was revving up to spout nonsense at him, but before his aerobics. The shot may have missed the exercise demo which happened later, but it is still a really funny image. You can see the manic look in my eyes, as Cliff looks at me and my notepad and seems to be sizing us both up. In the background lurks a partly hidden vicar and his dark shadow. It looks as though Cliff has conjured up some divine protection.

He could have done with a bit of protection when his family

Your award-winning Gazette team

The award-winning Gazette team in 2002.

Facing the hostility of the crowds with the rest of the world's media while covering the return of Diana's body to RAF Northolt.

Me and my teddy somewhere in Brum. I learnt to smile eventually.

My happy childhood home in Birmingham where, in case I got lost, I
was taught to say parrot fashion '256, Edward Road. Flat 2, I'm three'.
Sadly, the house was knocked down years ago.
No one's managed to lose me yet.

Me wearing the fair isle beret that kept me safe. Knitted by Nana
Parsons who had a hen called Matilda and a beautiful garden
in Great Barr with lavender and lupins.

Pushed forward by my photographer to be a guinea pig for celebrity
hair stylist John Frieda at a demonstration in Boots, Uxbridge,
I look as if I am about to be sick.

On location in Hayes with Minder star Gary Webster who took over from Dennis Waterman. As Gary was covered in fake blood he – and the photographer – thought being punched by me might make yet another great picture. Hmm…

Ten years after my lunch with the Queen, a nostalgic piece was commissioned by My Weekly magazine to mark the Diamond Jubilee. Sixty years on the throne!

A Learjet crashes on the A40 on deadline and a photographer and I had to physically go and find it. No internet to help us then.

It was a scoop for us when we discovered that an Uxbridge man, Peter Norris, was one of a group arrested in Greece as spies. He was there with a group of aeroplane enthusiasts and clearly innocent – so we did what we could to help.

Kissed by a Pitbull was the headline for this picture. It was truly an action shot as the dog bounded out and made a beeline for me as its owner came to open the front door. Photographers never miss a trick.

Tense times. A mortar attack on Heathrow Airport resulted in this press conference. I am on the left with my trusty notepad. The IRA had another couple of goes over the following days.

Back to Brum to celebrate our first wedding anniversary with mum and dad in La Dolce Vita night club. Very swanky – and yes, my hair really was that long, and Mike's was that black.

My friend Marg and me celebrating the new Millennium with … a mug? Of tea?

Me in the 1970s striking a pose before selfies or social network. And yes, I was that slim thanks to a practically no-calorie diet - not a route to be recommended. Although being slim is.

This sums up the sixties and seventies for me, as we partied our way through it. The photo was taken at Wapping at the Prospect of Whitby pub. I have parked a pint on Mike's head, presumably with a vague idea of putting in a claim. We hadn't yet become a permanent couple or come up with the novel idea of marriage.

Von, Jean and me at Butlins Holiday Camp Skegness. We went to work there for the whole of the summer holiday as chalet maids. We are pictured here in our droopy green overalls with our supervisor Mrs Eyles, (our version of Hi-de-Hi's Miss Cathcart.)

If it's Thursday it must be Greece. Mike and I at the Parthenon during our 2012 World Cruise. We'd just escaped from our long-winded guide and forced someone to take a photo of us.

I think we can safely call this an opportunity missed. I was inches away from Mandela when this picture was taken. Read it for yourself. I'm trying to forget it.

Actor Keith Michell, famous for his portrayal of Henry VIII, being interviewed LIVE by me at The Nave, St Margaret's Uxbridge.

Cliff Richard at The Nave… and me… and a vicar. And a strange shadow.

Trying to keep up with Jeffrey Archer (and get a good quote from him)
during the famous 1997 by-election in Uxbridge.
John Randall on right.

Interviewing Tony Blair in West Drayton in 1997. Alastair Campbell was in the background hurrying him up.

Screaming Lord Sutch at the 1997 by-election… err… screaming. He had been offering One Million-pound notes in Uxbridge High Street as bribes. I still have mine.

Newly elected Blair on a soapbox. He drew enormous crowds in 1997 –
it was like a rock star had arrived in Uxbridge.

Ken Livingstone surrendering. I wonder what I'd said…

Local police officer Clive Smith and his dog – a great partnership, and one of my favourite interviews.

Finding Phyllis – This article was published in 2011, five years before *Finding Tipperary Mary*, the Times and Sunday Times bestseller, was published by Mirror Books. My Weekly magazine recognised a good story well ahead of the book.

Teaching days – my class of 1972 in the quadrangle at Stanhope Junior School (now primary).

Zoe and her grandad Frank Fisher, which appeared in The Guardian Family section April 2013.

Zoe and Nick, (FJ – Fisher Junior and SiL – Son in Law in my column) at the Alhambra in Spain.

All scrubbed up ready to go to a Royal Garden Party at Buckingham Palace in May 2017. I am reminding Mr F – resplendent in morning dress – that I had decided against wearing a fascinator after realising it made me look like a potted plant.

brought him, aged seven, over from India where he was born. The new boy at school in England was so brown he was called names like 'Indibum' which compared with trolls' internet abuse today, seems rather tame. In any event he said he did not feel it was racist.

My friend Sheila, one of the crowd at West Midlands College where we were all training to be teachers, went to the same secondary school as Cliff, and she remembers him as a local boy. Apparently there was a primary school teacher, Stafford Young, whom Sheila had kept in touch with, who gave the young Cliff space to play his music – loud!

She said, 'Stafford never actually taught Cliff, but he opened a Boys' Club in Waltham Cross where he went. He told me many stories of Cliff's early life in music. He was responsible for Cliff's fame – he actually won a talent show at the club – and Cliff never forgot that and was close to Stafford right to his death.

'And yes, Cliff was called Indibum. I remember that. Name calling was rife back then.'

His musical interest was influenced by crooners like Frank Sinatra and Rosemary Clooney, but it was the King himself – Elvis – who inspired the young Cliff to open up his vocal cords and eventually find his own style and loyal fans. There was a spell though, when he became religious and lost interest in his career to such an extent that records were made without him. He would just turn up at the end and put his voice over the top. Eventually he decided that being a public Christian could actually help him. Asked if he was conceited he said: 'We all are in this business to a certain extent; we have to be. But I don't feel the need to talk about myself and my successes all the time.'

Cliff was amused by his record 'The Young Ones' being used over the titles in the sitcom with Rik Mayall and Adrian Edmondson, and said he had fun doing a new recording of 'Living Doll' with them. 'The stars of *The Young Ones*, about some unsavoury students, have immortalised me!' he laughed.

As he was then nearly 50, he said he knew he must recognise when his career was winding down. 'I don't want to end up in a heap,' he said. Twenty-five years later Rik Mayall is dead and Cliff is still working as I write, and as far as I know is not in a heap.

Jenny Agutter, November 1996

Jenny Agutter was interviewed by the Rev Alison Christian at The Nave, the arts centre in St Margaret's Church. She first played Roberta in *The Railway Children* on TV when she was only 14 years old, but was getting on a bit – 17! – when the feature film was made.

Asked why it is so popular and enduring she replied: 'The Railway Children is about everything we want life to be: the Victorian ideal, the possibility of innocence, the perfect life and good people,' she said. 'I'm not Roberta, but I wish I was that wonderful person.'

Following her early success on the big and small screen, she went on to learn the craft of the theatre, but it wasn't easy. At Farnham Rep, she appeared in *School for Scandal*. 'I knew nothing about Restoration Comedy and I didn't get a single laugh for the four weeks we did it,' she admitted. In *Arms and the Man*, with Tom Courtenay in Manchester, she learned the art of speaking out to the audience which, she said, was not a skill necessary for films. As I write this in 2017, I wonder what she'd say to TV audiences today who complain about mumbling actors, and have been forced to switch on the sub-titles to understand what is going on.

At 21 years old the biggest change came: Hollywood beckoned with a part in the film *Logan's Run*, but she never quite felt part of the glitzy scene. However, being married and having a child – her son was then five years old – made her more content than she had ever been. 'I didn't before have a sense of myself and a place in society,' she said.

She was appointed Officer of the Order of the British Empire (OBE) in the 2012 Birthday Honours for charitable services and has since gained a whole legion of fans through starring in the popular BBC drama *Call the Midwife*.

Jeffrey Archer, November 20 1996

Jeffrey Archer, the former MP and best-selling novelist was interviewed by Stewart Henderson as part of his An Audience With... series.

He said that as a young boy he was 'pretty intolerable. I always wanted to be number one.'

That year (1996) the film *The Nutty Professor* was showing at cinemas and Lord Archer of Weston-Super-Mare also had a whiff of eccentricity about him. He has a Bertie Wooster-type boyish enthusiasm, rather like a Labrador that has just come out of the rain and is shaking itself over everybody.

I remember covering a later visit of his to Mount Vernon Hospital in Northwood. He was happy to demonstrate a new scanner for our photographer by climbing aboard and waving his arms about. I asked a medical question of the experts present and Archer was suddenly next to me whispering in my ear. 'You know someone suffering with that, don't you?' He was right – and I was surprised he picked up on it. Not so self-centred then, or just a good observer, I wondered? Vital for a writer of course.

At The Nave, he admitted his great annoyance about the snobbish reception his books received then – and still do. 'If I sold no books they would be described as masterpieces, but because I sell millions, snobs say I'm an 'airport reader'. I have 150 million readers and every time they insult me, they insult them,' he said.

He was a Conservative MP from 1969-1974 and deputy chairman of the party from 1985-86.

Asked about the demise of Mrs Thatcher he said she had

misread the poll tax outcry. 'We got it badly wrong. Also, her great weakness is that she will not turn back. She should not have gone to Paris that weekend. Cecil Parkinson begged her not to go. Norman Tebbit asked her to stay, and then I rang her.'

She said, 'You're ganging up against me.'

Mr Archer told her, 'No, we are ganging up for you.'

He is adamant that she could have gone on to win the next election.

When quizzed on the Tory stance on sleaze he said they had to be very careful about taking the moral high ground 'unless the position we are in is so pure.' Hmm…

The following year he was back in Uxbridge supporting Conservative candidate John Randall in a by-election.

Five years later Jeffrey Archer's political career ended with his conviction and subsequent imprisonment (2001-03) for perjury and perverting the course of justice, which followed his second resignation. He was made a life peer in 1992, and his books have sold at least 330 million copies worldwide.

Janet Brown, April 1991

Mentioning Margaret Thatcher reminds me of the mimic Janet Brown, who was interviewed at The Nave by Paul Gillingham in 1991. Famous for her impersonation of the prime minster who resigned in 1990, she said that mimicking Margaret Thatcher had changed her life. 'When I started watching her she was the Education Secretary, but I never dreamt she would become PM. I was startled by her approach on TV and the way she answered questions, so I began to study her.'

At the height of her career, Janet was invited to tea with Mrs T. Surprisingly, she didn't find it daunting. 'She was very motherly, asked me if I got nervous in front of a camera, and admitted she did. As I left, I asked her not to change because she was so good to impersonate. "Oh no," laughed Mrs T, "I mustn't deprive you of your livelihood!'"

The audience applauded as Janet broke into routines, one minute wrapping her top lip around her teeth to be Esther Rantzen, the next adopting a Liverpool accent as Cilla Black. Detail, she said, was important and victims like Hilda Ogden from *Coronation Street* had to have the right colour and texture of lipstick as well as the correct mouth shape to bring the character alive.

Janet was married to Carry On actor Peter Butterworth from 1947 until his death in 1979. They had two children. She died following a brief illness in a nursing home in May 2011, aged 87, and is buried alongside her husband in Danehill Cemetery, in East Sussex.

After her interview, I had a chat with her about my father-in-law Frank Fisher, who had been in the same Prisoner of War camp as her husband during WW2. They were in the same compound in Stalag Luft III when the Great Escape happened. Peter Butterworth was one of the vaulters on the wooden horse which was placed in the same spot every day while digging went on underneath. My father-in-law was one of the men who got rid of the sand/dirt – immortalised in a Monty Python sketch many years later where they shook it from their trousers, which was pretty accurate! Frank was not impressed with the film *The Great Escape* though; not even Steve McQueen. I think especially not Steve McQueen.

After he died I had this piece – a brief account of his story – published in *The Guardian* Family section, alongside a photograph of Frank with our daughter, his granddaughter.

The Guardian April 27 2013 – A Great Escape

Looking at this photograph of an elderly man, peacefully sunning himself in his garden with his granddaughter, it is hard to imagine that 70 years ago he was a young RAF navigator with Bomber Command.

Born in Hove in the final year of WW1, Frank Fisher lived in north London as a child. His family always holidayed in Bournemouth and he often hoped he might live there someday.

Plucked from the safety of a job in insurance, Frank Fisher – my father-in-law – was on his 33rd mission when he parachuted out of his Halifax, after it was shot down on April 16 1943. He was taken as a prisoner of war to Stalag Luft III, where The Great Escape happened and remembers many of the characters portrayed. He said it was not at all like the film version!

An only child, he married Gladys, a WAAF, after she fell for him – literally – when he knocked her off her bike in Wales, or so the family tale goes. After the war, he trained as a teacher, eventually becoming a headteacher, and they fathered two sons. The boys bucked the trend by producing three granddaughters between them.

Once, to entertain the girls he decided to be a Dalek by sticking a rubber sucker on his forehead. He ended up in the doctor's surgery with a sore head and it took weeks to heal. I'm sure his pupils would love to have known, when he faced them in assembly after the weekend, the real reason for the strange alien mark.

When I turned up from Birmingham to marry his elder son he could not have been more welcoming. I always remember his kindness, particularly saying we should value and preserve regional accents (mine was quite strong then). I loved discussing current events with him, particularly on education, as we were both teachers.

After Gladys died in 1988 he was lost for a while, but insisted on continuing to provide family teas on Sundays – unusual for a man then – including making the red jellies that the girls adored.

Occasionally we could coax this modest man into talking about the war: what it was like to jump from a burning plane, finding his way in the dark (in what he hoped was France or Belgium until he found a tombstone with German writing on it); later his sadness at hearing that many of the escapees had been shot on the direct orders of Hitler.

But he was happiest putting all this behind him, leading a quiet life, later with his second wife Doreen, whom he married in 1995.

When the newlyweds moved to the coast, his long-term goal was achieved – to live in Bournemouth where he had felt so secure as a child. He also acquired a step-family of whom he became very fond.

Frank played the piano, ate very healthily before it became fashionable, always went for a daily walk – and could still fit into his old RAF uniform in his 90s.

He died in August 2012, aged 93. His three grandchildren and three step-grandchildren all made it to his funeral and his eldest granddaughter, also a teacher (pictured with him in the Southbourne garden about ten years ago) read aloud from his war diary, written in the POW camp. She pointed out that, typical of his generation, 'granddad never complained about risking his life.'

I think this picture, which we keep on the door of our freezer, sums up the peace he felt, to be alive and with his family on a sunny day in the garden; contentment he richly deserved.'

Fiona Phillips, 2008

I met the then GMTV presenter Fiona Phillips at the Beck Theatre where she was to present awards to Uxbridge College students. She remembered the Beck bomb, planted by the IRA in 1991, from her time at Sky News, but I don't think she'd visited the Hayes theatre before.

Now she was leaving GMTV after fifteen years to spend more time with her family (literally, not in the politician sense), so she was happy to have a quick chat with me, before dishing out the certificates.

That morning she had interviewed *Baywatch* star Pamela Anderson who she said was fun 'as she was able to laugh at herself'. She also enjoyed meeting Charles and Camilla – 'delightful and very well-suited' – and a whole string of desirable interviewees from Brad Pitt to Mel Gibson. But she awards the title of hottest man to David Beckham, saying he is: 'Lovely, so nice. He's just never changed. I don't know how he and Victoria handle some of the publicity they get. If they sued, they'd never be out of court.'

Fiona will always be remembered for the interview with Heather Mills, when the then wife of Sir Paul McCartney went into melt-down, venting her fury on the media and its treatment of her.

'I felt so sorry for her, she was breaking down, but she's a human being and something just tipped her over the edge. Heather had specifically asked for me to interview her and it was nice to feel she trusted me.'

On a lighter note, she accepted her time on *Strictly Come Dancing* in 2005 was memorable for her disappointing performance, which led to her being voted off in the fourth week. She said: 'I was quite staggered about how awful I was. I used to practise about six hours a day (with partner Brendan Cole) but when Saturday night came everything just went out of my head.'

A patron of The Alzheimer's Society – her mother died from the condition and her father was then developing it – she appeared in a programme, *The Killer in Me*, in 2007 where celebrities agree to tests for 11 major diseases to review what is lurking in their genes.

She said: 'I chose not to know about Alzheimer's because even if you know, there's nothing you can do about it. I was told I was prone to heart disease and obesity so I went and had a heart scan. But when my scan was clear I went out and stuffed myself with fat!'

She was then writing a column for the *Daily Mirror*, owned by Trinity Mirror which also owns my paper, so we had a bit of a chat about being columnists for the same group.

She said: 'I love writing it and I don't feel you have to be nasty about people to be interesting. Also, so-called soft sofa interviews are not an easy option. Jeremy Paxman has it easy – being nasty.'

Fay Weldon, 2008

When author Fay Weldon came to Uxbridge she agreed to be interviewed on the stage of our local university. I was in the audience, reporting on it for the paper.

There was great excitement that one of Britain's most successful writers, with more than 20 novels and five collections of stories under her belt, had just taken up a post as Professor of Creative Writing at Brunel University.

Vice-chancellor Prof Chris Jenks quizzed her in front of a big audience made up of people from the university and the community, from serious fans to the simply curious. As she took her seat the writer – now in her eighties – cast a mischievous twinkle at her audience giving a hint of what was to come. Though every bit the icon I wanted her to be (I've read all her books, having just finished *She May Not Leave* and *the Cloning of Joanna May*), she was also someone you could imagine living next door to. I was thrilled to hear that she had written a sequel to the 1983 novel *The Life and Loves of a She-Devil*, which was published last year (2017), and can't wait to get my hands on it.

Fay described her post at Brunel as her 'first proper job' even though she had worked for the *Daily Mirror*, the Foreign Office and in advertising. Fay produced the famous slogan 'Go to work on an egg' for the Egg Marketing Board long before Jamie Oliver started the healthy eating bandwagon rolling. It encouraged us to eat an egg each morning and became one of the most remembered and applauded advertising campaign ever. However, her 'Vodka gets you drunker quicker' never saw the light of day as it was deemed unsuitable by her superiors.

Although she came from a family of writers they didn't inspire her to make it a chosen career, as they 'all died poor', she said.

'It didn't necessarily seem the best thing to be but I found I could use language easily. After all, I had worked in the Foreign Office where I used to write fiction – or propaganda.'

She said she believed her 'fiction' was true. 'You make it up but it is according to the world around you as you see it.'

Born in England, but brought up in New Zealand, the ten-year-old Fay felt a bit of an outsider but she said she felt this was probably good for writers. When she got her job in advertising she found she could 'handle words'.

'I then worked in a TV department making commercials and in those days, you did everything yourself; you wrote it, edited it and delivered it by bus, or taxi if you were lucky. I eventually thought it might be a good idea to write a long story so I started with TV plays. Not many women did it in those days (mid-1960s) but Fay attributes her bravado to coming from an all-female family – she lived with her mother, sister and grandma.

Asked about her label as a feminist she said she prefers to think of herself as 'a writer who gave women a voice'.

'I was a feminist but I didn't see it as that. I just assumed women were human beings and wrote about them. Feminism is a continuing good idea but you have to make it up as you go along. There's no headquarters.'

Many years on, however, she said there have been significant breakthroughs and she felt it was ridiculous to go on blaming men for everything. 'Women, who had no choice before, now have a lot of choice,' she said.

Post-feminism, women are expected to work when they have babies and she felt that this should not necessarily be regarded as the norm. 'I hope what women want is a happy, useful and fulfilled life, not particularly lots of money. Women who do not have children have higher jobs but the opportunities are there if you are willing to sacrifice a part of you.'

She looked at the audience and said, to laughter, 'I get into trouble for saying things like that.'

Other examples of her outspoken views in the past have included her praise of glamour model Jordan, her criticism of the Spice Girls, and her approval of women faking orgasms. The Spice Girls, she said, had been synthesised into these 'extraordinary creations' – girl power – without the ability to sustain it. Pushed on the subject of Katie Price (Jordan) she thought her a nice person with a great appetite for life. She wished her luck, particularly trying to sell her DD cups on eBay. What she thought of Katie putting her old implants up for sale in 2016 – hoping for a six-figure sum, I've yet to hear.

Her generous nature did not extend to upholding the widely held view that everyone has a book inside them, just waiting to come out. She said: 'Everyone has experiences, but not all people can join up the dots and write about it. People who want to write should never study English Literature. Those who do, tend to write five words and then go into a spiral of depression. Writing can be learnt and encouraged but not everyone will have a bestseller in them.'

She said the students on the university's creative courses were very nice to each other – 'in fact it's very hard to get them to criticise each other's work. They have an aptitude for writing but they can only do it if they read a lot. When I write a book, I write something I would want to read myself. The students' desire to learn is astonishing. I must be careful not to constrain it.'

I didn't know then that the following year (2009) I would be doing an MA course in Creative and Professional Writing – and the iconic writer would be one of my lecturers.

Jo Brand, 2007

Another big name to take to the lecture theatre at Brunel was stand-up comic Jo Brand. A former student at the university, she had received an honorary degree of Doctor of Social Sciences from her alma mater in 2006, the previous year. Again, I was in the audience taking notes for an article for the paper.

Introduced as 'Dr Jo' she returned to give an insight into her life, from her days as a psychiatric nurse to stand-up comic and television star.

Jo kept the packed lecture theatre entertained, illustrating how she survived on the comedy circuit in its heyday when there were only 15 women to about 300 men.

She admitted, 'I played up to the whole thing of being a man-hater – a violent, psycho lesbo. I had a lot of contact with lesbian groups and eventually they would ask me to make it clear that I was heterosexual, as I was giving them a bad name!'

Admitting she spent most of her four years at Brunel drunk, she looked out at the audience who'd come to hear her speak and said she was amazed to be asked back to lecture such an academic group.

After getting her degree in social science and nursing in 1982, she went on to be a staff nurse at Maudsley Hospital clinic, eventually spending her off-duty moments doing open spots at London comedy clubs. After a TV appearance on *Friday Night Live*, she left nursing and took a chance on a career in comedy.

In the early days of her stand-up career the unrelenting jibes about her physical appearance, such as being called 'a hideous old boiler' were sometimes difficult to deal with. She said, 'I got used to it but my parents didn't. Imagine relentless abuse seen by your family. If you complain it seems so petty. You are performing, you are doing well. Why are you moaning about it?'

She said the press had been kinder to her since she got married and had two daughters and they realised she was not going to go on the Tube 'shooting people's testicles off'.

Nevertheless, Jo said she would recommend having a go at being a comedian, adding wryly, 'The worst that can happen is being totally humiliated in public.'

Jack Wild, 1991

After the *News of the World* featured the story of a well-known child actor who was getting help for his alcoholism in our area, we wanted the story for our own paper.

The fourteen-year-old Jack Wild, who played the artful dodger in the 1968 film of *Oliver!*, was a huge hit with those of us who saw it then, and thanks to endless TV repeats, his portrayal became the definitive version of Dickens's cheeky chappy.

Now that he was an adult with serious problems I didn't hold out much hope of him agreeing to an interview. It was more than 25 years ago, and well before it was de rigueur for celebrities to parade their drink or drug problems in glossy magazines, almost as a badge of honour, and for readers to sympathise with them.

So, it was a big – and a very welcome surprise – when Jack agreed to see me at St Nicholas's Church in Hayes where he was attending weekly meetings for alcoholics.

He looked older – of course he did, he was all grown up, in fact middle-aged – and rather careworn, but underneath there was still something of the mischievous young lad I remembered from the film.

The group at the church was called Alcoholics Victorious. It originated in America and is an offshoot of Alcoholics Anonymous. AV believed that prayer and Bible teaching, as well as swapping experiences, were important in beating addiction. There were only four AV groups in the UK at that time; the other three were in Bristol, Gloucestershire and Nottingham.

Born in Manchester, Jack moved to Hounslow when he was eight, and at the time I met him he was living with his fiancée Lisa in Hampton Hill.

His big break, he told me, happened while he was a pupil at The Barbara Speake Stage School in Acton, where he was friendly with, amongst others, singer and drummer Phil Collins. He said: 'I was in the stage show of *Oliver!* as one of the gang – they said I was too small to be Dodger, but I got the film role. Then they had to find an Oliver who was smaller than me (Mark Lester). Even then I had to wear two-inch heels. It was great fun. I didn't treat it as a job but it certainly paid more than a milk round!'

After the film, he really hit the big time, ending up in Hollywood where he was surrounded by superstars like Sinatra, Charlton Heston and Paul Newman. 'I just walked around with my mouth open,' he laughed. Unfortunately, fame brought problems, too, in the form of his alcohol addiction. 'I couldn't walk past a pub or off-licence without going in,' he said. 'Then that depressed me and gave me a reason for drinking more.'

When I met him, thanks to the support group at the Hayes church, he had kicked the habit. 'It was a miracle to me. I am so much happier and now I have peace of mind. I now know what God wants for me. I'm sure I'm a better person – but still nowhere near perfect,' he added hastily.

At that time, he was tackling roles such as Much the Miller's son in Kevin Costner's film, *Robin Hood, Prince of Thieves*. Most of his part may have ended up on the cutting room floor, but it was 'great fun' he said. He had a pantomime lined up in Crewe for Christmas and was looking forward to the future.

Jack died in 2006, aged 53 from oral cancer, which he had blamed on his drinking and smoking.

Jayne Torville, Jeff Rich, Paul Daniels and Sooty

Looking through my old cuttings in 2015 it was funny to see that 20 years previously I was interviewing Jayne Torville about her 'retirement' from ice skating. The year was 1995 and she was on a farewell tour with Christopher Dean. In the interview, she told me she was looking forward to swapping a glittering career on the ice for the chance to put her feet up and defrost the fridge – just like everyone else.

Well, she must have got fed up with defrosting the fridge and putting the rubbish out, since in 2006 the dancing duo became huge stars again when they headed the hugely popular show *Dancing on Ice*, which ended up running for nine series.

At one time, it was enjoyed by 13m viewers, but it was taken off in 2014 after Torville and Dean decided to quit while they were still at the top of their game. Now, in 2018, the show has returned with them as judges. It looks like we'll never let them retire.

So, back to my interview in 1995, when I was I admit, rather excited to be interviewing half of the nation's chief national treasures. They are, of course, best known for their sensuous skating to Ravel's *Bolero*, which projected ice dance into an art form and earned them nine sixes at the Sarajevo Olympic Games in 1984. I watched the nail-biting moment on TV, and have never forgotten it.

When I spoke to Jayne she was on a gruelling tour called Face the Music, which was being staged everywhere, from Belfast to Birmingham. It was going down very well and they were getting a great response. Bolero was always a must on the programme and it inevitably stirred an emotional reaction. She said they never thought when they did it in 1984 that it would become like a signature tune. The other routines which were equally loved by fans were 'Mack and Mabel' and 'Let's Face the Music', the latter only getting them a bronze at their third Olympic Games in Lillehammer.

During the tour, it was clear that audiences were still cross about that and showed their loyalty by holding up cards with six on them or shouting out 'You were robbed'. This more than compensated, said Jayne, but admitted she was puzzled by the mark, as they knew they skated really well and couldn't have done any better.

At the time, the pair had been featured in a documentary for the BBC which showed them in training. It attracted the biggest audience for the *Omnibus* series at the time. We are all now very familiar with the pitfalls of reality television, particularly in the slanted editing, but Jayne told me she was not happy that so much emphasis was placed on a scene where she was in tears at her partner's taunts during a difficult rehearsal, saying it just wasn't representative of their relationship.

She described it as a 'false interpretation', as it only happened one day but it looked like it happened all the time. They were only human beings, she said, and that was one of the worst days. They had a lot of work to do, were tense, and having the cameras there made it worse. They had thought the programme makers would have respected certain things; they were also disappointed that they didn't pick up on some things, like showing a routine from the beginning, the changes it goes through, and how it ends up.

Jayne was looking forward to increased leisure time after the farewell tour but said it was not the end of the partnership and they expected to appear on other people's shows from time to time. She was looking forward to enjoying simple pleasures like television, shopping or the cinema and they both wanted to spend more time in their homes, ordering newspapers and milk like everyone else. And of course, getting rid of the surplus ice from the fridge!

***

When celebrities are not on the road they can be found in unusual places. The week after my chat with the ice queen I reported on Status Quo's drummer hosting a master class at a Harefield school. Jeff Rich, who played with Def Leppard and Elton John before joining the Quo in the 1980s, talked to the pupils at John Penrose School (now Harefield Academy) about his rise to fame, the history of drums, and the qualities needed to get to the top. He did emphasise, however, that students who were keen to follow in his footsteps should stay at school and take exams first. He told them that to play drums you need FAT; not the usual advice young people are given these days.

Before they ran for the crisps and full-fat chocolate, Jeff explained that this was advice for drumming, and stood for Fitness, Attitude and Timekeeping. Another important requirement was 'independence' – this meant the left hand should be able to do something different from the right. He showed them African drums, a tabor and a snare; and compared an early hollowed-out log with a modern drum kit. Some pupils played the school drums accompanied by Jeff on his own kit. The drummer told me though that, although he'd been to around thirty schools, it was not easy talking to an audience of 300-400 youngsters. In fact, it was more nerve-wracking than playing in front of thousands.

Most celebrities are co-operative and willing to chat if they are keen to promote a book or a tour. Some surprise you, though. I took my young daughter with me when I went to quiz Johnny Morris, who was appearing at the Beck Theatre. He was well-known on children's TV as a genial storyteller but from the minute we entered his dressing room he was grumpier then Scrooge at Christmas. I didn't know what to expect of Paul Daniels but he proved to be the opposite. After welcoming me to his then home in Denham, he settled me with a cuppa, then sprawled on the sofa while I interviewed him. He was very relaxed and when he heard I was originally from the Midlands he did an impressive Brummie accent for the rest of our interview. His wife Debbie McGee wasn't there, but he spoke fondly her. The pair of them still kept in the public eye even though at one time they seemed to be falling out of favour, which made me think unfairly that I wouldn't warm to him. It taught me never to go with pre-conceived ideas.

Another famous face I'm glad to see is still hanging on in there is Sooty, who came out of retirement to entertain a new generation of children. In my time, the puppet's innocent pranks were admired as the height of mischief. Sadly, many of today's children think that 'naughtiness' is something entirely different and Childline is being inundated with calls from youngsters who are disturbed by images – both sexual and violent – that they see on TV and on the internet. What puzzles me most is why so many parents appear to have stopped protecting their children from adult material. It isn't that long ago that it was normal to put children to bed before the watershed and parents complained vociferously about the possibility of kids glimpsing top-shelf magazines in their local newsagents. Have people just reached saturation point and given up?

Back to Sooty, and it's easy to forget how fascinating puppets can be to children. During my years working in primary schools I used to get my pupils to make shadow puppets. Mr F rigged up a 'theatre' for me from an old-fashioned wooden clothes horse – that's the sort of thing expected of you if you marry a teacher. We stretched a sheet tightly across the front to make a screen, which was then backlit by an angle-poise lamp. Some Chinese-sounding music accompanied the children as they operated the puppets to act out the willow pattern story to the class. Magical.

Fisher Junior's first trip to the Beck Theatre was to see the Sooty Show, and she was immediately hooked, insisting on calling it the 'Sooty Centre' for a while. Later she joined the Beck Youth Theatre and took part in Summer Youth Projects such as *Alice in Wonderland* and the *Wizard of Oz*.

I must admit though, I found it disturbing years later when, as a reporter, I had to interview Sooty. The little bear, of course, doesn't speak, but his 'keeper' Matthew Corbett expected me to shake paws with him while Sooty nodded or shook his head at my questions. I felt ridiculous.

I suppose I was lucky he didn't squirt me with his water pistol or bash me over the head with a hammer. All good innocent violence, eh?

***

I mentioned that I was chief reporter in the early 90s, and a few years later when I was deputy news editor, it became harder to fit in writing time. This was particularly of course when the news editor was away, as I then took over the helm and was (not literally, thank goodness) glued to the desk.

I have always enjoyed organising and working with a team, and I think I have a reasonable amount of common sense, but not having had a formal training in journalism – you will remember I came from teaching and learnt to be a reporter 'on the job' – I didn't always cut the mustard when it came to editing, which was not just a simple matter of checking spelling and grammar. Thankfully editor Anthony Longden (probably in despair) eventually sent me to Hastings on a news editors' course in 2000.

I was the oldest on the course but it was great fun – as well as informative – and the fledgling, prospective news editors included me in everything, most memorably slipping away one evening to see the film *Billy Elliot* at the local cinema. I hope they are all now in top jobs in the media. If not famous ballet dancers.

The news editor – the job doesn't seem to exist now, as staff on local papers have been cut to the bone – used to be responsible for what went in the paper and, as this was a hefty task, they no longer wrote stories. As I was deputy, I still tried to find the time to write news, and continued doing the schools' page until 2007. It was dropped while I had a prolonged spell off work for two operations. I had been doing it every week since 1984, the first five years as a teacher before the change of career to full-time journalism in 1989, so I was sorry to see it go.

By 2007 I had gone part-time – working three days a week – in order to visit my mother who had severe Alzheimer's, in Birmingham. I left as a staff member in 2009. I still do my column as a freelance, emailing it in each week to the subs, who are now based in Guildford.

Our old office in Uxbridge is now a food bank.

The news desk was the first base for the reporters' copy, before it was sent on electronically to the sub-editors, after checking for accuracy, fairness and balance. The news editor would send a story back to the reporter if necessary, often with a note on the top with suggestions (or orders!) as to how the story could be improved. These comments could be cutting, rude, even soul-destroying, but there was no time to indulge in hurt feelings when a space was being held for a story that was too long, over-written and already late. Reporters soon stop being precious about their stories and harden up.

But the comments could also be good-humoured, such as a gentle reminder that a 300-word story was required – 'not War and Peace'.

At that time, the news editor's job included finding a lead, an anchor (the next biggest story), then shorts and nibs, plus a picture, for every page. They were big papers, with four editions, so it was not an easy task. When I used to do talks to pupils in primary schools about the paper and its production, I would ask them what they thought nibs stood for?

It actually means News in Brief, which are those tiny fillers you often find in the side columns of newspapers or filling up small spaces, rather like parts of a jigsaw. Once the adverts, then the lead and anchor were placed, short stories and nibs had to be found to complete the page.

One clever child suggested it could stand for Not Important Bits. I was impressed. However, it was my cue to say that everything we put in the paper was important, not just the big stories. That may sound glib, but the lifeblood of a community paper was not just the dramatic reports with national appeal. The children I was speaking to at that school, and their families, would remember the football reports, the street party stories and accounts of their grandparents' Golden Wedding in the paper, long after they had forgotten the headline stories.

Keith Michell, 1997

One of the jobs I was still able to fit in as a reporter was again on stage at The Nave, in March 1997, when I quizzed actor Keith Michell in a public interview.

He was the first man to be famous to a wide audience for playing Henry VIII, and in the 1970s he had the whole nation glued to the TV screen for weeks. Few people knew that this very English gent was in fact Australian and had made his mark in many musicals as well as serious dramas. He was also a talented artist, most famous for his Captain Beaky illustrations.

When he came to England he found life at the Young Vic gruelling, doing ten or twelve performances a week. For this he earned £9 and had to find his own accommodation. To supplement this, he painted portraits. He had met Noel Coward and Bette Davis, who was a big fan after seeing him in the musical *Robert and Elizabeth*. He had also worked with the legendary Vivien Leigh and Laurence Olivier. The latter, he said, taught him a lot. His Oz accent was 'beaten out' of him at the Old Vic School, but it was singing lessons that finally saw off his twang, he said.

Playing King Henry, he said was a marvellous part but no-one in the cast realised how huge the series was going to be. He said, 'It was just a job of work.' It was when the crew, who usually couldn't wait to get home, were hanging on to give the cast a round of applause that it started to dawn. The part made him an international star but he did not collect the well-deserved Emmy that he received for his portrayal of Henry.

'I wasn't expecting to get it so I didn't go to the ceremony. That sort of thing doesn't happen to me. My agent picked it up for me.'

He was the definitive Henry on stage and screen – they even brought him back to TV in the 90s to play the King in the *Prince and the Pauper* but he had no qualms about being typecast 'as long as they pay me'. Henry, he said, is everything he'd like to be: omnipotent and ruthless.

So, if he'd played one of his six wives, which would it be? Without hesitation, he said: 'Anne of Cleves (whom he divorced). She was the cleverest one of all.'

Wendy Craig, 1996

I was only a guest interviewer at The Nave but if a particularly popular figure was appearing, the editor would make sure we got press tickets to sit in the audience and take notes for a write-up. Unfortunately, they were normally on Tuesdays, just after our deadline, so the story wouldn't appear for a whole week.

Actress Wendy Craig appeared in March 1996 and was interviewed by the Rev Alastair Cutting. The star of Carla Lane's hit sit-com *Butterflies* was originally from County Durham, but she told the audience, like Keith Michell, she had the accent 'knocked out of me at drama school'.

'You couldn't get a part then if you had a strong northern accent and now you can't get one if you haven't!' she laughed.

Though for three years she was voted the funniest woman on television, the actress insisted she was not naturally funny. She said she had a sense of humour but couldn't tell jokes. 'I like to laugh,' she said, 'but I'm a very serious person really.' It was refreshing to hear a star admit that her success was a lot to do with having good writers.

***

We are not given scripts for our lives so there was no way of knowing when I first met Mr F at a party that we would end up together. It would be fun if we could turn over to the next scene, as an actor would, and see what's next for us.

I met Mike at a bonfire night party in Loughborough. We were both students and it was the 1960s, a great time to be young. Once we got a whiff of a party my friend Marg and I would be off – even if it was fifty miles away and a three-hour bus journey via Leicester, as it was that night. It doesn't sound that far now, but none of us had cars then – and we didn't always fancy hitching. We did hitch sometimes; everyone did.

It is funny to think that drivers stopped regularly to pick up hitchhikers and on the whole treated us properly. If they got a bit frisky we'd just match their banter, but if they did behave inappropriately (as we'd call it now) we gave them short shrift.

I do though have a distant memory of a car-load of lads who decided they would take us with them to Blackpool, even though we'd asked for a lift to Manchester.

Clearly, we should never have got in their car in the first place. Some of them were hiding, so we didn't realise how many there were, until we got in and we ended up sitting on laps because there was nowhere else to go. I confess we considered it a laugh at first.

It was fun – until it wasn't, and they started to want more, and got bolshie. We scarpered as soon as we arrived in Blackpool (you couldn't see us for dust!) and continued our journey by public transport, unscathed, and having learned a salutary lesson.

So... back to our journey to Loughborough by Midland Red bus, and my first meeting with Mike. I've never forgotten that night as, from our seat on top of the double-decker, we saw the most wonderful display of fireworks in people's gardens. It was actually November 6, which was a Saturday when most people would be celebrating the fact that the Houses of Parliament were not blown up in 1605 by Guido Fawkes and co. Things haven't really moved on much in 400 years as people are still fighting and killing in the name of religion or politics. If anything, it seems to have got worse, but that may be because, with modern technology and 24-hour news bulletins, we are so in tune with the news.

Of course, we didn't worry much about such things like that in those days of peace and love and parties. It was actually a birthday celebration we were heading to – Pete Devey's 20th, and all we had to do when we got there, was find The Wheatsheaf pub where it was to be held.

My friend Marg and I didn't pack a bag but just took a toothbrush. Well one each... we did have some standards. There was always a floor to sleep on, which I'm sure is the same for students now.

All Mr F remembers is that Marg and I were both wearing green coats. Hmm. Not love at first sight then. We remember his raven black hair and Donovan hat. He was 19 and he had a girlfriend with him. We didn't speak that night, although I always remind him now that there were fireworks when we met!

A couple of months later, Mike Fisher (as he was known before he morphed into Mr F) appeared in my local pub The Stone in Northfield, Birmingham. He was staying with our mutual friend Pete Caswell, who was a Brummie like me, and who'd invited us to the party in Loughborough, where he was also studying. He'd invited Mike for New Year.

Later, Mike walked me home through the snow (time to remind you that no one had cars in those days). He came in for coffee (I was back with my parents for the holidays) and he told me he came from Greenford.

'Where on earth is that?' I asked. Strange to think that four years later we would be living there together as a married couple.

There was no clue as to our future together that night in our 'romantic' parting. He kissed me goodbye with the immortal words 'See you around' and set off into the chilly night.

How he found his way back to Pete's I'll never know, but as the *Birmingham Mail* had no reports the following day of a lad being dug out of a drift and asking the way back to Northfield, or even Greenford, I assumed he hadn't done a Captain Oates.

We both went out with other people in the intervening years, but always had a great time when we met up, with others, in different parts of the country.

In London, we knocked back pints of bitter or Guinness at the Prospect of Whitby in the docklands, always with a crowd of friends. There was much drinking and smoking against a background of the Beatles, the Stones and Bob Dylan. For me, Marg and Thelma, it was Tamla Motown too.

We all walked everywhere once the pubs closed, sometimes falling into a midnight movie, other times the whole group crashing on someone's floor. Mike and I were easy together so it was natural that our friendship evolved into something more. Eventually I simply couldn't imagine living the rest of my life with anyone else. I still can't.

We married on a sunny March day at St John's Parish Church in Longbridge, Birmingham. I think his relatives thought they were travelling to the other side of the world. Auntie Blanche from Bournemouth was heard to say about Mike's choice of bride, 'Couldn't he have found anyone who lived nearer?' She didn't brave the mammoth trek to the Midlands.

I wore a long white velvet dress trimmed with marabou, which went well with the smattering of snow that lingered by the side of the road. Mike looked gorgeous in his suit.

Marg, from Twyford in Bucks, who had accompanied me to meet the great author Alan Sillitoe, and was with me when I first met Mike in Loughborough, was my chief bridesmaid. The other two bridesmaids were Birmingham girls: Thelma, part of The Stone and Prospect of Whitby crowd, and Jenny who joined our singles crowd later. They wore deep pink velvet.

Among the many friends and family were my schoolfriend Von who shared the Butlins experience and whose mother was a Labour MP, later a peer, who introduced me to politics. Von was by then married to John, a school pal, and also part of The Stone crowd.

The best man was Pete Caswell, now married to Denise, who got us together in the first place at that Loughborough party. All of these people, though now scattered around the UK, are still great friends. We have even recently made contact again with Pete Devey, whose birthday celebration provided our first meeting. And I am still in touch with my West Mid College friends.

My lovely dad gave me away, and my mum, who adored weddings more than anything, couldn't believe she was actually Mother of the Bride, and positively glowed all day.

Much to the surprise of passengers, a number 41 Birmingham Corporation double-decker bus stopped outside the church when they spotted us being photographed. The driver and conductress (the latter had chatted to us on the shopping trips Mum and I had made for the wedding) got off the bus to come over and wish us luck. We have it on film!

Our first home together was in Mornington Road, Greenford, in the West London borough of Ealing. My dad drove me and my few belongings to the flat a few days before the wedding. There was no room for my mum so, not wanting to miss out, she travelled by train.

It was a furnished flat – well, actually half a house with a shared bathroom – and I was thrilled at last to have somewhere we could settle; we'd been travelling back and forth at weekends between London and Birmingham for many months. I'm not sure Mike felt the same way, as he then went on a residential course for a month. He was a civil servant working in London then, and getting fairly rapid promotion.

We had a variety of housemates during our two and a half years at the flat, but the most bizarre were a family of clowns. During the summer, their appearances at fetes meant we were exposed to the full scary regalia on a regular basis. Luckily, they didn't pretend to throw buckets of water at us, or leave strings of sausages in the bathroom.

I was teaching – on supply at first – then a permanent job down the road at Stanhope Primary School, which were then separate infant and junior schools. I loved teaching my junior classes, I loved our flat, I loved Mike. It was one of the happiest times of my life, although at first, I missed not bumping into anyone I knew, as I had always done in Brum. It was so weird when shopping not to be greeted by family, neighbours or old school friends, although Mike's parents and brother lived nearby. Teenager Dave and his friends were notable in the area for driving around in a black van with a massive box fixed to the roof rack. This macabre construction was useful for squeezing in extra passengers. As they all lived on baked beans it didn't bear thinking about.

I soon made some friends at Stanhope School – many are still great mates to both of us. We ended up as part of a very lively circle, many involved in amateur dramatics, and Carole Lewry hosted some fab fancy dress parties. Our friend John Griffiths went on to make a successful career in the theatre.

One of the last of the fancy dress parties that I remember – many years later – was to celebrate St George's Day. We were all given a role in a Mummer's play and instructed to find our own costumes. Mike was rather pleased to be given the part of George, while I was just 'a nurse'. Little Zoë was a mini-nurse.

In the very early days of our marriage, much to our amusement now, I decided to give Mike a cooked breakfast each morning. That was until I realised he didn't want it, and I didn't want to cook it. We then snatched a piece of toast – or ate nothing – like everyone else. It was my only nod to the Stepford Wives. This was the emancipated seventies – what was I thinking?

I enjoyed adding some 1970s flourishes to our little flat – typically oranges and browns: cushions, nick-nacks, anything to make our mark on the place. Our meals mostly came from *Cooking for Two*, a book given me by my school friend Thelma, who married Martin after meeting him at a hop at Birmingham University. She had cooked for her father after her mother died when Thelma was only seventeen, so she was our go-to cooking expert. My favourite meal from her book was Pork Chops Italiano, the sauce made from tinned tomato soup, lemon juice and bay leaves. We thought it very exotic.

During this time, I lost several stones in weight. I'd always been fairly chunky (although when I look back on photos then I look OK – thinner than I thought), but I made a concerted effort to get really slim. I started counting calories and still do – often these days to stay the same. But in the 1970s I was eventually so slim people were telling me to put on weight. I was even able to wear hot pants, a memory which my friend Marg can't shake off, and often reminds me of (she assures me 'in a good way!').

Over the decades my weight has gone up and down. After losing two and a half stone since I stopped being a staff reporter in

2009 (too much time spent at a desk for twenty years), I am more or less happy with how I am. But it will be a surprise for many to hear that I was slim for about twenty years, so I made sure that I included a photograph in this book!

We got our first mortgage and first car by the time we moved to a ground floor maisonette in Harlington, and five and a half years after our wedding, we had Zoë. We had decided to wait that long, and to our astonishment I became pregnant immediately I stopped the pill.

Zoë decided to arrive two days early. Mike spent all day polishing our pink Ford Capri, while my contractions got closer together. Eventually, at about 6pm they were every three or four minutes, so we set off for the maternity home in Harlington.

Maternity homes were cottage hospitals where you could be tended by midwives, with your own GP on call if there were complications, or you needed to be stitched up.

We had only travelled a few yards down our road when the clutch went. Unbelievably, the car wouldn't move. Mr F transferred me and my case to a startled neighbour's car, after a frantic knock on their door which interrupted their dinner.

Apart from a disgruntled dragon of a midwife – Sister Marriot – (not her real name) who clearly didn't want to deliver a baby at 1am, or be working at all, it was an amazing experience.

When my waters broke it was a shock, so I immediately told the dragon. She said 'What do you expect me to do about it?' I was lying in a soaking wet bed. Hmm. When I finally gave birth, she didn't even bother to tell me the gender. Luckily Mike did. We had a lovely little girl.

My friend Marg had given birth to a baby boy ten days previously and so we spent a few hours together in hospital, which was very comforting. Sister Marriot never improved, and I was glad to get home. I never complained about her. I just wanted to forget.

Thank goodness our baby has turned into the best daughter

we could have hoped for. It was certainly worth the effort! She is now married to lovely Nick, and is teaching A-level psychology and living in Wales. They tolerate me writing about them in my column as FJ and SiL (Fisher Junior and son-in-law), for which I thank them.

13

Politics – not boring

During the 1980s I joined a new political party, the now defunct Social Democratic Party (SDP). I'd always felt there were parts of all the main parties' manifestos – Labour, Conservative, Liberal – that appealed to me, so when the SDP was formed by the four rebel MPs Shirley Williams, Roy Jenkins, David Owen and Bill Rodgers, known as the Gang of Four, I was keen to get involved.

Our local Labour MP for Hayes and Harlington, Neville Sandelson, was one of the first to defect and there was great excitement nationally and locally about the new party, which drew members from all the old ones. Those of us who joined from nowhere were dubbed 'political virgins'. You will remember I had joined the young socialists while at school, but, although I remained interested in current affairs as an adult, I'd taken no active part in politics since then.

Now I was a teacher, wife, mother, and fledgling writer, and very ready to get involved in something new.

I stopped being a novice the day David Owen, the leader of the party, who had been foreign secretary with Labour, came to Hayes to speak at a packed public meeting. I was tasked with walking him from his car while belting out at double speed a history of the

178

political situation in our area. He had to be well-informed by the time he got to the platform so I gabbled while trying to keep him dry under an umbrella as the rain poured down. He was a doctor in a previous life and a very attractive Mr Darcy-like character.

Shirley Williams was also a great figure in the party. She is still admired for her common sense, and is one of the few people who gave measured responses in her occasional appearances on programmes like the BBC's *Question Time*.

Labour members felt particularly aggrieved, as the SDP dug deep into their party, taking more members from there than from anywhere else. As new, shiny, naive supporters, we enthusiastically started canvassing, only to be taken aback on the doorstep by being called traitors and worse, by staunch Labour supporters. It was frustrating for those of us who had not betrayed anyone, but it did stop us from getting too complacent about the SDP's growing popularity, which could be seen by rapidly rising support in the polls. It was clear that not everyone loved us.

I was still teaching in Ealing borough, but during the time I got deeper into politics, I had also started to write a schools' page, first for the *Hayes News*, then for the *Gazette*. At one time, I was secretary of the borough party and in 1986 was agent for all the Liberal and SDP candidates in Hayes after the SDP–Liberal Alliance was formed. Later the parties merged to become today's Liberal Democrats.

As an election agent for the first time I had to learn very fast. There are many legal requirements, including keeping accounts of each penny spent on everything, right down to paperclips. Leaflets had to be approved by me and nomination forms scrutinised for mistakes. I was constantly being reminded that if things went disastrously wrong I could end up in prison. When I took my huge pile of papers to the civic centre after the election Peter Fagan of the Labour Party was standing there, ready to warn me he was going to scrutinise my accounts with a fine-tooth comb.

Unfortunately, during the frantic form-filling stage for

nominations, I didn't notice that one very experienced candidate had muddled up two questions: her status/job and the party she represented. When the list of candidates was published, unlike all my other candidates who were SDP or Liberal, she was standing for the 'Housewife Party' which of course didn't exist. She didn't win.

Writing for the paper, albeit in a small way as a freelance at that time, while being involved with local politics, did cause ripples for some activists in Hillingdon. However, I only wrote about schools and did the odd theatre review, so any worries of bias were unfounded. Convincing them was a different matter, since I discovered that political people see plots everywhere. If I did have to wade into political waters such as interviewing councillors on the education committee, I was very careful to be fair. Later, as chief reporter, I covered many of the big political stories, but by then my political past wasn't a problem; in fact, many of my previous rivals are now friends. Also, I had agreed with the editor when I went to work for the paper full-time in 1989 that I would not be signed up to any party, and I kept to that. I re-joined the Liberal Democrats when I became freelance, but to date – nine years on – have not been active politically. I can still see reasonable ideas coming from all parties and am actually in favour of coalition government. Probably the only person left on the planet who is!

As far as the electorate was concerned, it was frustrating that so many people continued to sign up to (and still do) so-called ping-pong politics, where everything said by your opponents is automatically wrong. To me, not to accept that some of your rivals' ideas might be worth considering, is just ditching the baby with the bath water.

Which reminds me of something that happened when I was canvassing in Hillingdon for the SDP. I was getting so depressed by how many women, when asked on the doorstep how they were likely to vote at the next election, said they would have to ask their men. One of these, who certainly owed nothing to the Suffragettes, said she was unable to answer me because her husband was in the bath and couldn't be disturbed.

'I'll put him down as a floating voter then,' I muttered between gritted teeth.

The Alliance was all set to get lots of seats in the local elections of 1982 – everyone said so, even the cynical broadsheets. The old parties looked tired and dated compared with the shiny new SDP, and PM Margaret Thatcher was extremely unpopular. Then, just before polling day, the Falklands War broke out, and everyone rallied round to support the Government by voting Tory. Over the years the SDP did return several MPs, but the party never really recovered from this setback. For me, it was certainly one of the most exhausting periods of my life.

Hillingdon has always been an interesting borough politically but this is not the book to give a detailed history or analysis of the past decades. Others can do that. It is a vast subject and needs plenty of detail to do it justice. A whole book, not just part of a chapter.

After my short period being involved in the fledgling new political party, the SDP, in the 1980s, I had developed a keen interest in local politics and so enjoyed my years reporting on the council's many committees, and following the activities of our MPs. During this period 1989-2009 I did not belong to a political party and, as with all the reporters, tried to make sure my copy was fair and balanced. But there were inevitably always those who felt they were short-changed.

As I said earlier, we would regularly be accused of being biased to either Labour or Conservative members, but we would point out that as both parties complained it looked like we had the balance right.

It was good to see democracy at work – the arguments thrashed out before us in council committees – but now, with the cabinet system, there would not be the same opportunities. Decisions are mostly made by the leader of the council with high ranking members of the cabinet.

Some people complain that public accountability has been diluted as a result. Others say it has saved a lot of time-wasting. With staff cuts on newspapers there would not be enough reporters to cover all the old-style committees now anyway.

In the days when we covered everything, the dates of upcoming council meetings would be written in a large diary. The sub-committees ran on a cycle leading up to a meeting of the full council, where final decisions were made (but now, as mentioned, with increasing delegations the full council decides very few things).

At the paper, a reporter's name would be written next to the meeting they were assigned to cover. These could be anything from housing, planning, leisure or environment, to the rather exciting-sounding Whips or Urgency sub-committees. If you'd arranged to go out that night you'd have to find a kind fellow reporter to cover it for you; it would normally be a swap. It was preferred that reporters specialised – I tended to do the education and social services sub-committees, but not exclusively.

Going back to the same committees benefitted us journalists too. We became familiar with the topics that came up, and began to understand the history of the arguments from all sides. Also, councillors got used to seeing the same person perched at the press table and we could hopefully build up trust with the chairs of our committees and their opposite numbers.

Agendas would arrive at our offices a few days before a meeting and items of particular interest marked in them by the news editor, or editor. Sometimes a reporter would need to ring the council press office to check on the background to a story before the meeting.

But it was often something that was said or decided at the actual meeting on the night that made the biggest story. Councillors would bend our ears, and residents would alert us to items on the agenda that they were particularly concerned about, particularly when cuts were threatened, or schools up for closure.

One of the biggest protests I covered was about the proposal to build on school playing fields.

The Tory group was split on this and there was real drama when the mayor had to use his casting vote (for the status quo) – on his 80th birthday!

On occasions like these, extra committee rooms were opened for the larger audience, with monitors to watch the action in the council chamber.

I remember once a massive screen was set up outside the civic centre. The resulting Big Brother photo that appeared in the paper remains one of my favourites. Very 1984.

The council was ruled by Alderman John Bartlett's Labour administration from 1972-1978. He is mainly remembered for his expansive council house programme – mixing private and social housing – and for building the Civic Centre. Opinion remains divided on both, but I can't be the only one who thinks that architect Andrew Derbyshire's building is a beautiful design; a welcome change from the grey concrete blocks of the sixties. Inside it is a different matter, and many staff say it is like a rabbit warren, with too little daylight.

Ray Puddifoot MBE has been the leader of the Conservative administration for 18 years (since 2000), but I wonder how many people realise that he started out as a protester. He was part of a group who were prepared to stand in the path of bulldozers to save Uxbridge open-air pool if plans for a giant Warner Brothers Movie World complex went ahead.

Residents felt the area could not cope with so much extra traffic. They also wanted to protect the land for popular local activities which were regularly held there.

Councillor Puddifoot, who was then chairman of Hillingdon House Farm Action Group, visited the exhibition in Uxbridge which aimed to bring a film studios and theme park to life.

His scepticism at the Warner Brothers attempt to woo residents by giving more information, is clear from the quote he gave to the *Gazette* at the time, after visiting their exhibition.

He scoffed: 'Warner Bros has provided no more information than on day one. There were cartoon figures and information about rides, but no models or detailed plans.'

Warner Brothers eventually abandoned its plans.

In between the Labour and Conservative administrations, Hillingdon 'tolerated' or 'enjoyed' – depending on your point of view – hung coucils in which the Liberal Democrats held the balance of power.

The two periods of no overall control were from 1986–90 led by Tony Little, and 1998–2006 when Steve Carey was the group leader.

In 1986 no committee chairs could be appointed so the mayor or deputy mayor shared the majority of them. By 1998 the cabinet system had replaced the old committee system. In 2006 the smallest party went down to two councillors, led by Mike Cox.

Mike later stood unsuccessfully against Boris Johnson for the Uxbridge and South Ruislip parliamentary seat in 2015. The Labour group is presently led by Councillor Peter Curling. There are no smaller parties represented on the council now, and the present make-up, as I write in May 2018, is Conservative 44, Labour 21. The next local elections will be in 2022.

BNP, February 1992

I suppose my most dramatic political experiences were as a reporter, with the most surprising being a brush with the BNP on a sunny Saturday afternoon in West Drayton. Looking now at the cutting, I am shocked again by the headline 'Abused – for doing my job'. Here is my report as it appeared in the *Gazette* on February 19 1992:

On Saturday, I went to West Drayton to report an Anti-Nazi League (ANL) rally – and got more than I bargained for. The job of a reporter on these occasions is to remain neutral – no matter what our personal feelings. If there is trouble of any kind, the task is still to interview both sides, and leave readers to make up their own minds.

When I turned up at Station Road at noon, the meeting time the paper had been given by the Anti-Nazi League (ANL), their leafleting was finished and they had moved to the De Burgh Arms, a nearby pub. I followed them there, and spoke to one of the organisers who told me they had started at 10.30am – I suspect to avoid any problems. Any potential troublemakers would, like me, have turned up too late (not that I was going to cause any trouble). They gave me a handful of leaflets to study in my own time and some badges, and I left to go to a job in Hayes.

For me, it looked like there was no story. I had been sent to report on any clashes so, although my editor would be disappointed at the lack of drama, I was quite relieved. As I left, head down thinking about my next assignment, I had no idea that the BNP had got wind of the ANL being in the pub. Having missed them in the town centre, they were waiting outside and getting impatient. I'll never forget what happened next.

As I left the pub alone I was faced by a group of up to a dozen youths who, I quickly realised, were waiting for the ANL supporters to leave. Innocently forgetting the literature, I was holding, I was shocked to find myself surrounded, and the subject of a torrent of abuse.

One moved close to me, and I flinched as he roughly tore the papers out of my hand, ripping some of them. I was met by a stream of venom as the young man, who appeared to be the leader, accused me of supporting the IRA. As he continued to goad me, I tried to tell him I was from a newspaper, covering the demonstration. 'Why have you got all this then?' he demanded, waving the literature and pointing at the badges as I desperately fumbled in my bag for identification. Their attitude changed when I produced my press card, and I tried to slot swiftly back into reporter mode. It was difficult after such extreme intimidation, and my hands shook as I held my pen. The leader said he was from Hillingdon and they were indeed members of the BNP. He admitted they were responsible for (racist) posters and stickers in

West Drayton, but not graffiti. He pointed to the pub and said: 'We're the voice of the working class, not them. We want the return of capital punishment, an end to immigration and a start on repatriation.' I was told they would be putting up a candidate in Uxbridge at the general election. I just hoped my experience was not a taste of their canvassing methods.

This happened more than 25 years ago when UKIP was only a gleam in Nigel Farage's eye, but it is not difficult to imagine where this group would have stood if the 2016 referendum had happened then. Maybe their political views have changed dramatically since then, but many still feel the same way, and a majority of the UK voted to leave Europe.

Now in 2018, Brexit negotiations are being carried out for leaving the European Union and we are all holding our breath for the future. We could never have predicted any of this in 1992.

Tony Benn, February 1991

One of the best speakers I saw interviewed at The Nave was MP Tony Benn. He was witty, interesting, and every bit the committed politician you imagined him to be. What surprised me, though, was that in front of a live audience he shed tears over the victims of war. It was February 1991 and it was the war in Iraq, which had just been invaded, that upset him. This was long before reality TV, and showing raw emotion was highly unusual, particularly for a man, never mind a politician. Speaking to interviewer Stewart Henderson in front of a packed audience, he described a letter he had received from a woman whose father was killed in Iraq in 1917. His voice cracked, his mouth trembled as he said, 'These are real people. We live in such a tiny globe. If we can't find a way of living together...'

He believed socialism was about being brothers and sisters. 'It's why Jesus was crucified – it was a new idea and not even popular then.'

There was no disputing that this was a man with genuine beliefs and even those who turned up to dislike him could not have failed to admire his conviction. The tabloids were not his greatest allies, but remarks like the one in *The Daily Star*, in which he was called 'a treacherous swine' because of his stand on the Gulf War, he said did not bother him. What he did find particularly upsetting was the way we watched real scenes of carnage on TV (quite new in 1991) as if it was spectator sport. 'We watch it and then we go and have a cup of coffee. I find it personally distressing,' he said.

No-one should be given power unless it could be removed – and everyone misuses it, he said. 'Brotherhood and internationalism is what we want. I am frightened by nationalism and racism.'

The interview wasn't all serious. My favourite of his anecdotes was in 1931, when he saw Gandhi in London. 'What do you think of Western civilisation?' the Indian leader was asked. 'I think it would be a good idea,' Gandhi is supposed to have replied.

He also amused the audience with revelations of 'the biggest growth industry' – the secret service. He was well aware that his phone was tapped and letters opened. 'They're sometimes put back in the wrong envelopes!' he told the audience to roars of laughter.

Uxbridge is put on the map: The 1997 by-election

The 1997 Uxbridge by-election was brought about by the death of our MP, Sir Michael Shersby, only seven days after he was returned to parliament. He had held the seat for nearly 25 years, and it was a terrible shock for everyone. This was following the General Election in which Tony Blair and New Labour triumphed for the first time. I had seen Mr Shersby at the count. His colour was high and he had looked severely stressed. Labour was making huge inroads all over the country and the Uxbridge MP could see his healthy majority of 13,179 slipping away to just 724. In the event he held on to his seat, but it took a terrible toll on him.

The new government was still celebrating its victory when the news broke about Mr Shersby's death. At the paper, we thought there must have been a mistake, what we'd now call fake news. But there was no Facebook – it started in 2004 – or Twitter (2006) and the internet was not widely used. If it were true, it was up to us to relay the shocking news, so we had to make sure we had got our facts right. These days everyone considers themselves a 'news'-gatherer, and rumour and innuendo are spread as fact on social media without a nod to accuracy, sensitivity or responsibility. There is no news editor to tell them to write objectively and check their facts over and over again. Can you imagine any of today's bloggers – or anyone spreading 'news' on social media – listening to advice?

I attended Michael Shersby's funeral for the paper – it was held in Harefield, where he had wanted to be buried – and also, later, a memorial service in Westminster, attended by Tory dignitaries, including Margaret Thatcher. His family were dignified in their grief but there was still an air of shock and disbelief. Harefield 'boy' Russell Grant sat next to me at the local service at St Mary's, which was naturally a sombre affair. I still have a vivid image now of Michael Howard, who was Home Secretary from 1993-1997, standing at the graveside. Mr Howard was eventually Tory leader from 2003, until 2005 when David Cameron took over.

New Labour may have taken over the Government from the Tories but, with this unexpected by-election, they had no time to rest on their laurels. Its victory machine under Peter Mandelson and Alastair Campbell went straight back into top gear, as this would be their first test as a credible power. They had slashed the Tory majority in Uxbridge; now, with the eyes of the whole country on our town, they were determined to win it.

That was when New Labour made a fatal error. Changing the candidate from popular local man David Williams, who had done very well in the General Election, to Andrew Slaughter from West London New Labour territory, was a huge mistake. Local party members claimed angrily that Slaughter was 'parachuted in' against their will. The two sides of the same party – left and right – were pitted against each other and it helped the Tories retain the seat.

Conservatives had cunningly put in another popular local man, John Randall, who had been Mr Shersby's election agent. His family had owned a store in Uxbridge for generations. He won, and went on to have a brilliant record as our Uxbridge MP, rising to be deputy chief whip, and eventually receiving the ultimate accolade: a knighthood in 2013. He was a superb constituency MP and was respected by people of all parties. Boris Johnson was voted into Sir John's seat in 2015 and Mr Slaughter eventually found his natural home as an MP in Hammersmith, which he won in 2010.

It may have ended in tears for Labour, but both sides had put up a good fight during the by-election, and I had some of the best experiences on the paper during the run up to the result.

Labour dispatched their heavyweights to Uxbridge, including John Prescott, whom I accompanied on their battle bus to West Drayton. It was then part of the constituency, but is now in John McDonnell's area, following boundary changes.

I remember the night John McDonnell – now shadow chancellor – was first elected in 1997 with a majority of more than 14,000. Victory was extra sweet as he had been defeated by the Conservative sitting candidate Terry Dicks in 1992 by only a slim 53-vote majority. His agent was Julian Bell, who masterminded the victory in 1997, and who was himself elected to Ealing Council in 2002, and is currently its leader. His daughter is the well-known TV presenter Angellica Bell.

But back to Uxbridge in 1997, where Labour was fighting its second election in a matter of months. 'Things Can Only Get Better', the anthem by D:Ream, which helped the victory for New Labour only weeks before, blasted out from the bus as we stopped for John Prescott to address a crowd. Unfortunately, there were some wind-up merchants there who were pressing all his buttons (not difficult) so he had to be persuaded back on the bus before a fight broke out. He has a very short fuse, and of course only a few years later, in 2001, Mr Prescott punched a protestor in Rhyl, after he'd thrown an egg at him.

On another occasion, I, and other reporters, were allowed a few words with Gordon Brown. I found him rather chilly, and very reluctant to address the problem posed by an unpopular candidate. He seemed generally a bit fed up about having to talk to anybody about anything. He did however admit the by-election would be an uphill fight for them.

As reporters waited for our five minutes with candidates from either side, some of their aides were continually buzzing in our ears. These were the new breed of spin doctors – the smiling assassins – dripping their views, and sometimes venom, about opposing candidates. They were mostly playground tales, rather than credible tip-offs. I tried to help national journos who bent our ears for insider local knowledge to give their pieces more colour, and we were also able to help them navigate their way around the borough (while of course not giving away any stories that we might have found for ourselves). Exclusives are always sought after – be it for local or national newspapers. It was a two-way thing, and they in turn let us know of anything they'd heard, unless they'd netted an elusive exclusive.

Labour, probably by then getting a bit desperate, wheeled in popular TV celebrities. Michelle Collins was pleasant enough, but fellow EastEnder Ross Kemp was very unhelpful. I asked him cheerfully, with the expectation of a supportive response for his party, 'So why are you here today?'

It would be obvious to anyone that I wanted a quote about why he was backing the Labour candidate – and the new PM, Tony Blair. He gritted his teeth, refused to make eye contact and growled: 'Why do you think?' Charming. He was being deliberately unhelpful as, any way you look at it, this was not a quote I would be able to use in my piece, and he knew it.

The Tories sent mainly big-name politicians to Uxbridge

such as novelist Jeffrey Archer, and Cecil Parkinson, beloved of Margaret Thatcher. On the other side of the political coin, I found myself enjoying coffee and croissants with Lib Dem leader Paddy Ashdown, while interviewing him at a supporter's house.

Most startling was the announcement that Tony Blair would be coming to Uxbridge. Prime ministers historically never appeared at by-elections; there was too much danger of sinking with a defeated candidate. Better to keep a safe distance.

But Blair was extremely popular then: unstuffy, with a young family and a whiff of celebrity, so it seemed a good decision to send him on a charm offensive to Hillingdon borough.

Uxbridge was buzzing on the day he arrived. Even the sun came out. I'd never seen the pedestrianised area so packed – it felt like a rock star was about to arrive. As his car drew up, there was cheering and screaming as the crowds surged forward. I wriggled my way to the front to get a good look and by a sheer fluke found myself right in front of his car. As he stepped out he shook my hand and said a cheery hello. In the absence of any formal welcoming party I felt pathetically obliged to mumble a weedy 'Welcome to Uxbridge'. He seemed to forget he was still holding my hand and so for a few rather awkward steps we trotted along together like primary pupils on a school outing. I could see how it happened to our Prime Minister Theresa May with Donald Trump when she was photographed in a hand clinch with him earlier this year.

After Blair had addressed the crowd from a soapbox, I was ushered into a car with various advisers and Number 10 staff to set off for West Drayton, the bit of the constituency where John Prescott had had a good rant at a protestor. We arrived before the PM, so it was arranged by radio contact that we would 'hide' in a quiet side road until he joined us. It was very strange to see Tony Blair eventually draw up behind us, chatting to his fellow passengers as the two cars – his and ours – waited for the signal to move off.

Squeezing through more enormous crowds in West Drayton, and a sea of red flags, we were ushered into the Labour campaign office – a shop, which was very small so only a handful of media were allowed in.

Even with our lower circulations, local reporters are not the poor relations you might imagine on these occasions, compared with the big political reporters from TV and the nationals. We were always courted, as our papers were what the electorate would mostly be reading. One of our reporters was even sent to Downing Street to interview the PM.

So, back to West Drayton, where the handful of journalists who were allowed in were granted a few minutes with Blair, before he was to be interviewed for lunchtime news. My photographer captured the moment for me. This was of course long before the selfie generation, so it is great to have the photograph as a memento. It would have been very naff to have asked for one.

The moment for Blair to be interviewed live on TV was to do with a national problem (I can't remember what it was now), but as the camera was trained on the PM we were commanded to be completely silent as he answered questions, direct from the TV newsroom via his earpiece. There was a weird, long silence while he listened to whoever was interviewing him. We of course could not hear the questions, only the answers. Alistair Campbell stood a few feet away from the PM, eventually doing an impatient wind-it-up signal to his boss when he felt it was time the interview came to an end. When Mr Blair continued to answer questions, the Campbell commands became more frenzied.

The Monster Raving Loony Party (MRLP) candidate, Screaming Lord Sutch, made the nearest comedy club his headquarters when he arrived in Uxbridge. He handed out fake £1m notes as bribes (I still have mine) to astonished passers-by, and announced plans for a victory party the night before polling day! The MRLP Party founder 'Lord' David Sutch spoke to me at his party at the old Continental pub in the High Street.

He said: 'There has obviously been a loony here before me who designed the traffic system in Uxbridge.' He promised to build a bridge to the channel tunnel, and turn Uxbridge into Loonyland. As for Uxbridge open air swimming pool, he said, contrary to local desires, 'I promise to put a lid on it.'

Election night on July 31, 1997, was very exciting – and we even had Mr Elections himself, David Dimbleby, covering the results live from Uxbridge. John Randall and his wife Kate were generous to a fault and always made sure, even when the nationals were clamouring, that I was constantly kept up to speed with what was going on. They remained very loyal to their local paper, and to those of us who worked for it.

Sir John, as he is now, held the seat for the Conservatives by a large majority, gaining over 50% of all votes cast, while the Labour and Liberal Democrat vote fell sharply. It was the first time the Conservatives held on to a seat at a by-election since the Richmond (Yorkshire) by-election in 1989.

Their victory was celebrated at The Turning Point restaurant in Cowley, where Conservatives celebrated in brilliant sunshine next to the Grand Union Canal. We were all after an interview with the then Tory leader William Hague. The Randalls, ever mindful of their loyalty to the *Gazette*, steered me into the cool interior of the restaurant and, as I got my notepad and pen ready, the four of us sat down at a table together.

It is well known and accepted that new governments normally enjoy a bedding-in period where they are congratulated and given a chance to draw breath. I therefore asked Mr Hague about the honeymoon period. Would it (referring to the government's popularity) last?

He looked slightly shocked. What had I said? Then he laughed and said: 'I'm not telling you that!'

Then I twigged. Of course. He was about to get married to fiancé Ffion and thought I was asking about their honeymoon plans and whether the marriage would last (it has).

Oops. The four of us laughed then, which really broke the ice, and we continued the interview in a more relaxed mode.

I found Mr Hague, now a life peer, very approachable and pleasant, but I discovered many years later that some of those around him didn't do much to help sustain his popularity.

I was at a Conservative conference in Birmingham, with a press pass, when I saw Mr Hague chatting easily to his supporters. As even more came up to be photographed with him, I heard one of his group sneer, so that they could definitely hear, 'You sad people'. Charming.

I still get to election counts. The national papers and TV pay us to phone in the results.

They use local journalists, whom they call stringers, from all over the country. Before mobiles they used to post unwieldy landline phones to us, which we had to plug in at the count (and post back later). It seems very primitive now.

Most recently, fellow journalist and friend Liz Driscoll and I have shared responsibility for ITV and the Press Association, at the counts for the three Hillingdon constituencies. Votes are counted at Brunel University. We also phoned in the EU referendum result. We like to make sure that if one of us can't make it for any reason, we are covered. They can't NOT have a vote phoned in. The Press Association provides the information to all the national newspapers, and ITV (and BBC of course) are waiting to have the result to put at the bottom of your TV screen. It is always a great atmosphere and I love being there even though it means being alert all night – often going home bleary-eyed at dawn.

There is good camaraderie amongst the journalists and press officers, and many are even prepared to share their Pringles or Haribo. Fat and sugar are needed when you're up all night.

Europe pre-Brexit, 1995

I wasn't always confined to my desk in Uxbridge; our MEP, Robert Evans, invited me to Brussels in 1995, so that we could see that life wasn't all Beaujolais and bonhomie. How could I resist?

We (Mike was also invited – probably so our MEP didn't have to entertain me all the time) were as excited to be experiencing our first trip on the Eurostar train as much as anything. At Brussels, we were met by our host and escorted to his place of work. Here we were photographed and processed like sausages through security.

It was interesting to see Robert on the job. Nothing in Euro politics is straightforward, even just communicating with fellow politicians in the corridors, as there are at least eleven languages to cope with. And they are only the official ones. English was widely spoken of course, and Robert's French was surprisingly good. The smattering he started with had improved thanks to special lessons in Brussels, which were provided for all MEPs who wanted them. This was not just schoolboy stuff like 'la plume de ma tante' or even holiday phrases like 'où sont les toilettes?', though the latter would definitely be useful. The tutors covered vocabulary that was useful for the job.

Bumping into MEP Glenys Kinnock did not present language problems of course (even though she's Welsh!). We were introduced and she made me laugh when she showed an interest in the fact I had taught in Ealing borough before switching to journalism. She had also been a teacher and said: 'You escaped too, did you?'

We then passed a much less jolly looking, harder-edged MEP. Robert said you normally could not miss him because he was usually being barracked by Socialists, who made up the largest group of Euro MEPs, wherever he went. He was the righter than right French politician, Jean-Marie Le Pen, who has since been succeeded by his daughter Marine, who is now president of the National Front in France.

In the two days we were his guests in Brussels, Robert Evans attended the European Parliament and several committees, often accompanied by us. Every session was a complicated affair, even down to the smallest committee. On the back of each seat were headphones which members and visitors could use to select their own language. Mike and I selected English (number two) and settled back to hear the debate on Slovenia's proposed membership of the European Union. It was great to be able to understand what Italians, Germans, French and Scandinavian speakers were saying, but my brain found it hard to cope with the conflicting images relayed by listening and looking. Just imagine a German with a harsh voice and aggressive stance being interpreted through your headphones by a Barbara Cartland trill.

Central to all this were the interpreters who were an impressive, and apparently well-paid, breed. They sat in glass-fronted boxes around the parliament chamber or committee room and made switching languages look as easy as changing chaussettes (socks).

At times, it must be nerve-wracking for the interpreters as they never know what is coming next. While we were there one interpreter prepared to translate from Danish to English but quickly stopped as the Scandinavian speaker changed to English. Presumably somewhere else in another glass cage a Danish interpreter was frantically translating the words of her fellow countryman back from English into his native language for any non-English speaking Danes.

Subtle political statements were being made everywhere if you were astute enough to find them, or like us, had a friendly guide. For instance, MEPs against nuclear testing had stopped ordering French wine in the European parliament restaurant. Even the line-up of flags told a story. There were then only 15 countries in the EU and enlargement was being negotiated for some eastern European countries and the Baltic states. Not included in the proposed expansion was Norway, which had voted to stay out. An empty flagpole in the line-up of countries signified its dramatic snub. It's interesting to look back now and see how the enlargement has led to so many debates about free movement, particularly to the UK from Eastern Europe.

During our trip one of Robert's meetings was with the Indian ambassador to help prepare for a European parliamentary trip to India. Unimpressed by a suggested itinerary of banquets and handshaking, former headteacher Mr Evans asked if they could visit schools (not 'show' ones). He also wanted to find out what was being done to improve India's 'appalling' record on child labour and prostitution.

At that time, the Euro parliament was a moveable feast – meeting three days a week for three weeks in Brussels. Then, just as everyone was organised and comfortable, they all moved to Strasbourg. The trunks which sat outside the MEPs' offices were a constant reminder of the shifting population. Papers were dropped in these, ready to be transported when it was time to move on.

At a parliamentary session on small businesses Robert spoke up for his constituents in North West London, saying he would like to see the European Commission take a more targeted approach and give more access to information to help them. He told them that a questionnaire sent to 1,000 small businesses across his constituency revealed that sixty-five per cent of them did not want a single currency. In hindsight – and with our present knowledge of the near collapse of the Euro – it was clearly a good view to have had.

And now, more than 20 years later, the UK has voted to get out of the EU altogether.

14

Vocal Locals

I have reproduced here only a small sample of the features I wrote about local people during my time as a reporter at the *Gazette*. Hillingdon is full of interesting people with fascinating tales, so my apologies to anyone I wrote about who is not specifically mentioned in this book. It doesn't mean your story is any less important. To choose from such a rich seam was difficult, and there is just not enough room to include them all.

I've not only included stories of high-profile people but have included a police dog handler, Brownies, a mounted police officer, firefighters, and young performers from the Beck Youth Theatre.

***

One of the best spin-offs that fell into my lap, from being steeped in the local community, was being asked to help set up the Beck Youth Theatre (BYT). I was closely involved with it for only a short time but have remained a fervent supporter ever since. At its 25th anniversary in 2013 I was asked to cut the cake with Phil Brewin, the prime mover in its set-up in 1988. It was great to see many original members returning to perform, as well as technical experts, costume and marketing bods and co-ordinators from the past who'd worked on BYT prods and summer projects, including the early 'mothers' of the BYT, Marian Ockendon and Wendy Brackley.

The Summer Youth Project (SYP) happened annually. It was open to all and a big show was produced in only two weeks. It not only gave kids something to do in the summer holiday that didn't involve fast food or computers: it also gave many of them a first look and a lasting love of the theatre. They weren't expected to find a career in the theatre – the main spin-off was confidence, team work, and social skills. All good for any job.

Many, however, have gone on to work in the theatre, and down the decades phone calls, letters, drop-ins to the office by former BYT-ites, have kept me up-to-date with the exciting things they're doing. It was always great when my editor agreed I could write a piece on them so we could let others know about them too.

Luisa Bradshaw-White, who was in 31 episodes of *This Life*, as Kira, was also a regular in *Bad Girls* and *Holby City*. However, she is probably best known for her role as Tina Carter in *EastEnders*.

Three local lads I particularly remember are Matthew Robinson (stage name Matthew Stirling) who gave me the ammunition for a fascinating piece about becoming a stuntman; James D White on filming the role of the Rolling Stones drummer Charlie Watts, and Gareth Walker who landed the plum job of choreographing Take That on their comeback tour. Many many more members have gone on to make steady careers in luvvie land, and a bit of me envies them. I could never have been an actor though, as I said previously – I can't remember the words, which is a bit of a disadvantage.

Matthew got into the exciting business of being a stuntman by accident. In 1996, then 24, he told me: 'I was always interested in that side of things, but it wasn't until I was working at the Royal Opera House doing fight work that I thought of trying to get on to the stunt register.'

Matthew was one of three fighters – stand-ins for less fit (even portly) opera singers when their role required climbing up towers or swinging from ropes – who was plucked from Covent Garden to appear in the film *Rob Roy*. Matthew laughed when I asked about the glamour of film work.

A film set in Scotland in the late Autumn was not the most glamorous of places, even when rubbing shoulders with stars like Liam Neeson and John Hurt. 'It was November and freezing cold. We had to be up at 5am, in costume by 6am, on set by 7am and filming by 8am,' he said.

While in Scotland he met people who were on the stunt register – a list of highly qualified stunt men and women. He couldn't have guessed the gruelling training and specialisms required then when he decided he'd like to have a go.

Before being accepted, Matthew had to achieve a high standard in several specialist areas. His categories included karate, fencing, horse riding, swimming, trampolining and water. As if this wasn't enough, each of these categories was broken down into further areas called 'set skills'. 'For instance, an exam for horse riding involved riding three different horses, riding bareback, cantering, trotting, galloping and riding with a sword and shield.'

Did he ever feel frightened when tripping over tables, falling out of windows or jumping from a great height? 'Sometimes, such as when I was diving 35ft at Crystal Palace, I thought, what am I doing here? It can be dangerous but if you can trust the equipment it is all right,' he said.

Clive – actor and police dog handler

One of the dog handlers I accompanied on the round-up of dangerous dogs in the early 1990s was more familiar to me as the romantic lead in many roles with a local musical society. That's one of the great things about being a journo on a local paper; you bump into people in unexpected places or recognise them from past 'lives'. A mayor may, in a former 'life' have run a local business, such as Albert Kanjee, who ran a dry cleaners, or Steve Panayi, who had a hairdressing business. Pat Foster, who was PA to the manager of the Pavilions Shopping Centre, turned out to be a faith healer who has since written her own book about her fascinating life.

It was particularly great to spot a tough-looking cop like Clive Smith wearing fancy costumes in shows like *Barnum* or *Singing in the Rain*.

I can't remember in which place or time or role I cornered Clive to ask him for an interview about his job as a police dog handler but in 1997 he agreed, also promising to bring his current canine chum Gerry. At that point, he had completed twenty-five years as a Metropolitan Police dog handler.

Dogs are traditionally man's best friend, but for a police officer he can also be his last defence against criminals. When I interviewed him, Clive's dog Gerry was also there. The three-year-old may have been hardwired for action but he sat patiently as his master chatted to me. All Clive's dogs have lived with his family since he took the first German shepherd, Luke, home in 1976. His daughter Anna was only three, so Clive admits he was a bit apprehensive as the dog had never met a toddler 'running around and squeaking' but they soon worked out a peace treaty. Luke won the Black Knight trophy in 1992 for the most successful street dog in London, which, said Clive proudly, was 'well-deserved'. Even after retirement, Luke remained with the Smith family until he died aged twelve. He was followed by Robbie, another champion who won trophies in working dog and police dog trials, then Buck, who was sadly run over by a car in the early 1990s. After Buck came Jet, who retired early because he was not 'socially acceptable' and could not be approached. Being people-friendly when required can be just as important as being ready to spring to the attack, as dogs often accompany their handlers to schools and fetes.

'The children think it's hilarious when you take them out into the playground, hide the headteacher's handbag and get the dog to find it. And of course, they love it when you get "attacked".'

This stage-managed attack – and Clive's am dram background must have come in handy here – was far removed from the real world of a police dog handler. He and Gerry could be sent on a drugs raid, attend an armed robbery, chase criminals or search for lost children or confused pensioners. They are also sometimes required to accompany RSPCA officers on a job if they need a warrant or think a dog may be dangerous.

Clive admitted: 'We're probably more scared than them. When I'm staring a Rottweiler in the face, I think, I know what they're capable of.'

He also patrolled the grounds of the royal palaces at night – his favourite is Buckingham Palace – but he has never spotted any intruders.

One of his scariest moments of his career was in Hayes when he arrested an armed man who was drunk and threatening to kill his wife. 'I was glad my dog was right next to me,' he said.

July 2001 – Mounted Police officer

Most of us only see mounted police officers from a safe distance, relying on them and their horses to keep order for us. They are on our TV screens at football matches, trying to calm a riot, or protecting the Royals, but I didn't know anyone who'd met one personally. So, I was excited to be invited to interview a local man who was then retiring from the police force, particularly as I was to meet him at Hammersmith police station where the horses were kept. Michael Plowright turned out to have a fascinating catalogue of stories from his career.

After joining the police force at the age of twenty-four, he became a trained armed officer and served in the CID – at one time under Det Ch Insp Jack Slipper, who pursued the Great Train Robbers – as well as in the uniformed branch.

As an armed officer, he also spent time protecting the former Home Secretary and Northern Ireland Secretary Merlyn Rees, who lived in Harrow.

Before he was a mounted policeman Michael's experience was restricted to donkey rides and pony trekking, but his move to the mounted section in 1977 was the right one, he said. Although he 'knew nothing about horses' in those days, you were pressured into specialising in something.

When he was a boy he had seen the mounted police at football matches and was impressed by their smartness, and how the horses were so well kept and behaved. There was no denying he was thrown in at the deep end.

'You rode on your first day. Most of us were in the same position [novices] and we had a laugh, but the horses had a bigger giggle. They were aware it was our first day, and they knew they were in charge. We spent most of the time on the floor!'

The first thing the riders had to learn was how to move the horse, and stop. They were also tutored in the horse's physique and in grooming and stable work. They were even taken to see a horse destroyed. The officers cared for the horses themselves and exercised them in Hyde Park, Barnes Common or Richmond Park. He discovered that the horses are all individuals with their own characters.

'There have been a lot of brave horses and a lot of chicken ones. The brave ones lead the others. The horses are not taught to push or provoke – in fact quite the opposite. Officers learn to control crowds safely by turning the horses sideways – the horses should be restrained. They have to learn to trust us.'

Most of the time the people they meet at fetes and sports events are friendly. They admire the job and the horses, and officers are happy when people, particularly children, crowd around. But of course, there are times that they are in the thick of it, and it is far from pleasant.

'It is horrible. In the 1970s and early 1980s there were big clashes with the National Front and Anti-Nazi league, and at football matches there was always fighting. At Wapping [there were big clashes] when the print workers on strike, and when there were striking miners in London, it got nasty.

'In the 1990 poll tax riots – when people were protesting against Prime Minister Margaret Thatcher's proposals – there was a lot of violence. We were taken away from a football match at Chelsea for that one. In the carnage and the chaos, it is the violence of the people that you notice. They will throw anything, from dustbins, ladders and scaffolding posts to bricks and cobbles.

'You see the hate in their faces. Some are just rent-a-mob who have no sympathies either way. They are simply there for a good fight and to have a go at the establishment.'

In the first May Day protests the anarchy rioters trashed the city. The Mounted police were there to protect Buckingham Palace as the rioters were not just against the Government, they were anti-monarchy too.

He had been hit by flying missiles but the protective gear – body armour, helmet, leg protectors and visors for officers – 'generally do the job', he said. Following the death of one horse after a brick was thrown in Wapping, the horses now have proper protection on their heads.

Being on duty at many Notting Hill carnivals, where there has been little or no trouble in recent years, sounds like fun, but it is very noisy for the horses. 'Some horses are fine one year, and the following year they've had enough. It is deafening for them and hurts their ears,' he said.

Michael was also involved in many ceremonials, and regularly took the horse Bachelor Gay to Buckingham Palace for the Queen to ride, in her brown leather boots with gold spurs.

He said, 'I would put the mounting block by the horse so she could ride side-saddle around the grounds. She is a very nice lady, and far more attractive than she appears on television.'

Bachelor Gay (I kid you not) was also ridden by the Duke of Edinburgh during Trooping the Colour when someone took a pot-shot at the Queen in 1981. Michael was relieved the Queen was unhurt but also proud that Prince Philip, who was riding next to his wife, reported that the horse, though startled, was 'very well-behaved'.

Before he retired in 2001, he told me, I was a bit apprehensive in the job at first, but I've had a great time. My faith in human nature is still there. The job has not changed me or hardened me, though people said it might, and I have lots of friends outside the job. I have seen some horrible sights, experienced more of the bad side of life – death and serious injury – but I have seen good as well. A lot of things happen which restore your faith in human nature. You feel proud of the horses when they are not frightened and do as they are told.'

Michael was given the Lloyds Bank Black Horse National Award in 1996 for achievement as a mounted policeman.

David Brough

ONE of the best-known people in Hillingdon borough, and a great contact of the local paper is David Brough, once described by David Dimbleby as 'devoted to democracy'.

The son of a factory worker and a hospital cleaner, David Brough was the head of Hillingdon Council's democratic services until he retired in 2007. I say 'retired', but he has been knee-deep in community stuff ever since.

After being the first in his family to pass the 11 plus exam, he went on to be head boy at his grammar school, and a degree in economics followed at University College, London.

Though his family were natural Labour voters, the real seeds of the young David's future interest in politics and local government were sown when he stood in a mock election at school (and lost); but he was elected for real to Harrow Council in 1971, one of the youngest councillors in London.

His time in Hillingdon will be remembered for a fierce commitment to the democratic process, including making council decision-making open to the public. He developed rules to limit the number of decisions that can be taken in private and these were taken up nationally to form a key part of the Access to Information Act.

He also devised the council's petition procedure, which gives the public the right to speak to a cabinet member and address meetings, and he drew up the first council-wide complaints procedure.

He said: 'I believe the council, because it is closer to people, can also transform people's lives, provided it is open and efficient. Local democracy is so important and I don't think it is always valued enough. The forces of national government have got so immensely powerful; it's now all about power and finances. It was one of the biggest mistakes making central Government the funder of local government. We have lost something. The old adage about the piper and the tune springs to mind.

'We should not have our affairs run by faceless Whitehall mandarins who don't know where Hayes or Ruislip or Uxbridge are, it should be more about local people knowing what's best for the area.'

David was one of five people who took the Government to the European Court of Human Rights on the issue of freedom of speech and, despite winning in the penultimate court, the case was finally lost. The law was changed to ban senior government officers being involved in politics in areas other than the one in which they worked.

He turned his attention to running elections and became Hillingdon's Returning Officer in 1993.

The importance of voting is obviously very dear to his heart and when he visits schools he describes the first day of voting in

South Africa when there were long queues of people waiting to cast their vote for the first time. He says the youngsters are moved by the power of democracy without revolution, the means to kick out people who misrepresent their views and the fact that a road sweeper's vote is of equal value to a millionaire's.

He set up the Hillingdon Community and Police Consultative Group – now replaced by Safer Neighbourhood Boards – and has spearheaded community safety in Hillingdon, working with police and other bodies to fight crime and anti-social behaviour, look at the causes of it, and generally improve life in the borough.

'It was realised that police can't tackle crime on their own, and all of us working together, including the safer neighbourhood teams, has really benefited the community.'

David met inspirational freedom fighter Aung San Suu Kyi in 2012 when he was invited to train pro-democracy activists in electoral best practice ahead of Burma's first democratic elections for 20 years. He dined with Dr Suu Kyi, a Nobel Peace Prize winner who had been under house arrest for the best part of two decades.

He said: 'She has an amazing serenity, but you can see she has a core of steel.'

This has been seen in recent news reports where she has been highly criticised for not taking on Burma's military to stop the violence against Myanmar's Rohingya minority.

David worked for Hillingdon Council for 38 years and was made a Freeman of the Borough when he retired. He also has a Police Community Safety Award – and a cycle route! – named after him.

He is a great supporter of local papers which he described as 'allies of local democracy'.

'There will always be friction between the council and local newspapers but I believe they have a mutual interest in working for the local community. They need each other. I can honestly say, in all the years I have worked with local papers, I have never been misquoted.

'However, I would criticise all media for being too negative; it would be good to see more positive coverage, as this can bring a community together.'

Anna Kennedy

Many parents will go to extreme lengths for their children but one woman was so determined to see her autistic sons get a good education that, against enormous odds, she founded her own school.

Anna Kennedy remortgaged her house, leased a disused school, fundraised with help from the community, recruited an army of volunteers to transform the building, then staffed it and made a huge success of it. I first started writing about Anna when I saw her at Hillingdon Council meetings. Later, in April 2013, I had a two-page feature about Anna published in the national woman's magazine, *My Weekly*.

Her fierce determination to make a better life for her sons (Patrick who has Asperger's Syndrome, and Angelo, who is autistic) has resulted in a string of awards, including getting an OBE from the Queen in 2012 and being voted Tesco Achieving Mum of the Year 2013.

Born in Middlesbrough of Italian parents she says: 'The fire started in me when the kids had suffered bullying and ridicule, and there was no school that was suitable for them. We set out to establish a centre of excellence for children with Asperger's and autism which would be as near to mainstream education as possible, so that as many families with similar problems could benefit too.'

When Anna and her husband Sean started what must have seemed an impossible quest to found a specialist school they could never have guessed that Anna would also write a successful book about her experiences and have many appearances on TV.

Along the way Anna has unflinchingly taken on people in power – the movers and shakers, from politicians to Simon Cowell, in order to see her dreams come to reality.

'I'm like a dog with a bone. You can achieve anything if you put your mind to it. I left school at 16 and haven't got a degree, but my passion and love of my sons drove me on. If I got a no from anyone I'd just go somewhere else. I was told I couldn't use the title Autism's Got Talent for my show at The Mermaid Theatre, but I said we're not competition, we're not using your logo and we're not a problem. I kept going until they agreed. I wouldn't back down even when they phoned and offered seats at the Britain's Got Talent final. I turned their tickets down and stuck to my guns, and eventually media company Freemantle issued an agreement with the support of Syco, Simon Cowell's company.'

Her first school, Hillingdon Manor, an independent school for children on the autism spectrum between three and a half and nineteen years, opened in 1999. Since then she has set up a community college in 2001, a respite home for adults in 2004 and a second specialist school in Kent in 2011.

Anna is also pivotal in offering support and advice on the internet to struggling parents. Demands on her are enormous but as she has been through the same problems she never wavers in her wish to help her followers on her own website and helpline, Twitter and three Facebook pages.

'Some families are desperate, particularly those trying to get a diagnosis. Their kids are often at home and may have been excluded from school and you can feel very isolated. We have built a virtual autism community all over the world. They want tips on dealing with their particular situation or maybe just a listening ear. It's not all serious stuff though; we also swap cupcake recipes!

'I think it helps that women are good at multi-tasking. I can be talking on the phone to someone and they won't know that I'm in the kitchen. I say, if you hear a bang it's because I'm making dinner. I'm quite good at switching on and try to act immediately.'

Even though there is more awareness about autism and other special needs there is still room for more sensitivity, says Anna. She is sceptical about TV programmes like *The Undateables* which tries to find partners for those with conditions like Down's and autism, and says she has had several people contact her because they were concerned, sometimes distressed, about what feels like voyeurism. 'It is obviously done for the "watch" factor and I am uncomfortable with it,' she says.

So how did Anna ever find the strength to see her vision through while her sons were little, and she was dealing with challenging behaviour during the day and getting little or no sleep at night?

'You have got to go with your gut instinct. Autism has changed my life. I used to be quite shy but I'm more vocal now. Looking back, it was scary, often frustrating, taking on the council and fundraising for such an enormous amount, but in the end we did the whole thing on £90,000. Most of the time we were on automatic pilot.'

In her book which charts the whole amazing story, she has acknowledged the help and support eventually given by Hillingdon Council, even though at one time she feared being strangled by red tape. However, after our interview Anna was off to yet another council meeting to speak about getting permission to expand her original school.

She said: 'I'm always looking to the future. I get a real buzz from new projects.'

It seems that for this tireless campaigner and great mum, the end of the marathon – the finishing line – is still not in sight. And that's how she likes it.

Anna's charity website www.annakennedyonline.com is fast becoming a global charity with its very first overseas ambassador hailing from California. She has almost a hundred thousand followers across social media and the website. Her book, *Not Stupid,* is available on Amazon in paperback and on Kindle.

The support group Hillingdon Autistic Care and Support

(HACS), which helped lead the way is now run by Chief Executive Toni Mullally, and is still very active for families. As I write (Sep 2017) they have just been awarded a £25,000 grant from The Masonic Charitable Foundation following support from the community who voted for them.

Brownies and Rotary

What do I have in common with Glenda Jackson and Lorraine Kelly? Well, not much, except that they were all Brownies or Guides in their youth. Visiting the bouncy Brownies of the 11th Hayes for a feature I would be writing for the Gazette took me back in a flash to my past as a pixie (Brownies were put into groups like elves, imps, gnomes etc).

Brownies have always been subjected to strange names. When I arrived to meet the modern Brownies I was greeted warmly by adults with titles like Brown Owl, Tawny Owl and Barn Owl. The very youngest girls – Rainbows – are looked after by their leader, known as Woodpecker.

The guiding movement began in 1910, a year after some gutsy girls insisted on being noticed, by turning up at the first Boy Scout rally at Crystal Palace. In 1914, a junior section for eight to eleven-year-olds was launched called Rosebuds (oh dear) which was later renamed Brownies. Baden-Powell had apparently asked his unmarried sister to organise a group for girls.

My own memories are centred on my Brown Owl, Miss Silver (remember older women didn't have first names in those days). She was very old with white hair to match her name, a sharp nose and a constantly exasperated look which meant she really did look like an owl. I don't think she liked little girls very much.

I loved Brownies but Miss Silver scared me to death, particularly as she would pounce on me because I never had my beret on straight. I would freeze as I watched her chins wobble with indignation as she, yet again, rearranged the offending article on my head. No such problems now – I looked enviously at the outfit today's Brownies wear, which is now much softer and less military. They can choose from skirts, trousers and sweatshirts, and the badges that they earn from doing different activities or learning new skills, are attached to a sassy sash.

The girls told me that it was fun to be a Brownie in 2007 and that they particularly enjoyed the pack holidays – that's camping to you and me – where they cooked (Shepherd's Pie was the favourite) and cleaned for themselves. The highlight, it was generally agreed, was on the first night, when they always paraded in their PJs (the grown-ups too) as if they were on a catwalk. The lowlight was cleaning the toilets.

Brownies are still put in groups of half a dozen called Sixes, but a big difference is the challenges set for Brownies who get badges for their achievements. My generation were expected to polish up their skills in laying the table or skipping. Hmm. Today's youngsters can get them for horse-riding or gymnastics. Circus skills, crime prevention, recycling, fire safety and disability awareness, are also on offer. Brownies do still brush up on cooking and cleaning, skills which are always needed by all of us. This applies to Scouts too, of course.

I'm a bit bemused by Scouts opening their doors to girls – I don't think it works the other way around does it? I'm all for equality but still think there's a place for gender specific groups if they are set up honestly as single-sex organisations.

This will surprise some people who may remember that I and a friend caused a bit of a stir when we became the first women in Hillingdon to become members of a Rotary group. Historically only open to men, when the membership rules changed from the top, Shifa Yusuf and I were invited to make history in the borough. Acceptance of this modern mix wasn't unanimous, however, with members of Hayes and Harlington Rotary club.

A few men, and several of their wives, did not approve. Some resigned. The women said they were happy to wave their husbands off for the night knowing they were going to an all-male group, and anyway there was a spin-off for wives called Inner Wheel.

Females from the world of work, they thought, could be a distraction.

Why was this rather startling change happening? Rotary, locally and nationally, needed new members. The business world was changing and was not now populated by a majority of men, so it was a good opportunity to swell the numbers. Shifa and I were put forward by Phil Brewin who was then chief executive of The Beck, our local theatre.

As I was then a reporter for Hayes and Harlington my editor was keen for me to take up the offer. He knew it would be a good story and would give me new contacts for the future.

I said earlier that I think there is still a place for single sex organisations, from boys' brigade and girls' brigade, to hard-drinking rugby teams. We need women's centres and refuges which offer a place of safety away from abusive (usually) partners.

However, when it came to an organisation solely set up for business people to get together and do charitable work for the community it seemed wrong that in the 20th century it was still admitting only men, so I, and Shifa infiltrated the ranks. Because of time problems we are no longer members, but many women are Rotary members now; several have become presidents of their clubs.

Firefighters

There is no doubt that firefighters enjoy the risqué image perpetuated by strippers at hen parties and their own oily-torsoed calendars. In October 1998 my job for the paper, I was relieved (disappointed?) to hear, that was to veer away from the stereotype to find out more about the day job.

Two men at the opposite end of their careers welcomed me

to Hayes fire station where Green Watch, fully clad, was on duty: Harry with nearly thirty years under his belt and new fireman Mark.

Though at the start of his career, I discovered that Mark was not a raw recruit straight from school, having worked at BP as a fire officer for seven years. He was previously in security. When Harry joined, most recruits were ex-servicemen and the search was for younger people to join the brigade.

He joined the Junior Fireman's scheme when he was 15 in 1966 – a residential course for two years. 'It was the first time I'd left home,' he told me. 'We learned about firefighting and also did college studies. We were training in five-foot-high grass and carrying people up and down trees.'

Fast forward 30 years and Mark's initial training lasted only 16-20 weeks, but it was followed by a probation period at a fire station lasting up to four years. This hands-on experience he said was key to learning the job. 'The training was pretty physical, but the worst bit was travelling up and down from Southwark Training School. Eighty-five per cent of the course was practical, learning how to pitch ladders and so on.'

Both men welcomed the fact that the service had opened its doors to women. 'We had about four female recruits at training school and I was impressed with them,' said Mark.

Harry admitted that, rather like my experience at Rotary, some older firefighters had reservations at first. 'But I have been out on jobs with women firefighters and they are just as good as blokes. They have proved themselves. The service has opened up, which is good as it is becoming more varied with race and gender.'

He said the service had looked into why there were not more Asian people in the fire service and discovered it was because it was a uniform job, like the police. At the time, their parents wanted them to be lawyers or doctors.

To most of us, it is the unexpected aspect of the job which is most frightening. Firefighters never know what they are going to discover when summoned by a 999 call. I have twice been in a fire – the first time when I and my mate Marg were doing one of our student holiday jobs at a hotel in the Isle of Man in the 1960s. A guest had been smoking in bed and his room was gutted.

It happened in the early hours of the morning and we had only just got into our basement beds after being out on the town. I wanted to ignore the fire alarm and go back to sleep but it had the opposite effect on Marg – she was frantically packing her bag. We both joined the staff and guests on the pavement in our nighties and later enjoyed some hot toddies with our rescuers.

The second occasion was many years later when Mike's car caught fire as we drove down the Uxbridge Road. The first flickers grew into alarmingly real flames as we shuddered to a dramatic halt. Behind us a very welcome fire engine had appeared from nowhere, thanks to a thoughtful motorist who'd spotted our flaming car and made a hasty 999 call. Hurrah for mobile phones (again). And firefighters, obviously.

We must have looked a bit sheepish when they discovered the blaze was caused by the car's instruction book which had fallen down the side of the radiator and got wedged there!

Mark once had to rescue a horse, after the RSPCA summoned the fire brigade. The tethered horse had its foot caught in a chain. Using bolt cutters, he managed to free the animal but it was very frightened and kicked out in all directions.

Harry told me about an incident at Euston, where he was part of a crew attending a hotel fire.

'There were lots of Americans staying there and when we arrived the tourists all wanted to have their photos taken with a firefighter. Smoke was coming out of every window and we were trying to get into the building while they were trying to grab us for a picture!'

One of the hardest experiences for any firefighter is when the casualties include children. 'It is hard when you find children huddled in a cupboard. You can't believe parents have just left them. We have known some people who have taken their TV sets out first from a fire,' said Harry.

'It is sad when children have died, but you just have to get on with the job.'

It made me think again about the tragic story I mentioned earlier in which two children died in a fire. And particularly about the courage of their mother who spoke to me about what really happened in order to put the record straight.

Youngsters are also involved in funny incidents, such as two children rescued from the roof of a community centre. The five and six-year-old were scared when police were called, and wouldn't budge because they thought they were in trouble. However, when firefighters arrived they were more relaxed – and positively enjoyed being transported down on the hydraulic platform in a cage.

The firefighters enjoy their visits to schools where pupils are allowed to inspect them and their engines. This is an important part of the job and can take away children's fear of the unknown.

Both men agreed that one of the best parts of the job is the camaraderie at Hayes station, where there were then five fire engines and 18 firefighters. They would both recommend the job.

Harry said they were not heroes. 'You just enjoy the job. You don't think about the dangers. As people are running out, you're running in and you always have back-up. If you thought of the dangers you wouldn't go anywhere.'

This was never better illustrated than in the Grenfell tragedy last year (2017) when a tower block fire in London claimed the lives of around 71 people.

15

Victims and Survivors

One of the most difficult jobs I had to do was to interview the mother of a boy who had died after being run over by a car. I didn't do the original story when it happened, which appeared in the *Gazette* in May 2000 following the inquest, but I had the job of following up when the Green Party member on the GLA, Jenny Jones, came to the area to look at road calming options where the accident happened in Royal Lane, Hillingdon.

I immediately warmed to the mother, who had other children, but who clearly (and obviously) had never got over the loss of her son, William. She was actively involved in the charity RoadPeace after her son had run into the road and was killed.

The verdict was accidental death, and no blame was apportioned to the driver, who would also have to live with the dreadful incident. Police confirmed that she had not been speeding.

I had learned many years before that there are many victims in this kind of accident.

I once quoted a case when I did a talk to a victim support group at Townfield Community Centre – Chief Inspector Ken Wise was there, a man respected and loved by the community. If ever there was a case for keeping police officers in the same area – he was definitely it.

The accident I spoke to them about happened in Birmingham in the 1970s on the morning of Christmas Eve when a happily married, popular, law-abiding, middle-aged couple were heading for work. Their car was loaded up with presents ready to take to London after work where they would spend Christmas with their daughter, son-in-law and baby granddaughter. It was a very cold day so the driver went very carefully. A witness later said he wasn't doing more than 10/15 mph. They hadn't even left their estate when a woman stepped into the road immediately in front of them. The car skidded on black ice and she was thrown on to the windscreen and killed instantly.

Again, no blame was apportioned to the driver – his car was checked by police at the scene and there was no fault found, including the brakes. He had done all he could to avoid the accident. The couple were eventually told to continue with their plans for Christmas and drive to London. He later said it was the hardest drive of his life.

On that day, I was at home in West London, cooking up some Christmas treats and looking after my one-year-old, when my mother phoned from a stranger's house. Her voice sounded strange. 'Barb, something terrible's happened,' she said. My heart stopped. 'Is it Dad? Is he OK? What's happened?' 'He's killed someone,' she said.

I still find it hard to believe that the driver I described: the man who had such a terrible thing happen to him, was my lovely careful, kind, good-humoured, patient dad who had never, would never, hurt a fly. It shouldn't have happened to him. It shouldn't have happened to the woman who died. It shouldn't have happened to her family. It shouldn't have happened to us. Not on Christmas Eve. Not ever.

Mum and Dad arrived. We let him talk about it. We let him be silent. We were all in shock. The presents remained unopened on

Christmas day. Nobody ate much. How could we celebrate? The only saving grace was our little daughter who was oblivious to the tragedy and just happy to point at the Christmas tree. Her first word gave us hope. It was 'light'.

Much later, at a coroner's court inquest with a jury, both fire and police officers spoke in my dad's favour. They said that their vehicles also skidded on the ice when they arrived at the scene. The jury recorded a verdict of Death by Misadventure. I still find it hard to talk about it. Most people don't know it happened to our family. If William's mother reads this she will be surprised to hear my story. She and her family are a lovely unit and I know she will understand why I never mentioned my experience to her. It wouldn't have been appropriate and there was no need.

Later, when I gave that talk at Townfield Community Centre about victims, I made the case that sometimes a driver can be a victim of circumstance too.

Readers will always rally round when they feel someone has suffered an injustice. One of the biggest responses came after we published a story about an 85-year-old woman who was wrongly accused of shoplifting.

While filling her trolley in Tesco, Uxbridge, she felt dizzy and looked for a seat. The only place was beyond the tills, so she had no choice but to go there, taking her shopping with her.

Although she was clearly unwell, not trying to hide anything, and had money to pay, she was stopped by a security guard, and police were called. She was given no chance to explain, or pay. She had arrived with Dial a Ride so there was no way she was going to get back on the bus, which is used by elderly and disabled people, with a trolley full of goods, and no receipt.

Many people who read our resulting story called for a boycott of Tesco.

Her grandson, who rang me at the paper, when it happened, said, 'Nan had been going to Tesco for many years and they must have known her. I was determined to see her proved innocent.

'Going to the newspaper is good when you have nowhere else to turn. Tesco decided that she was guilty of shoplifting when she just felt ill and needed a seat. They didn't give her a chance. The Gazette did.'

After several attempts, we managed to get an apology from Tesco saying, 'We are genuinely sorry for the embarrassment caused.'

We never heard of it happening again.

Magistrate

Our local magistrates' court in Uxbridge is the nearest to Heathrow Airport, so occasionally there is a big stir when a famous person is hauled up before the beak. In 2012 the barriers were set up to hold back the press when Ronnie Barker's son Adam appeared on child porn charges (images on computer). He was later found guilty and imprisoned for a year. Previous bods in the dock have included Linda McCartney for possession of marijuana, footballer turned actor Vinnie Jones for air rage and Gerry Marsden for attempting to evade customs duty on a guitar bought in Germany. All were found guilty and fined.

Though I didn't do court reporting myself, I was keen to get the lowdown on the day to day job of a magistrate – which not many people know is voluntary. Eventually I got the chance to interview one of our local magistrates.

Richard Bristow's interest in the judicial system had been sparked by reading reports in the old broadsheet *Gazette* newspapers. By the time I quizzed him for my feature he had spent more than 20 years dealing with similar cases himself, ranging from domestic violence to drugs offences. He was then bench chairman.

Uxbridge Magistrates' Court was celebrating its 100th year in 2007 when I interviewed him. It was about to open its door to the public for an open day, but Richard remembered his own nervous steps on his first day as a magistrate in 1985.

He said: 'I did feel a 'new boy', but I was fascinated. One of the first things I had to do was sign a warrant for the arrest of someone who had not appeared in court. I was aware what a big thing this was, taking someone's liberty.

'Then in my first case, someone was sentenced to prison, and the experienced magistrates I was sitting with wanted to give him six months. I said why six? Wouldn't he have learned his lesson in two? They agreed with me and changed the sentence. That really impressed me and showed how open-minded they were.'

About 95 per cent of criminal cases are started and completed at the magistrates' court, including theft, motoring and environmental offences. There is however one aspect that Richard found very difficult.

'Domestic violence cases are the hardest and these days it is always taken very seriously. Thirty years ago, the police wouldn't usually have attended court; nowadays they do, and they always charge. If the accused, who is usually a man, is in custody he has generally been in the cells overnight and is asking for bail. If we get the decision wrong we could have a dead woman on our hands; if he is sent to prison you could be depriving children of their father and the mortgage may not be paid. Often it ends up with us making an order for him to stay away. We can ban him from the borough altogether, but we will always put someone inside if we think anyone is in real danger.'

The job also has its lighter side and Richard proved they are not all po-faced judges with his tale of a man who stole a fish-pond from a garden centre. In court, the man apologised for his crime and explained he took the pond, which he wore on his head, because he was drunk, adding, 'I haven't even got a garden, I live in a flat.' The court was amused but he was still fined.

There was good camaraderie among magistrates, whose average age was fifty-seven. People could apply if they were between 18 and

65, and at that time the 110 magistrates at Uxbridge included retired people, teachers, a firefighter, full-time mothers and several airport workers. They covered five court rooms, which each required three magistrates for 75 sittings a week, and were expected to do a minimum of 13 days a year. The average stint worked out to twenty-five to thirty days, with some doing many more.

Customs cases from Heathrow Airport kept them particularly busy and these could be anything from illegal deliveries of drugs to transporting big dogs in small containers.

The compressed canines may have been shipped by an individual in a far country but the airline is still held responsible for the cruelty and will be duly tried for the offence.

Richard said: 'Once we fined BA £6,000 for shipping four dogs in under-sized boxes. The next day I couldn't help but smile when I flew BA – and got an upgrade. Fortunately, they didn't put me in a box.'

One who bore a grudge against our local court was the lawyer and writer John Mortimer QC, who also wrote the *Rumpole of the Bailey* series. 'He used to defend many of the stars being held for drugs offences at Heathrow Airport and liked to get his cases hurried along so that he could get away for lunch'. This usually had the opposite effect, said Richard, and he had to hang around. He got his revenge by often making derogatory references to Uxbridge Magistrates' Court in his Rumpole series.

Like many, Richard was concerned about the increased number of juvenile cases – the numbers of days in youth courts had doubled – but he felt the now defunct ASBO had a place and could reap positive results. He said at best they were a useful tool but 'we must be careful we don't set people up to fail.'

He said he would recommend being a magistrate to anyone. All that is needed is common sense, integrity and a commitment to serving the community. 'It is being fair that's important, but it is fascinating and a huge privilege. Being a magistrate, you really affect people's lives.'

Methadone baby, 1995

One of the saddest stories I covered at the *Gazette* was about an eleven-month-old baby who died from a massive overdose of methadone. I first heard about it from the baby's father who lived in the north of Hillingdon borough and was not implicated in the tragic tale. Two of his three children, including the victim, were living with their mother and her new boyfriend when the baby girl lost her life, just weeks before her first birthday.

Tragically, it happened three days after the children had been placed on the 'at-risk' register by Berkshire Social Services.

These cases are not as common as it seems from reading the national news, certainly not in Hillingdon borough; but before I changed from teaching to full-time journalism I, like many people all over the country, was shocked by the death of Heidi Koseda in 1984. I never dreamt I would one day be covering an equally macabre story. Heidi had been starved to death in a locked room in Hayes, not far from where we lived.

The methadone baby story began for me when the father, whom I called Steve in my subsequent articles so as not to identify the children (and even now they are grown up I think it's right to do this) contacted me, as he was concerned to tell his side of the story. This, of course, could only be used after the verdict so as not to risk contempt of court. Learning the job 'on the job' had not always been easy for me, as the young reporters who had come to the paper by the usual route were already well-briefed in law. I learned as quickly as I could, though, and it was constantly drummed into us all that any mistakes may not only upset the families or mess up the legal system, but could result in serious problems for the paper. There was plenty of expertise at the paper to draw on and sometimes legal advisers to the paper also went over the copy before it was published.

I was invited by Steve to attend the baby's funeral where the mother, bent double with grief, sobbed all the way through. Her cries pierced the strains of that children's hymn 'All Things Bright and Beautiful' which I, like the entire congregation, struggled to sing as we gazed at the tiny white coffin. Steve's family were not only grief-stricken but understandably pale with anger at what they saw as an avoidable death. Steve felt that the authorities had not listened to his pleas to remove his children from the child's mother and her new partner, from what he saw as imminent danger. One relative said to me that the family felt that the children had been taken away from people who loved them, to be battered, abused and killed.

Having lived in a children's home himself, Steve was used to having his life ordered by social workers. Three days earlier, the family had come to the attention of Slough social services after the baby's two-year-old brother was taken to hospital with severe scalding following a mystery accident. A meeting was held with the mother and her boyfriend, the children's father Steve, and two of his three children. Steve told the social services meeting that he was not happy with his children being left in the care of his former partner while she was living with a drug addict. However, he didn't want to see his children split up, and feared they would be taken into care if he challenged the decision. After the hearing, Berkshire Social Services Department placed the three children on the Child Protection Register and agreed to do a more detailed assessment of the whole family.

Three days later a police officer called on Steve with the terrible news. His baby daughter was dead. Told at first it was a cot death, he arrived at Hillingdon Hospital to hear from a nurse that it was being regarded as a suspicious death, and police were investigating. The next morning Steve was told he could apply for custody of both his surviving children.

At the Old Bailey, the court heard that the baby's mother and her boyfriend had given the helpless infant enough methadone to kill an adult. The couple had only been together for a few months before the baby died. Most poignant was when the prosecutor said that the children had all been in good health when their mother had taken them from Steve.

On the day the baby died, the little tot was wheeled around shops for several hours while suffering the effects of the drugs. The mother claimed she noticed nothing.

The pair denied manslaughter charges, each claiming they had no idea how the baby had been drugged, but the jury convicted them both. After the trial, they each admitted criminal neglect of the boy who was scalded – they did not seek medical help for his burns for at least 24 hours. For this they received three months jail to run concurrently with their sentence for manslaughter.

However, the biggest blow was to come. The mother only received 18 months for her crime; her partner thirty months. Nine years previously her boyfriend had been sentenced to five years in prison for robbery with an imitation firearm. For the baby's death, he received only a third of that.

The punishment for the couple in the Heidi Koseda case was very different. Her stepfather was jailed for life for her murder while her mother was found guilty of manslaughter and detained in a high security psychiatric hospital. A private inquiry into her death found that the senior National Society for the Prevention of Cruelty to Children inspector allocated to her case failed to investigate a complaint of child abuse made by a neighbour. He also tried to cover this up with a fictitious account of a visit to see the child.

For Steve's surviving children life would never be the same again. The boy who was scalded in a hot bath wouldn't get into the water until his father had taken off his shoes and socks and tested it first, while he watched. His five-year-old daughter was deeply affected – attention-seeking one minute, shy and withdrawn the next. The children visited the grave of their baby sister regularly. Hopefully, now as adults, their lives have moved on.

In my Bm@il columns for the Gazette, which started in 2008, I have often defended health and social workers over the harsh criticism they receive about child cruelty cases. After all, they are the good guys trying to help, not the perpetrators of abuse.

However, details which came to light in another part of London in 2009 made me worry about some professionals. In one case, I couldn't believe that a doctor did not examine a child with horrific injuries and in terrible pain. Why? Because he was crying so much. I would hazard a guess that this would be from the pain he felt after his spine was cracked by his abuser. A quick examination could have eventually stopped his screams and saved his life.

And in a column, I wrote then (Bm@il 9.9.09), I wondered why some social workers believe no-one is at home when the bell isn't answered, or, when they do get a foot in the door, swallow ludicrous lies about the reason for a child's horrific injuries. It is gullibility at best and incompetence at worst.

Most worrying, though, was and still is the lack of community watchdogs – that's all of us.

You would think that neighbours would be aware of a suffering child long before any authorities were involved, although this can go horribly wrong if you try and intervene at the wrong time.

Stepping in can be awkward, as my mother discovered in an incident many years ago when we lived in a block of flats in Birmingham. My mother and her friend heard a child crying pitifully behind a locked door. They were concerned that he'd obviously been left home alone, so they persuaded him to drag a stool to the door where they soothed him through the letter box and tried to get him to let them in. Their eyes peering through the slot must have doubled in size when the toddler's dad came storming up the hall – without a stitch on – and demanded to know what on earth they were doing peering into his home. It turned out the family had all gone to bed early, but the youngest member had got bored and was stomping around looking for a bit of attention. Which he got!

A serious thought though: these two women would never have turned their backs on a distressed child and eventually, when they calmed down, his parents were grateful for their concern.

In another Bm@il column (7.8.13) after a similar child abuse incident – a boy called Daniel in Coventry – I confessed I was curious about where schools stand in these types of cases.

It made me think about when I was a young, inexperienced teacher my school was concerned that two brothers were being ill-treated by their father. One boy was in my class – he was seven years old, pale, very disturbed, drew violent images and flew into rages in the playground. One day the family disappeared and I felt terrible that I hadn't taken any positive action. It was only months later when watching a TV documentary about the first women's refuge (Chiswick Women's Aid) that I spotted my ex-pupil playing happily with children from other families – all victims of domestic violence – and I could stop feeling guilty.

Years later I was a mother, and back in teaching, when I found out about one pupil at my school who was about ten years old, fending for herself in a bedsit in a house owned by a male landlord. This was not a case of cruelty; she was much-loved by her single mother, who was in hospital and had left plenty of food and instructions. Nevertheless, the school was worried about the girl's safety, so this time I didn't hang about. I asked if she could come and stay with the Fishers, which she did for a while.

I know that these days you'd be strangled by red tape before you could pluck a child to safety, but how could Daniel's teachers let him go home each night when he was eating out of bins and stealing his classmates' packed lunches? He weighed 1stone 7lb when he died and his body was compared to that of a child in a concentration camp.

Drugs, 2008

The thorny problem of drug-taking is worldwide and well documented, but many are unaware of the good work being done closer to home to combat the illegal trade and help its victims. In

National Tackling Drugs Week in 2008 I discovered that a wide network of people exists in Hillingdon borough. They support police action to clamp down on growers and suppliers, while quietly helping drug abusers get back on their feet.

While I was gathering information for my article, I was told that the last quarter of that year, in Hillingdon borough, more than 60 police warrants had resulted in 26 arrests for possession with intent to supply both class A and C controlled drugs.

One inquiry alone resulted in seven arrests of people concerned in the cultivation of herbal cannabis in 'cannabis factories' and more than ten of these were closed down.

Astonishingly, at least 20 other possible factories were identified by police as a result of these searches.

In National Tackling Drugs Week, the spotlight is on all the agencies, from council and police to drugs action teams, who are working together to get these positive results. One young man who had benefited from this was a former crack cocaine and heroin addict from West Drayton; he said he had been helped to turn his life around.

The 24-year-old, who did not wish to be identified, said he first became involved with petty crime on his estate, mostly car theft and commercial burglaries, when hanging around with older lads.

He said: 'I then had money in my pocket but couldn't spend it on things like new clothes because my parents would ask how I had paid for them. So, I bought cannabis, coke and crack.'

With his life clearly out of control, he was sentenced, at 21, to four years for importing drugs, of which he served two, in an adult prison. It was his fifth time behind bars.

He said: 'I got on to heroin in prison. Everybody has it but I started to realise how bad I felt when I couldn't get it. There is help in prison if you want it, so I joined a course and was drugs tested every week.

'When I came out in December (2007) I was arrested a couple of days later for having drugs. It was then I decided I'd had enough.

I have two children but had spent most of my adult life in prison. I was told by my probation officer if I didn't take a two-year Drug Rehabilitation Requirement (DRR) I would be in for a long spell in prison.'

The last six months had been difficult, but the help he received at Blenheim CDP (the London drug agency), for substance-misusing offenders from Harrow and Hillingdon, had transformed him.

A DRR is an alternative to a custodial sentence which gives offenders the chance to work through their drug problem in the community. DRR orders last between 6 and 24 months depending on the offence, and the programme includes group work and one-to-one sessions, focused on breaking the cycle of drug use.

This sits comfortably alongside therapies like Indian head massage and acupuncture, and support is also given with sorting out things like benefits, housing, and working towards training or work.

The 24-year-old was aiming to help others who had gone off the rails like himself. He said: 'I can't believe how I feel now. Straight away they make you fit in, as they are friendly and don't judge you. Before, I had felt very alone.

'It made me think a lot, and find out about myself. I couldn't blame what I had done on my childhood as I came from a good home.

'I am not on any drugs at the moment, but am still fighting it every day. They give you the knowledge and tools to overcome the cravings and deal with things.

'You can't come here and take the mickey. People are respectful to the staff and have respect for each other. I haven't seen one argument since I have been here.

'I'm normally very bad at attending things but I have made sure of attending this twice a week, as well as going weekly to report to my probation officer and to the Hillingdon Drug and Alcohol Unit in Uxbridge once a fortnight.

'Within the next month I will go from someone who needed help, to helping other people.

'I was very low but now I feel like a human being and can look people in the eye again.'

Assisted Dying, 2003

Fifteen years ago, I interviewed a relative of one of the first people to go for assisted suicide through the now famous Dignitas organisation.

Sisters Lesley and Margaret accompanied their brother John, who had Motor Neurone Disease (MND) to Switzerland. It was a big story for me as a journalist, but was particularly poignant, as I know the family well.

Marg is mentioned in this book many times. She was my college friend (we met Alan Sillitoe together), we were each other's chief bridesmaids, and we had our children at the same time. Our lives have been intertwined for decades.

Of course, I had met John and Marg's younger sister too. It was Lesley who agreed to be interviewed when they returned from Switzerland. Then a patron and spokesperson for Dignity in Dying, she has campaigned tirelessly, supported by her sister, to get the UK law changed to allow this to happen here. Her case that the terminally ill with the mental capacity to decide their own fate should no longer have to make that difficult journey abroad if they wish to end their lives is laid out in a book, co-written with Jo Cartwright.

When John was diagnosed with MND in 2001, he was told his condition was fatal, untreatable and irreversible, and, after doing some research into Dignitas, he made the decision to end his own life.

He had read about Reg Crew from Liverpool, who in January 2003 was thought to be one of the first UK citizens to end his life through Dignitas.

John's message was simple. He tapped the words, 'That is what I want to do' into his computer.

Lesley said, 'I was dumbfounded, but we said it was his life, and we would support him in anything he did.'

As John's needs increased, he had the help of a full-time carer from Australia, but when her work permit expired, he was less than happy with the care given by a succession of untrained staff from agencies.

In his last days, Lesley and her partner Michael, who had been very proactive in his care already, took over completely.

She said, 'With MND your body fails you but your mind is still active. We could see his isolation, helplessness and dependence. One of the cruel twists of the illness is that although John could only take liquids and medicines through a tube, he still had an appetite.

'He loved his food and on the Friday before he died he wanted to be taken to a chip shop just to smell them. We sat outside and put some on his lap and he breathed in the aroma very deeply.'

John became a member of Dignitas, which then cost about £25, and just joining it made a huge difference to him, giving him a sense of being able to do what he wanted.

'It was a guarantee. He had thought of taking his own life, but he didn't have the medicines and he dreaded coming round in hospital with a well-meaning doctor having saved his life.

'By this time, he could only communicate through his computer, and by face and hand signals, but when he joined Dignitas he felt in control again.'

In April of 2003 he expressed a desire to go, and eventually he was offered a date: May 26.

Though Lesley said she felt 'sad and sick', John emailed her to say, 'It is a good date'.

Flights from Luton were arranged for John, Lesley, Michael, Margaret and Peggy, a friend, and an emotional farewell party was arranged at Willen Lake in Milton Keynes, two days before the trip.

As John sat in his wheelchair facing the water, friends and colleagues came up in ones and twos to say their farewells. Poems and messages were read out and there were many tears.

Lesley said, 'He was always firm in his resolve but he knew he could change his mind at any time. We left the flat exactly as it was so he could easily have come back if he chose. He didn't want to. He was amazing.'

The flight to Zurich was uncomfortable for John but his sense of humour shone through. Referring to his window seat on the plane he tapped into his computer a message for Lesley. 'You can have my seat on the way back.'

Dignitas founder Ludwig Minnelli met them at Zurich, and accompanied them to their headquarters, where documents from passport to birth and wedding certificates – John was divorced – were checked. Details of his four companions were also logged.

John was questioned on his own about his desire to die. When asked if he was tired of life, he replied, 'No, tired of living.'

Later, alone with a second doctor at a second location, he was again asked if he was certain he wanted to die. The doctor told him it was his duty to keep people alive but in Switzerland he could also help people who chose to die. 'I am prepared to do this for you,' he said.

John was very, very tired but was able to relax now it was guaranteed it would happen that day. The final move was to a flat in Zurich, near the city centre.

When they were all left alone with John, he spotted some chocolate which he had always loved, on the table.

Lesley said, 'I saw his eyes light up, so I unwrapped a square and cut it in half. He licked and smelt it, and I had the other half. It made him smile.'

With his family by his side John took an anti-nausea drug to stop a reaction to the fatal dose. He was told it would take twenty minutes to work.

He asked to be left alone for five minutes. During this time, he wrote a poem which he signalled should be read after his death.

A nurse brought in a syringe of barbiturates. John still had a small amount of movement in his left hand, and he pushed the syringe into his feeding tube, attached to his stomach, while still sitting in his wheelchair, as he wished.

Lesley said, 'We were told it would take two or three minutes for him to drift off to sleep. We held his hands and said goodbye. We were all crying and in my head, I was saying 'No, take it back'. But I knew that was for me, not for John. He went into a deeper sleep and was utterly peaceful.'

The nurse then came in to say it was her duty to inform the authorities. Seven people soon turned up, including a police chief and medical staff, who examined the room and John's body. Twenty minutes later they said everything was in accordance with procedures, and no investigation was needed.

They went back in the room and saw John's face one last time. 'He looked so peaceful,' said Lesley. 'We all kissed him. We didn't want to go. He never should have had to go all the way to Zurich. I am sure the safeguards needed could easily be drafted here so that people cannot be exploited. Anyone who is terminally ill, and wishes to die, should be allowed to with dignity in their own homes.'

John's compassion for his relatives and friends – and his gratitude to those who had accompanied him on his final journey – was apparent right up to the time of his death.

'At the end we were obviously upset, but as he died he patted our hands to let us know it was all right,' said Lesley.

Below is John's poem which was written while waiting for the anti-nausea drugs to take effect, twenty minutes before he took the fatal dose. He asked to be left alone for a few minutes to write something on his computer, and signalled this should be read after his death.

I am tired
in the spirit and the body
if they carried me back to
the taxi
I would soon be a corpse
anyway
no more faxes
no more emails
no more reasons for living
I do think though
it seems sad to have come to
such a grand city
and such good people
only to die
– these thoughts are those of a weary, terminally ill man
out of joint
they have no proper form
or ending
but thankfully
his life has

June 1992

Rape victim/survivor

Interviewing a victim of rape was an experience I shall never forget. In spite of the obvious trauma suffered, the woman, who was in her 50s, had agreed to speak to me to help highlight the services and support available. She had suffered what I imagined to be the worst kind of personal assault. She was the victim of stranger rape in broad daylight, while out for a walk.

Bob Borwick, the DI in charge of serious and major crime investigations, based at Uxbridge Police Station, said this is very uncommon, but emphasised 'date rape' or rape by 'someone you know' can be equally traumatic.

The woman, who we did not identify, was helped by a whole team of people. They included the female police officer, who first chaperoned her at Hillingdon Hospital.

Attitudes were changing at that time, and the Juniper Suite, where Alison (not her real name) was taken, had been opened twelve months before at the hospital, specifically for people who had suffered rape and sexual assault.

Having a specified area where victims could be treated – meant no more hanging around, distressed and half-clothed, or wrapped in a blanket, in a police station or A and E, as had happened in the past.

Staff in the Juniper Suite – named after the herb signifying peace – had already dealt with thirty cases that year. Decorated in peach and blue it was a cosy, not clinical, space, in spite of the necessary bath/shower and examination room and facilities for vital forensic specimens.

Victims could present themselves to the suite, I was told. They didn't have to go to the police first, and in the end, it was up to them if they wanted to bring charges. 'Rape is a crime of violence with sex as a weapon,' said DI Borwick. 'We would always like people to report it because the rapist could strike again. The women have been violated but, when they see someone being punished by the courts, it can restore the balance of power.'

Following her ordeal, the woman was met at the suite by Angie, the police officer. She admitted she was nervous too as she waited for Alison to arrive, saying how to deal with victims was not always straightforward. Her first instinct was to provide comfort.

'You feel like grabbing them, but you have to be careful because some wouldn't want that. Everyone is different. Though we are strangers there is an immediate bond. We may be the first person they will confide in.'

As no-one is pressured to report the incident to the police,

Angie said, 'in the end it is only me and the nurse who knows, but after being in the Juniper Suite, even if they take it no further, they will know they are OK physically and will have had AIDS and pregnancy tests.'

The brave victim that I interviewed had been to the police station first, so had reported the rape. 'At first, I wondered whether I'd done the right thing,' she said. She must have dreaded what was likely to happen next, as the wheels by then had been set in motion.

But she told me it was a haven after the horror. 'At the Juniper Suite, I saw the kettle, an armchair and a sofa. They didn't examine me straight away. It was home from home. I just sat down with Angie and had a chat.'

The final member of the team who helped Alison was Carol, from Victim Support. Her role, which is voluntary, is to accompany any victims to hospital, the police station or to court, or simply fill in the compensation forms.

Carol said when she listened to rape victims it could be distressing – 'but it is important I don't let it show. I can't let the victim see the anger I feel on their behalf.'

The rapist was eventually caught, charged and pleaded guilty. A DNA test was conclusive evidence.

16

Finding Phyllis

Sometimes a chance meeting can lead you on an extraordinary journey; my involvement with the publication of the *Sunday Times* Bestseller began when I met the author Phyllis Whitsell in 2004.

My mother Nora Parsons, who had Alzheimer's, was being cared for at a nursing home in Birmingham, where Phyllis was a nurse.

One day when I was visiting mum at the home, Phyllis stopped me, and shyly asked if it was true that I was a journalist. 'I have a story I think you might be interested in,' she said.

This simple statement eventually led, in April 2011, to my writing a two-page feature about Phyllis for a national women's magazine, *My Weekly*. But the longer we chatted, the more I could see there was enough material for a book.

But to rewind for a moment.

How did we get here? The last time I mentioned my mum, she was the lively all-singing and dancing parent, which she more or less remained until she hit her 80th birthday.

We had a surprise party to celebrate the big birthday in her favourite restaurant in Harborne, Birmingham, with many friends, relatives and former work colleagues, but it was clear that she could not remember many of them.

It all went wrong for her when she was widowed in 1990 when she was 69. It was a terrible shock, as it happened after she had been out with my dad Gordon for dinner with friends.

He developed chest pains during the night but, not wanting to worry her, he didn't tell Mum until it was light. She then rang me in Uxbridge at 8am to say she thought he was having a heart attack and had phoned the GP.

Frantic, I told her – even though the country was in the middle of an ambulance strike – 'Mum – dial 999.' She said Dad was putting on clean pyjamas. I said, 'Tell him to keep still and not move around.' Mum was adamant that she would wait for the doctor and rang off.

I quickly phoned my parents' very good friends in Brum and asked them to pop round and see if they could help. I was a hundred miles away – and I felt so helpless. And so scared.

The next call came quickly. The GP had arrived and had told her to dial the emergency services. By this time, he was trying to resuscitate Dad. Only a few minutes later she phoned to say 'He's gone.' It all happened within half an hour of my mum's first phone call to me. My dad, a young seventy-three, full of life and hope for the future, had died. The worst thing is, he probably could have been saved.

It was then, as we prepared for the miserable journey to Birmingham, that we heard that an army ambulance had arrived. There is no room for passengers in these vehicles so Mum would not have been with him if he'd died on the way to hospital. Don't ever ask me how I feel about emergency services going on strike. It still makes me very angry that anyone could put lives at risk in this way.

Mum's Alzheimer's had slowly developed from that terrible experience, although it wasn't officially diagnosed until some time later.

I was making the trip up the M40 weekly. Visits from three carers a day meant my mother was safe and still leading an independent life. She visited friends, enjoyed walking and going to the theatre and to church. At weekends I would stock up her freezer and take her out to lunch and the cinema, which she loved. Sometimes she stayed with us (I fetched her) and we even had a few more family holidays.

But by 2004, after a hip operation, she had deteriorated to the point where social workers would not let her return home from hospital, insisting she needed 24-hour care in a nursing home.

What followed was one of the most challenging times of my life: working in West London during the week and travelling at weekends to Birmingham, where I visited Mum in hospital, checked on her house, and then called at many nursing homes – all of which I refused to even consider for her.

It was a huge relief to find the nursing home where I met Phyllis and the other staff who looked after her so well during the five years she was there.

Mike and I bought a flat in the Midlands where we could take Mum out of the home for a visit and I could stay when emergencies came up. It was also halfway to North Wales where Zoë and Nick were living and working, so we had some lovely times there with them too.

By the time she was in her late eighties, mum could no longer walk, speak or feed herself. She had no idea who any of us were. With the flat not much used, Phyllis and I started to meet there, so that I could interview her to get information for the book we intended to write.

We had started the process together: her telling me her story, me recording and writing it down but Phyllis had a clear writer's 'voice' and a detailed, vivid memory.

She would often turn up to our meetings with pages and pages of handwritten notes and I began to realise that I must give her story back to her. It wasn't my tale to tell.

I told her she should write her own book and when it was complete, I would help her get it ready for publication. Very surprised, and just a little unsure about this unexpected development, Phyllis nevertheless bought her very first laptop and set to work.

It wasn't until 2014 that Phyllis came back with the finished book, which was mainly written during her stays in Greece. My mother had died aged 89 in 2009, and I had started an MA in Creative and Professional Writing at Brunel University, so my visits to Birmingham were rarer. But over the next year I helped her knock it into shape.

We met regularly at a pub in Gaydon, a convenient stop for both of us and roughly half-way between Birmingham and Uxbridge. We also spoke into the early hours on the phone, painstakingly going through her book page by page, only stopping for tea and toilets. Eventually it was time to offer *Finding Tipperary Mary* (Phyllis's brilliant idea for a title; much better than *Mother Love*, our original one) to the outside world.

We were impatient to see her book in print so, after being turned down by one agent and one publisher (who must be kicking themselves now), we decided to go down the self-publishing route. We planned on five hundred copies and a modest celebration launch at the Midlands Arts Centre in Cannon Hill Park. The invitations were drawn up, and we were getting very excited by the prospect of seeing Phyllis's story in print. Then everything changed.

Before the invitations were printed, never mind sent out – before the book was even published! – it took off in an extraordinary way. This was thanks in the first place to the then news editor of the *Uxbridge Gazette*, Steve Bax.

He had let me write a piece in the *Gazette* about the impending book and had then passed the story on to one of our sister papers, the *Birmingham Mail*, also part of the Trinity Mirror family. It was reproduced over three pages in its *Sunday Mercury* newspaper on September 13 2015, and this was followed by a big story in the *Daily Mirror* the following day.

I sat down at my computer on that Monday, first putting on

the TV to see what was happening in the world. The panel on the *Wright Stuff* on Channel 5 were discussing that day's news.

To my amazement I suddenly saw Phyllis's story flash up on the screen. It was included in their round-up of that day's top stories in the national newspapers. Presenter Matthew Wright picked up the *Daily Mirror* and said it was an incredible story and that it had got 'film written all over it'.

I now understand the phrase 'jaw-dropping' as mine slipped to the floor with a mighty (metaphorical obviously) crash. I knew then we were in for an interesting ride although I've never been tempted to describe it as an emotional roller coaster. (Readers of my column know that cliché affects me like a knife scraping a saucepan.)

Phyllis's story went on to appear in *The Times*, *Telegraph* and Mail Online – and I hadn't even printed out the manuscript at this point. Eventually the whole thing got too big for us, and thankfully Mirror Books, an arm of Trinity Mirror, became interested in taking over the publishing and marketing from us.

I didn't know what to expect of my first meeting with Fergus McKenna, who was then head of syndication and licensing, and is now Content Sales Director at Mirror Group at Canary Wharf.

It was coffee on the South Bank (my idea – neutral territory), and, thank goodness it was a relaxed, friendly affair. Fergus was accompanied by his deputy Antony Schipani who was mostly responsible for film deals. They both blanched when I said that with our self-publishing plans, Phyllis and I had allowed for only five hundred copies. I said we weren't even confident about selling them! They, of course, were planning on many thousands, which is what eventually happened.

I gave Fergus a few chapters of the manuscript to take away and crossed my fingers. Antony already had an astonishing number of people interested in the film rights, including some big names.

Things moved swiftly after that initial contact, and the serious business began. Phyllis came up to London so that we could both attend a meeting at Trinity Mirror's head office in Canary Wharf –

the fifty-storey skyscraper which is the second highest in the UK after the Shard (which overtook it in 2010).

It's amusing now to think that the only thing that worried me about this important meeting was going up more than twenty floors (oh Lordy) in one of the thirty-two lifts. I stopped going in lifts a long time ago after getting stuck in one with my parents when we lived in our six-storey block in Birmingham.

My resulting claustrophobia means I avoid the Tube in rush hour and can't even sit in the middle of a row in the theatre, but I knew I had to do this. There are times, like when Mike and I were in New York, when there really is no option. No way was I going to go home without having been at the top of the Empire State Building, and on this occasion, with Phyllis's book possibly at the start of something big, I could not be a wimp!

I needn't have worried. The lift was so large and lush it was like walking into a lovely room. It was also quick and quiet, so we arrived at the correct floor before I had time to think about trying to escape.

There was great excitement about the book by the powers-that-be at Trinity Mirror, which thankfully turned out not to be over-optimistic. On that day details were ironed out, including percentages of royalties, paying off the self-publishing company, and legal considerations. We were pleased that Mirror Books were now in full control. It was getting far too big for us.

Phyllis was soon in great demand – and her book had still not yet appeared in the shops. The publication date was set for February 2016.

TV interviews included *The One Show* on BBC 1 and ITV's *This Morning*. Although this was my time to bow out of negotiations and the publishing process, I was invited by ITV to accompany Phyllis to the latter, her very first public interview – live.

The studio for *This Morning* was a barn of a warehouse, situated snugly on the South Bank, well away from trippers. Even so, when I turned up there on Monday September 28 2015, I was surprised that, inside, the set had none of the front room cosiness that you see on the screen.

Phyllis, accompanied by her grown-up daughter Hannah, was already getting her hair and make-up done, so I was ushered into the Green Room, where guests on the programme are offered coffee and croissants. *The Jeremy Kyle Show* was showing on a big screen, so I was very pleased when someone else turned up that I could chat to, rather than listen to his grim tales.

Falklands veteran Simon Weston was the first to arrive. He had been called in to comment on a story about a military man who, while visiting a hospital, had been asked to move out of sight in case his uniform offended people. Simon was very friendly, and very modest, in spite of being voted the nation's most heroic figure in 2014. While we waited, we had a good chat about the insensitive request he was to comment on later. Eventually we were joined by fellow Brummie and showbiz reporter Alison Hammond, money man Martin Lewis, and an adoption expert, who was to take calls after Phyllis had been interviewed. It all became quite a jolly group.

I was very surprised that presenters Philip and Holly didn't introduce themselves to Phyllis before she was due to appear, particularly as she had never done anything like this before – and she was about to appear live on TV. Daunting for anyone.

Phyllis turned up looking good and surprisingly confident, and she did a great job with her interview. In fact, I think Hannah and I were more nervous than her. As Phyllis said later, as we looked on from behind the camera, we had our 'hospital faces' on. Apparently, we looked as though were standing by the bed of a very ill patient.

Phyllis appeared on local radio and *The Jeremy Vine Show* on Radio 2 (interviewed by Vanessa Feltz) and Radio 4's *PM* programme where she was quizzed by Eddie Mair.

Eventually the film rights were sold, and it has also been a bestseller in Canada, published by HarperCollins under a different title *My Secret Mother*.

So why did this tale touch so many people? I suppose I should really ask you to buy the book, but here's a little to whet your appetite.

Phyllis's story began when her mother handed her over to an orphanage when she was only eight months old. She was adopted as a five-year-old into a 'good Catholic family' to be a sibling to their daughter and two sons. Told that her parents had both died of TB, she was instructed to never mention she was adopted. In 1974 Phyllis had broken free from her adoptive family and started her training as a nurse. Having always been convinced that her mother was alive, in spite of what she had been told, she set out to find her.

Phyllis's birth mother, was in fact very much alive. Bridget, or Tipperary Mary as she was known locally, was a chronic alcoholic. She was in a bad physical state, mentally unstable, volatile, abusive and well known as a troublemaker in the local area. Definitely not the fairy-tale mother Phyllis might have hoped to find.

It was after a long hunt over several years, when Phyllis was working as a district nurse, that she finally tracked her mother down at an address in Balsall Heath, which was then a very rough area. Then married, with children herself, Phyllis knew there was no way she should disrupt her own family with the abusive, down and out, alcoholic mother she discovered.

So, she made an astonishing decision – the part of her story which enthrals people and makes it very different to any other long-lost family stories you may have read or seen played out on TV. If you don't already know, I can't give that surprising twist away. When my mother died in 2009, it was Phyllis who had phoned at the end to say I should come to be with her. It was Phyllis who sat beside me when she passed away – Zoë and Mike were on their way. The little girl who had so craved affection from a parent but had never found it, helped my own mother have a good death.

Phyllis is a mother to three much-loved children and two grandchildren. She attended our daughter's graduation as part of our family, and she has never shown any bitterness about her past.

Most importantly, she continues to love and care for other people's mothers.

To date the sales of the book, hardback, paperback and digital, are in five figures, and the film rights were sold.

On publication day February 15 2016, Phyllis was signing books in Waterstones in Uxbridge. People were queueing out of the door and the shop sold out of copies. More book signings were arranged in Birmingham and Coventry. Now she has written her second book (with Cathryn Kemp) – a prequel called *Song for Bridget,* published in February 2018. I wish her the same good luck and success.

17

Preparation –
and the dangers of none

Preparing for an interview is vital, particularly where big names (and sometimes fragile egos) are concerned. If you don't know your stuff it can be very embarrassing. In my career, I've done both – been well ahead of the game and also pathetically behind it. I had time to research Sir John Mills, but was hopelessly unprepared for a brush with Alan Sugar.

My mother was an avid cinema goer, so I was brought up with the old film stars like Robert Mitchum and Tony Curtis. Over meringues and tea in Birmingham city, or over the washing-up or travelling on a bus, Mum would educate me in this glamorous world with important snippets, like Betty Grable's legs being insured for a lot of dosh.

She fancied my dad looked like Fred McMurray and people told her she was a dead ringer for Lana Turner – or was it Loretta Young? We often found ourselves at stage doors waiting for a glimpse of stars like Ingrid Bergman or Richard Chamberlain when they were performing in this country.

Naturally, many years later when I got the chance to interview

John Mills I was more than keen to meet someone from my mum's magical world. Sir John, who was then 84, lived in Denham, not far from Uxbridge. He was touring with his one-man show, and the local reporters were invited to interview him at the Beck Theatre. Three of us turned up but I was the only one old enough to remember him from his heyday. I wanted to crawl under the table when one of them asked one of our greatest stars what he was famous for!

When the veteran actor came in the room set aside for the interview I was pleasantly surprised to see he had the sprightly walk of a man half his age. When he spoke, he still had the clear tones of a thoroughbred Englishman but his sight was very poor and we had to get in close to ask him questions. He told us his show included clips of his old films such as *Great Expectations*, *Forever England*, and *Oh What a Lovely War!*, and these were interspersed with some humorous behind-the-scenes stories which didn't make the press. He had worked with a variety of co-stars, and admitted when pressed that his favourite was probably Celia Johnson, famous for her role as Laura in the 1945 film *Brief Encounter*.

He had even worked with Madonna on *Who's That Girl?* In fact, he suggested the film's title to her. She was 'a great trouper' he said. 'I enjoyed working with her very much indeed. She was very professional with a good sense of humour.'

He had appeared in more than a hundred films, but I particularly wanted to ask him about *Ryan's Daughter* in which he played a disabled Irish mute so brilliantly that it earned him, as best supporting actor, an Academy Award.

'It's one of my favourites,' he said. 'I spent weeks talking to doctors and patients who had brain damage on the left side. Then, because my character could not speak, all I had to do was sit in the pub in the evenings drinking Guinness, while the rest were learning their lines!'

It sounded like the perfect acting job to me. You will remember

I can't remember lines. (Sir John of course did not have – had never had – that problem!).

However, with such a complex role, he found it difficult to go straight in front of the camera – 'I had to sit on a rock by myself for a while' – but he praised the job done by make-up man Charlie Parker, to turn him into the character.

Charlie took only seventeen minutes to transform him, concentrating on nose, hair and a special set of dentures which twisted his face. 'I always say the teeth won the Oscar,' he laughed.

While my mother grew up with Sir John, my generation identified with his daughter Hayley Mills who became a star in her own right. Most recently she appeared in *Wild at Heart* on ITV, the vet drama set in Africa.

Working for the first time in a film with his daughter Hayley, in *Tiger Bay*, he said was 'weird'. 'She just seemed to know what to do and never looked at the camera. Afterwards she was snapped up by Walt Disney for *Pollyanna*. Then I became known as Hayley Mills's father!'

Sir John, whose last film was *Bright Young Things* in 2003, was enjoying his tour and was pleased to find his audiences spanned all age groups. He said work kept him young and he could still be found tap-dancing in the wings before going on stage. He was amused when he saw himself in his old black and white films.

'The voices are higher and more clipped. It is funny to see yourself at twenty. My grandchildren look at my old films and I see them looking at me and wondering, "Is it really him?"'

In the interest of balance, I'll tell you about a time when I stumbled spectacularly because of lack of preparation. I met Alan Sugar briefly at Brunel University where he was a guest speaker. He appeared a bit grumpy, I thought, and he also had his sidekick with him, who looked just as miserable.

That was Nick Hewer, I later discovered, who now hosts *Countdown*. I had never seen *The Apprentice*, and, because I was asked to cover Alan Sugar's appearance at the last minute, I hadn't had time to do my research. (Now, of course, I'd google it on my phone while waiting for him to speak.) Worse, in the time allocated for questions afterwards, I was the only person from the press so I couldn't ride on the coat tails of other reporters' questions.

'Er… was *The Apprentice* your own idea?' I asked.

Oh dear, if looks could kill. Quite right though — the programme had started in the USA with Donald Trump. It was a stupid question. He gave his answer between gritted teeth.

I wrote about my experience and the subs topped my piece with the witty headline: 'Sugar not so sweet'.

I never let that happen again.

18

Finally…

When I first moved from Birmingham I missed the place where my family had lived for centuries, and where I was born and bred. In those days, it was nearly a three-hour journey to get back there as the motorway system hadn't expanded. I never told anyone about my homesickness, as my default system for coping has always been to pretend it's OK. Which eventually it usually is.

My memories of Birmingham are still vivid. I missed the cheery people, the yellowy creamy coloured buses, even the noisy, smelly, starlings that roosted in the city at dusk.

People in the south of England pronounced words differently and didn't say pumps, mardy or troach, or that people had got 'a face as long as Livery Street' if they were petulant or sulking. But in time, the borough of Ealing where I taught, then Hillingdon where I became a reporter, was definitely home.

I remain fond of my roots, but Mr F is from here, our daughter was born here, and we have worked with great colleagues and made many valued friends over the years. I can't now imagine putting roots down anywhere else.

Fast forward 20 years from my beginnings at the paper, and in 2009 I am at a ceremony for Local Heroes which the

Gazette organised annually with Uxbridge College. It had been my job for several years to organise the newspaper side: the nominations from readers for categories like citizen of courage, carer, etc; arranging a morning of judging by the current mayor of Hillingdon, and then helping to coordinate the arrangements for the night – trophies, certificates – along with our promotions department and the mighty machinery of the college, headed for press purposes by two former *Gazette* staff: Eddie Duller, then Liz Driscoll.

At this particular Gala night, I was sitting in the audience, keeping an eye on the running order, pleased it was all going well, when I was suddenly shaken out of my complacency. Something had gone horribly wrong. A final award was being announced. My head spun: we had completed all the categories. Even the last one had been announced – the main winner – the overall Local Hero. What was going on? I must have made a dreadful mistake and forgotten someone.

Why was our MD Simon Edgley still talking? Why was Uxbridge College principal Laraine Smith looking relaxed and smiling? I was in a blind panic wondering who I'd forgotten, so that I didn't at first realise that Simon was telling the audience that I was leaving my job as a staff journalist, after two decades at the paper.

The final Local Hero award – a beautiful glass trophy – was for me. All I could think was, how had they managed to keep this wonderful surprise a secret, and, after the inspirational stories of the night, how embarrassingly unworthy I was. Believe me, after tales of rescuing, caring, and fundraising during the evening, that is not false modesty on my part. I had just been doing a job like many others.

But what a great surprise. A few words were expected, and all I can remember saying was how much I had enjoyed it all. All 20 years of it. Not just organising Local Heroes. It was true; I had.

I may have fallen into the job by accident, but being a reporter is something I have never, ever regretted, even the bad bits. (Oh dear, time to wrap this up before I start singing 'My Way'.)

Local hero? Hmm. I wasn't a hero then, and am not one now. But I met many who were, during my time at the Gazette. These ranged from police and firefighters, to ordinary people achieving great things, or acting with courage, compassion, or dignity in difficult, sometimes terrible, situations. They weren't all nominated or awarded local hero accolades but I know that they earned the title. You will have read about some of them in my book. My local hero is Mike who has supported me practically and lovingly through all the weird and wonderful things I've been involved in. And our daughter Zoë, who has always been a tower of strength to us both. And our pets, Sam, Fizzy, and especially Ben, her Cairn terrier, who was always so much part of the family it was the hardest thing to be parted from him in 2001.

Mike still seems to find it all amusing and is a good sport when I mention him in my column. And he is still my best editor and copy-checker.

I may not be a hero, but for me, the other word on my glass trophy was even more important. It made me feel that this Brummie was really accepted in her West London home as a fully-fledged local. A local! – and proud of it.

19

Thanks and Acknowledgements

There are so many people to thank (or blame) for this book, from editors, sub-editors and news editors who attempted to knock me into shape over the years, to family and friends who thought it was a good idea, long before I was convinced.

I'm particularly grateful to Eddie Duller who took the courageous (foolhardy?) step to hire a teacher in the first place; Ivor Harvey and Richard Parsons who thought journalism was possible for me as a full-time career, and Adrian Seal who introduced me to Local Heroes.

Special thanks to Anthony Longden who got the short straw in training me – which thankfully we both survived – and more recently for his valuable advice on practical editorial matters connected with this book.

To the newspaper photographers who were out in all weathers getting pictures for our stories, with particular thanks to those who gave me prints to keep, some of which I've been able to use in this book. Most recently these were taken by Chris Berry, Leigh Quinnell and Toby van de Velde. Further back, thanks to Chris Saville, Alison Holman, Graham Bowles and Dave Kettlewell.

A special cheer of course to the many reporters I've worked, laughed, cried, and drunk too much with over the years. I hope they've also hoarded stories for their future books.

I'm very grateful to the *Gazette* publishers – in particular content sales director Fergus McKenna for permission to use excerpts and reproductions of newspaper articles, photos and columns, courtesy of Trinity Mirror. Also Sally Hampton at *My Weekly* magazine.

I will always be indebted to the people I've interviewed, and to the many contacts from schools, churches, arts and local history groups, residents' and other community organisations, charities, WIs, Rotary and fundraising organisations.

To Roy Mills and many press teams at Hillingdon council over the years who have put up with us reporters asking interminable questions – and 99 per cent of the time giving us the answers! Also to those in the police and other emergency services who realised that we, like them, had a job to do, and helped us when they could.

Thanks to contacts at Uxbridge College and Brunel University, which we are lucky to have in our borough. Also Hillingdon Hospital and the borough's schools, not forgetting the Beck Theatre and Compass Theatre staff, and the numerous amateur theatre groups and musical societies who have all provided us with stories.

I have great affection for past pupils and staff at Stanhope Primary School in Greenford, who shaped my young adult years! I learnt more there than on any teacher training programme.

Of course many people in my working life – teachers and journalists – have also overlapped into my personal life and some remain an important part of it. Those not mentioned by name are no less valuable.

Claire Moreton has not only cheered me on, but has also provided me with godchildren Sophia, Hope – and Joshua. The latter, when only five years old said it was time to ditch my Nokia and get a smartphone. The best advice I ever had.

A big hurrah for my longstanding COW buddies (which is not as rude as it sounds): we have been friends for more than 50 years. Also, thanks to my Uxbridge neighbours and my old friend Shifa for cheering me on; the BBPs who encouraged me over several lunches, and more recently Rebecca Hubbard, my MA buddy.

Thanks to Phyllis Whitsell, nurse, friend and author, who inadvertently led me into the world of publishing. It's been quite an adventure! Of course The Book Guild Team deserves a very big thank you too for deciding to publish me, despite being presented with its title.

Special thanks to Lesley Close for permission to use her brother John's poem.

To the politicians of all parties in Hillingdon who've provided us with so many of our stories. These include present council leader Ray Puddifoot as well as the several opposition leaders over the years who are still (as I write) hoping to topple him. We've all been around for a long time!

Who could have predicted when I reported on John McDonnell's first victory in 1997 (and previous defeats) that he would today be shadow chancellor? Or that Boris Johnson, foreign secretary until recently would be MP for Uxbridge? A huge thank you to his predecessor John Randall for much appreciated help over many years.

To my many cousins in Birmingham (and beyond) who are the last ties with my family history and share many of my early stories. Not forgetting old schoolfriends from Bournville Grammar, along with English teacher Mrs Morgan who gave me a love of books and writing. They all helped shape this memoir.

I wish my parents Nora and Gordon Parsons were still around to thank personally for giving me such a happy childhood. My wonderful mum and dad taught me the importance of love and loyalty, being open to the views of others, and above all, keeping a sense of humour, even when things are tough.

And thanks to Birmingham itself, the lovely, friendly city

where I was born, bred and educated. Also where I was married (at Longbridge, to my Londoner who led me away to the south). Brum will always have a special place in my heart – and not just because of the Cadbury's chocolate – but I've been in West London longer and it now shares my affection.

A big thank you to our lovely daughter Zoë and son-in-law Nick. We are very proud of both of them and they are always great fun to be with, but I can put it in writing here and now that we are never going camping under canvas this side of the next millennium.

Zoë was a first reader along with my longstanding friend Marg. They are always there when I need them, and are both appreciated more than they know.

And of course Mike – or Mr F as he is known in my column – who has always been my first editor. He read this unwieldy tome many times, encouraged me when I was flagging, and gave me the last gentle push to the finishing post.

My first passion may have been Billy Fury, but my enduring love is the other Mr F; the Morecambe to my Wise. Thank you Mike for all your subbing, sharing and supporting the book wot I wrote. And for always making me feel safe.

As this is a personal memoir, the events described can only be how I saw them at the time, and how I remember them now.

With hazier recollections I've attempted to double-check facts. I have also updated stories where I've felt it was necessary.

The articles reproduced from my hoard of newspaper cuttings are of course a matter of public record.

While thanking everyone for their help in getting this memoir together, I stress that any mistakes, or memory failings, are mine and mine alone.

People will forget what you said, people will forget what you did, but they will never forget how you made them feel.

Maya Angelou
US writer and activist
1928-2014